Also available from Cassell:

M. Barber: *Education and the Teacher Unions*

J. Beck: *Morality and Citizenship in Education*

S. Cowley: *Starting Teaching*

A. Hargreaves: *Changing Teachers, Changing Times*

G. Helsby and G. McCulloch (eds): *Teachers and the National Curriculum*

S. Ranson (ed.): *Inside the Learning Society*

P. Ribbins and B. Sherratt: *Radical Educational Policies and Conservative Secretaries of State*

J. Sayer: *The Future Governance of Education*

The General Teaching Council

John Sayer

CASSELL
London and New York

Cassell

Wellington House
125 Strand
London WC2R 0BB

370 Lexington Avenue
New York
NY 10017-6550

First published 2000

British Library Cataloguing-in-Publication Data
A catalogue record for this book is available from the British Library.

ISBN 0–304–70562–4 (paperback)

Typeset by Kenneth Burnley, Wirral, Cheshire
Printed and bound in Great Britain by The Cromwell Press, Trowbridge, Wiltshire

Contents

Abbreviations and Acronyms

ACC	Association of County Councils
ACSET	Advisory Committee on the Supply and Education of Teachers
ACSTT	Advisory Committee on the Supply and Training of Teachers
ADC	Association of District Councils
AEC	Association of Education Committees
AEP	Association of Educational Psychologists
AHM	Association of Headmistresses
AMA	Association of Metropolitan Authorities
AMMA	Assistant Masters and Mistresses Association (now ATL)
APC	Association of Principals of Colleges
AP(C)T	Association of Polytechnic (and College) Teachers
APVIC	Association of Principals of Sixth-form Colleges
ATL	Association of Teachers and Lecturers (formerly AMMA)
AUCL	Association of University and College Lecturers
AUT	Association of University Teachers
BEMAS	British Educational Management and Administration Society
BERA	British Educational Research Association
CASE	Campaign for the Advancement of State Education
CATE	Council for the Accreditation of Teacher Education
CATEC	Campaign for a Teachers Council
CBI	Confederation of British Industry
CDP	Committee of Directors of Polytechnics
CEO	Chief Education Officer
CP	College of Preceptors (now College of Teachers)
CPD	Continuing Professional Development
CTC	City Technology College
CVCP	Committee of Vice Chancellors and Principals
DENI	Department for Education in Northern Ireland
DfEE	Department for Education and Employment
DTI	Department of Trade and Industry
EAZ	Education Action Zone

EC	European Communities (later EU)
EIS	Educational Institute of Scotland
ESAC	Education, Science and Arts Committee, House of Commons
ESC	Education Standards Council (proposed 1990)
FCFC	Free Church Federal Council
FEDA	Further Education Development Agency
FENTO	Further Education National Training Organisation
GMC	General Medical Council
GSA	Girls Schools Association
GTC	General Teaching Council
HEFCE	Higher Education Funding Council for Education
HMA	Headmasters Association (now subsumed in SHA)
HMC	Headmasters (and Headmistresses Conference)
HMI	Her Majesty's Inspectorate
HMSO	Her Majesty's Stationery Office
ILT	Institute for Learning and Teaching (in higher education)
INSET	In-Service Education and Training
IPPR	Institute of Public Policy Research
IS(J)C	Independent Schools (Joint) Council
ICT	Information and Communication Technology
I(T)T	Initial (Teacher) Training
JCH	Joint Council of Heads
Joint Four	Former AAM, AMA, AHM, HMA
LEA	Local Education Authority
LGA	Local Government Association
LMS	Local Management of Schools
NAE	National Australian Education Council
NAGM	National Association of Governors and Managers
NAHT	National Association of Head Teachers
NAEIA(C)	National Association of Education Inspectors, Advisers and Consultants
NAPE	National Association for Primary Education
NATFHE	National Association of Teachers in Further and Higher Education
NAS/UWT	National Association of Schoolmasters and Union of Women Teachers
NCE	National Commission on Education
NCPTA	National Confederation of Parent Teacher Associations
NFER	National Foundation for Educational Research
NGC	National Governors Council
NQT	Newly Qualified Teacher
NUT	National Union of Teachers
NVQ	National Vocational Qualification
OFSTED	Office for Standards in Education
PAT	Professional Association of Teachers
PCET	Polytechnics Council for the Education of Teachers
PGCE	Postgraduate Certificate in Education
QCA	Qualifications and Curriculum Authority
QTS	Qualified Teacher Status

RSA	Royal Society of Arts
RST	Royal Society of Teachers
SCAA	Schools Curriculum and Assessment Agency (later QCA)
SCETT	Standing Committee on the Education and Training of Teachers
SCOP	Standing Committee of Principals (Colleges of Higher Education)
SEO	Society of Education Officers
SHA	Secondary Heads Association
TASC	Teaching as a Career
TEA	Teacher Education Alliance
TES	*Times Educational Supplement*
TTA	Teacher Training Agency
TUC	Trades Union Congress
UCEC	Undeb Cenedlaethol Athrawon Cymru
UCET	Universities Council on the Education of Teachers
UKCC	United Kingdom Central Council (for Nursing, Health Visiting and Midwifery)
WJEC	Welsh Joint Education Committee

Part I: Introducing the GTC

Introduction

First, the good news. For nearly 150 years, teachers in Britain have been trying to secure a general professional council, and recognition as a profession taking a large measure of responsibility for the service they offer the public. From the year 2000, all teachers have the beginnings of that opportunity. All qualified teachers in schools maintained by public authorities, and all teachers in non-maintained special schools will register with the new statutory General Teaching Councils for England and Wales and will become electors of those Councils. All other qualified teachers, whether in other schools, in other parts of the education service, in supply agencies or indeed not at present teaching, will be encouraged to register; in reputable independent schools this is likely to amount to an expectation. A GTC for Northern Ireland is to follow shortly; whilst in the Republic of Ireland a sound foundation has been prepared to start the new millennium. This book will focus as a case study on the build-up in England and Wales, and on the recent detail of the GTC for England; but the issues are common across the UK, between the UK and the Republic of Ireland, and well beyond.

The GTCs will be independent bodies recognized by statute and performing a public duty on behalf of teachers and those they serve. For the first time outside Scotland, which has had a GTC since 1966, teachers will be part of a profession with a large measure of responsibility for its conduct. South of the Border, teaching has been the only major profession in Britain without such a professional responsibility. The GTCs will not be government agencies, but independent self-regulatory professional bodies governed by a majority of registered teachers elected or nominated by peers, working in partnership with parents, governors, teacher-trainers, providers of schools and others vitally interested in education.

Registration brings with it rights, opportunities and responsibilities: the right to represent or be represented by other teachers in the body which will determine fitness to teach and will be the body with a statutory duty to advise the government and public on all matters related to the teaching profession, including training, professional development and teacher supply; the opportunity to help shape the future of the profession of teaching; and the responsibility to sustain and contribute to professional improvement in the public interest.

The opportunity for teachers and co-educators to take the initiative in shaping policy for their work is new and different in kind from what has been tried before. The GTCs are not consultative bodies, but have the statutory responsibility to advise, and will speak with the authority of their profession. They should be expected to become the prime source of advice on the qualities and qualifications to be required for entry to teaching; on the criteria for recognition of initial teacher education and training courses; on the criteria for completion of induction as a teacher; on professional expectations upon teachers; and on continuing professional development and re-training qualifications. Whatever bodies may in future accredit, fund, conduct and operate such courses, it will be the GTC on behalf of teachers and their public which will advise the government on what should be the professional expectations, and on what should be the criteria for professional acceptability.

How has that opportunity come about? That story is the second part of this book. The story is told not just as a record, but to illuminate what has been sought, what have been the blockages, and what has still to be accomplished to match professional and public aspirations. The legislation of 1998 which establishes the Councils for England and Wales is not the legislation proposed by the GTC movement. However, it has been amended during its passage through the Houses of Parliament to make it into a just acceptable beginning; and it has been accompanied by ministerial assurances that the role of the GTCs will be expected to grow. Moreover, the past belongs to the present in the sense that without the concerted efforts, of teachers and associated bodies, particularly since 1983, there would have been no prospect whatsoever of any kind of GTC by the year 2000, and even less prospect of legislation which could pave the way for a professionally and publicly acceptable one.

The third part of this book is a critical survey of the legislation and of the consultations and regulations arising from it, and shows what are the gaps between hopes and initial reality. The book invites all teachers and those concerned with teaching to work to reduce that gap, and concludes with proposals for a programme of further legislation in response to political assurances already articulated.

THE TEACHING AND HIGHER EDUCATION ACT

This Act, which is considered in detail in Chapter 1, received the royal assent in July 1998, following a consultation document and passage of a Bill routed through the House of Lords in parallel with the Education Standards Bill via the House of Commons, and most noticed for its section on student tuition fees. Its first chapter, which was debated with relative ease, provides for a General Teaching Council, expected to become separate but closely related Councils for England and Wales at an early date. Similar legislation is envisaged for Northern Ireland. The position of the GTC for Scotland is largely unaffected, although it is also included in the updating requirement to have regard to the needs of disabled people, and will accommodate the new powers accorded to inspectors to inspect the teacher training offered by higher education institutions in Scotland, already covered by GTC visitation.

For England and Wales, each Council will establish and maintain a register of those qualified to teach in maintained schools and in non-maintained special schools. It has the power to lay down standards of professional conduct and practice for registered teachers, to investigate breaches of conduct and to exercise disciplinary powers including prohibition, suspension and re-instatement as a registered teacher. After initial funding from the public purse, it will be sustained by registration fees and in effect owned by its members, not a servant or agent of the Crown.

The Council will have the duty to advise the Secretary of State on standards of teaching, standards of conduct, the role of the teaching profession, the training and professional development of teachers, recruitment to teaching, and fitness to teach; and it will have the power to give and publish that advice to others as it chooses.

Another section of the Act restores in England and Wales the requirement that all new teachers in the relevant schools must complete satisfactorily a period of induction, that the GTCs once established should be consulted on the standards to be expected for satisfactory completion, and that they should be bodies to which new teachers should if aggrieved, have the right of appeal for final decision. The Act is more fully described in Chapter 1, and subsequent regulations in Chapters 8 and 9, which together with the concluding chapter also envisage what will be the work of its first Council.

IMPLEMENTING THE ACT

The Act requires regulations to be made for the composition of the Council which ensure a majority of registered teachers and which also have regard to the interests of employers of teachers, providers of teacher training, those with special educational needs, religious bodies, parents, commerce and industry and the general public. Regulations are to cover the process of election and appointments, including Chair and Chief Officer. Parliament decided that it wished to approve these regulations before they are applied, and did so on 15 April (Commons) and 10 May (Lords).

Further consultation documents on composition for both England and Wales were published during the later stages of the Bill, and the resulting draft regulations were made ready early in 1999 for the approval of Parliament. An additional consultation has been pursued between April and June 1999 on the detail of powers and functions of the GTCs relating to registration and de-registration. The first Chief Officer, a most welcome appointment, is Carol Adams, previously CEO for Shropshire and for Wolverhampton. A temporary Chair and a small support staff will have been appointed by the autumn of 1999, the first elections to the Councils will be early in 2000, and the first full meeting by autumn 2000.

LIMITATIONS

As will be shown, the GTC movement has always envisaged that the roles and functions of the Council will be assumed by stages, so there is no quarrel with making a limited start to a change of such potential importance. The main difference of view is that the GTC movement has always pressed for a statutory framework which will enable development by stages to an agreed long-term aim without recourse to further primary legislation. Chapters 7 and 8 will examine this in detail. The government is less clear about future scope, and more intent on fitting the GTC into its stated priorities to raise standards. This is why it is all too easy to slip back into the negative modes of disbelief which for the last twenty years have been prevalent as a response to governments. The General Secretary of ATL, which has contributed constantly to the creation of the GTC, was quoted without context in the *TES* as late as 19 March 1999: 'The Government is trying to pass off a quango of its own creation as an authoritative professional body. It will become a glove puppet – a Sooty's consortium – and will command cynicism rather than respect.' That had seemed to be a real danger in the debates a year earlier, as shown in Chapter 8, and no doubt there needs to be vigilance that the danger should not re-surface; but there is now a real prospect that the GTC can grow into the authoritative professional body to which so many have aspired over so many years.

There are more deep-seated doubts which go beyond the particular topic of this book, but which must inform interpretation and action, even if only to avert the dangers to which they draw attention. They have to do with the political 'third way' expectation of private or non-government corporative initiatives, which far from rolling back the frontiers of the State may be seen to constitute a different and more powerful means of central regulation, of harnessing the will to autonomy and making that a more effective instrument of government than direct and overt government control, of pacifying potential opposition. Whether these doubts are justified will depend on what the GTC actually does and is felt to do. Even if the critique were shown to be justified, it could be argued that this situation could be preferred to what has gone before; but that would certainly not satisfy me – or, I believe, teachers and the public generally.

Ministerial assurances about future scope are helpful, and no purpose is served by being doubtful about them; but both the pressures and priorities of parliamentary time and the pressures and priorities of those bodies from which new powers would be transferred to the GTC will constitute a troubled environment in which to move forward. It will require even more shared professional vision, public credibility and political acumen to achieve what could and should have been anticipated in the 1998 legislation. This is one reason why parliamentary utterances have been quoted extensively in this book; they form a picture not only of growing political understanding and support of the GTC case, but also of commitments made which will have to be remembered when the time comes for the GTC to extend its scope.

The Act does not give scope to broaden the definitions of what is a teacher and what is teaching. Its requirements are limited to the school sector, and within that to maintained schools together with non-maintained special schools. It does not apply to further and higher education, and meanwhile other bodies are being created as training agencies or institutes for those sectors of the education service. By providing for separate GTCs for England and Wales, it creates the need but not the framework for co-operative links between them, and indeed leaves powers of co-ordination if necessary with the Secretary of State. This would in any case be a question to be addressed by the new Councils at an early stage with the GTC for Scotland. The detailed discussion in the following chapters is about south of the Border, but the issues are those being faced in all parts of the United Kingdom, in the Republic of Ireland, parts of Canada, Australia, New Zealand, and in my view are applicable across a rapidly changing Europe.

The GTC will have to assert its professional authority in territory which recently-created government agencies have occupied. The relationship with the Teacher

Training Agency is the most obvious one to be worked out, and this is examined in Chapters 6 and 13. There will be less obvious but no less arduous areas of negotiation with the Office for Standards in Education, and perhaps less conspicuously with the Qualifications and Curriculum Authority. The GTC movement has been crystal clear in distinguishing between the role of a GTC and the roles of employers and unions; that clarity is not yet reflected in the legislation. Above all, the relationship with the Department for Education and Employment itself will have to work. Access to information and the research capacity of the GTC in those areas directly affecting its responsibilities will be crucial.

There has been much anxiety about the initial location of the GTCs, particularly the eventual GTC for England. A decision based on cost-effectiveness would have to be based on an understanding of the long-term effects envisaged, and that is precisely what remains unclear. The only location which will work will be in the heart and mind of every teacher in the realm. That requires a location to symbolize the importance and independence of the Council. The initial location or locations provided by the Government will have been announced by the time this book appears. It will have its professional and political base in London, with a regional location for some administration. It will then be for the elected Council to determine its future.

It is not only location but accessibility which will be important. How closely will teachers identify with the GTC? Will their access be to the central Council or also to elected members? There was a strange dichotomy between the regional elections initially proposed for Wales and the lack of regional dimension in those for England. This also is examined in Chapter 13.

A PERSONAL POSITION

This book is seeking to inform reflectively. It covers the progress towards legislation for a GTC, the starting position and prospects for the GTC as the hallmark of the teaching profession. It has been the privilege of the writer to have been at the heart of the debate over the last twenty years, and for much of that time to bring together and help hold together the different views of the main professional constituencies of the education service. That has been a privilege which this book will try to record and not abuse. There cannot be an objective study from an actor, indeed activist in the process: rather, this book seeks to acknowledge and engage with the hearts and minds and professional aspirations of teachers and those they serve. It is a story of ever-recurring themes in ever-changing contexts. The sketching of background is not intended to be a balanced historical account, rather it should be seen as a personal view of balance; but it draws out those events which may be seen in retrospect to have had a bearing on the present day and the future. Much of the material used is unpublished, and drawn for the first time from GTC archives. The documentation will be a valuable source for future researchers.

Over the last twenty years, the aspiration for a GTC is the one important matter on which all the major education associations have agreed, during a period otherwise pit-marked by enervating conflict and devitalizing differences readily exploited by others in power or in the public eye. The processes of agreement deserve and have here chapters in their own right. Conceptualizing, co-ordinating and consolidating are Charles Handy's three verbs for education (Handy, 1994), and that is what is recorded here for the GTC. This is a case study in the management of significant change.

In any agreement there are aspects which are emphasized by some more than others, and although the first personal plural will be frequently found as shorthand to mean first the UCET-hosted initiative, then GTC (England and Wales), this book is ultimately a personal view and not the responsibility of the GTC movement. For example, what has already been signalled about a regional dimension is a question acknowledged but not pursued by many who have worked together to bring about legislation, whilst to me it appears to be a future necessity in a participative profession. Where possible, the writer will hope to clarify where the position taken is personal and not necessarily consensual. Every teacher has been shaped professionally by personal experiences, and every reader of this book is invited to share professional insights across situations, sectors, and generations. *Sein ist werden* for each one of us as for the new organization; and this book is about the GTC's beginnings, origins and future.

Chapter 1

The Council Comes to Life

Something quite remarkable has happened quietly. From the year 2000, the General Teaching Council is recognized in law as the independent professional body for all teachers, and will be the authoritative voice of the whole schoolteaching profession. In England and Wales, no such statutory body has previously been able to represent and develop the teaching profession, whereas Scotland has had its GTC since 1966. With Northern Ireland to follow shortly, probably at much the same time as its neighbour the Republic of Ireland, there is a completely new opportunity for teachers themselves, together with those closest to them, to transform the public role and image of teaching in those countries of Europe where teaching is arguably a free profession.

The GTC's aims are, in the interests of learners and the public, to be the voice of the whole teaching profession; to maintain and enhance high standards of public service; and to enhance the public standing of teachers. This is what teachers want, what the public wants, and at last what the government and indeed all political groups have recognized to be essential. Through the GTC, teachers have the opportunity and framework to lead and shape and be partners in change, through a Council drawing on the experience, knowledge and commitment of over 400,000 serving practitioners and their public contexts.

WHAT THE GTC WILL DO

How is this to be done? Will the Council have real powers and responsibilities? The GTC now has the responsibility in law to advise the government and others on the recruitment and supply of teachers; on initial teacher education and training; on the induction of newly qualified teachers; and on continuing professional development. It has a legal right to be consulted on any future changes in the standards required for entry to teaching. It keeps the register of all those who are qualified to teach in schools; registration with the GTC has become a requirement for practising as a teacher in a maintained school or an independent special school; and it will no doubt become an expectation in any other school of public standing. The Council will determine what the profession expects of teachers, and is the body to set out standards of professional conduct and good practice. On behalf of teachers and their public, it now takes from the government responsibility for withdrawing or withholding registration on grounds of professional misconduct, and it is expected to advise on such action in cases of child protection and medical fitness. Outside Scotland, all this is entirely new. Government statements recorded in Parliament indicate the likelihood of wider powers, if need be through later legislation, once the GTC has become firmly established.

THE WORK OF COUNCIL MEMBERS

How can teachers and the public be sure the GTC is genuinely independent? After initial start-up government funding, it will fund itself: that is to say, teachers will fund the Council by annual registration fee. It will be as credible as teachers and other constituents can make it. Starting in the autumn of 2000, the Council of 64 members is to include at least 34 teachers either serving or with very recent teaching experience; 25 of them directly elected, and nine drawn from the six principal schoolteaching associations or unions. The national elections will ensure a spread of teachers from five constituencies: eleven teachers of children below the age of 12, eleven of learners between 12 and 19, one teacher drawn from a special school, one primary and one secondary headteacher. Election will be for four years. These 34 teachers are to be joined by 30 other members, some from within the education service and others representing key public interests: parents, governors, employers, minority groups. After the initial appointment of a Chief Executive and temporary Chair, who have worked to prepare for the first Council, the Council will elect its own Chair and appoint its own officers.

What is it going to be like to be a Council member representing fellow teachers or other related groups? That, at the time of writing, is about to be discovered by the pioneer group. It is a huge challenge. The experience of Scotland is an indicator, but the roles are not identical and the circumstances are very different in the much larger nationwide constituencies of England and again the more compact constituencies of Wales. The structures and initial arrangements for the first Council in England will have been informed by two years' work of the GTC Unit set up in the Department for Education and Employment, by a GTC Partnership group drawing on a membership broadly matching the interests to be represented in the elected Council, and by the Chief Executive appointed in the summer and temporary Chair by the autumn of 1999 to make ready for the Council. But there is no doubt that the council members themselves will now determine how they can most effectively work, and how they can ensure that future Council membership is fully accessible to active teachers.

Publicity was modest while consultation was continuing, and regulations on powers and duties were still being negotiated. An information leaflet for teachers was drawn up early in 1999 by the GTC Partnership group with the endorsement of member associations, and after an abortive DfEE shot was circulated again with their help. From the autumn of 1999, there has been a campaign and nationwide advertisements to ensure that all teachers eligible to register to vote in the teacher elections have the opportunity to do so. Until now, incredibly, there has been no effective way to trace the whereabouts and current activity of qualified teachers not employed as teachers or drawing teacher pensions; no wonder campaigns to return to teaching have not worked! The GTC can hope to involve, not just for casting their vote, those who are engaged in a break from teaching and may wish to keep up to date and re-enter. It is encouraging registration by all teachers qualified to practise in schools, even though they may be working in further or higher education or other parts of the education service, including the independent sector. Up to half a million may be expected to register and it could be more.

Invitations to nominate teachers to stand for election to the first Council include mail-shots to all schools, in reasonable time for those standing to make arrangements in their schools. Appointments by the Secretary of State follow advertisements and invitations to nominate or make application. The full Council was due to be announced in the late summer, and the first meeting and opening will be in the GTC's first premises, at the start of the first full school year of the millennium.

How will 64 members and their officials work? It can already be seen that the Council has both regulatory and advisory responsibilities, which sometimes overlap. The regulatory tasks are to do with registration and professional discipline. They include acting as a final appeal board for those who are judged by employers not to have completed satisfactorily the new induction period. This new function is not the same as in Scotland, where the GTC itself has responsibility for the two-year probationary period. Nobody knows how many teachers will not complete satisfactorily, how many of those will appeal, and whether these will appeal to industrial tribunals or the GTC or both. Until autumn 2000, this function is being handled by the DfEE, and some initial experience of numbers and case studies is being built up. The numbers are likely to be in three figures, and the regulations published in the autumn of 1999 provide for a statutory committee procedure for induction appeals. Some Council members will be found to focus on this responsibility. Discipline cases are also an unknown quantity. At present, the DfEE handles 400–500 cases each year which may or may not lead to listing under its Section 99 as people unsuitable to be employed as teachers. The GTC is likely to operate more openly. A committee is proposed to investigate complaints or referred cases and to decide whether they should go to a discipline committee. Both committees would include a majority of Council members. Both would be serviced by officers, with legal expertise or advice. Controversially, a further committee is proposed for cases of serious professional incompetence. This may well be changed.

What of the advisory role, considered in greater depth in a later chapter? In order to advise on standards of teaching, the role of the teaching profession, its training, career development and performance management, recruitment and teacher supply, the GTC will no doubt work with an overall teacher education committee, having sub-committees on each major area of initial training, induction, continuing professional development and supply, and with a research capacity; or it could have full standing committees on such key areas with perhaps a co-ordinating group of those chairing. Either way, there will be between four and six major areas on which to focus, each made up of Council members. The Council will be expected by teachers and the public to build up a significant body of authoritative advice in each of these key areas in the four-year span of the first Council, as well as responding to questions and providing advice requested by the government.

Add to these functions the organizational ones: probably some kind of executive committee covering administration, registration, finance, premises, public relations, negotiations; key external linkages, for example with the other GTCs; liaison, for example with government agencies, with FENTO, or with ILT; and the international dimension, particularly the European development work and comparability of qualifications. The pre-Council work of the GTC unit, Partnership group, Chief Executive and temporary Chair has been to put enough in place for the Council to start functioning; but beyond the statutory committees required by schedule or instrument to carry out regulatory duties, it will be for the Council to determine how best to manage its affairs. What is immediately apparent is that there will be a very strong commitment on each member of the Council, and particularly on the teacher majority, until it becomes clear how much time can be given by those appointed by representative bodies or by the Secretary of State, and what scope there is for co-option. Development work can be commissioned and preparatory or follow-up work delegated to officers; but it is difficult to see how the Council can function without each member being involved in at least two of the major committees and engaging in working development groups, as well as having an overall understanding and decision-making capability over the whole field. Each member will have the task also of communicating with the electoral constituency. This must be supported by GTC information, publications, media publicity and a web page.

How can this be managed at the same time as being a full-time teacher or running a school? There must obviously be scope for replacement staffing, and it may well be that secondment for at least one year of the four should be allowed for, if members are to be able to devote themselves to making this a Council which really becomes the voice of the profession, a dynamic and authoritative source of advice, with a major impact on the teaching profession and the way it regards itself and is regarded. These are some of the demands which must inform the decision to stand for election to such an important body.

ORGANIZING THE GTC

The GTC for England is a large new organization. Its Council members, mostly full-time teachers, require a dynamic organization, comprehensive service by officers, and resources for information, communication and development. The annual income from registration fees alone will by 2002 approach £10 million. The start-up period of three years is funded by the government. The Council will make additional charges for some work, such as induction appeals and applications to re-register. The Council may well decide to become a registered educational charity and attract further income by donation for particular purposes. From this income it pays for most of its activities: advisory service, registration, premises, equipment, staff salaries, meetings, communications, and the expenses of members.

The Chief Executive Officer was appointed by Nolan rules in the summer of 1999, initially by the Secretary of State, drawing on the advice of independent assessors. After an initial period of three years, it will be for the Council to decide on this and all other appointments. The job and person specification were drafted by the DfEE and modified after comment from the GTC Partnership group. South of the Border, this is a new kind of post. It is not to be compared with, say, the chief executive of government agencies like QCA or TTA, nor with a local authority CEO; these are professional advisers to politically appointed councils or elected committees of lay persons depending on the CEO for professional advice and leadership. By contrast, the GTC itself is the authoritative voice of the profession and incorporates the public interest.

Until the Council comes together and is able to determine its own activities, the Chief Executive and a small support staff have been consulting and planning for the Council to be able to discharge its responsibilities, drafting a corporate plan, appointing further staff, setting up shop. Inevitably, the Chief Executive has been drawn into public statements about the GTC even before it comes together; how else could teachers' and public attention be attracted? After inauguration, the task will be to:

- represent the Council's considered advice and carry out its decisions on professional issues;
- co-ordinate its activities in an effective organization with an agreed corporate strategy;
- connect the Council with a large range of other organizations;
- communicate across the Council and to the public.

Rightly, this was seen to demand high qualities of professionalism, leadership, strategic thinking and planning, effective management, communication, negotiation and representational skills. Again, Scotland provides an exemplar, and Ivor Sutherland, the Registrar of GTC for Scotland, has been a constant source of advice and inspiration; but again, the job is different in scale and function. Of other professional bodies, only UKCC is dealing with comparable numbers.

The Leader of the Council will be the Chair, as soon as possible elected from and by the Council itself. Again, this is not like the leader of an LEA or a Minister, who will be lay people providing political leadership but depending on professional advice from officers; this will be the leading elected representative of the professional council. Much will depend on the flexible working relationship established between the Chair and the Chief Executive, and the support and understanding they have from and for the Council.

Are we expecting too much of the GTC? That is of course a danger. On the one hand, if it is to symbolize a sea-change in the relationship of teaching and government, and in the profession's morale and public image, it has to represent that change in action, and to build confidence from the outset. On the other hand, gradualists will argue that it has to have time to grow, to learn from experience, to start from modest beginnings, and indeed not to exceed its brief. There is truth and urgency in both these views, and they do not need to be incompatible. It is important for teachers to have in mind what, after all the debate recorded elsewhere in this book, is actually on the face of the Teaching and Higher Education Act 1998 and the ensuing regulations, both as a framework for current work and in order to build and work towards future legislation.

THE TEACHING AND HIGHER EDUCATION ACT IN DETAIL

Part I of the Act is entitled *The Teaching Profession*. It has three chapters. Chapter 1 is headed 'The General Teaching Council', Chapter 2 'Head Teachers', Chapter 3 'Teacher Training'. In Chapter 1, the first seven Sections are headed 'The General Teaching Council for England', whilst Sections 8 and 9 on 'The General Teaching Council for Wales' make it clear that Sections 2 to 7 apply also to Wales as well as making specific provision. The Act requires that there shall be a GTC for England, whilst enabling the Secretary of State to make provision by order for a GTC for Wales. That textual difference derives from the stages of the Bill in which it was originally envisaged that a GTC would be set up for England and Wales, to be followed by the separate bodies. What remains does, however, appear to give greater powers to the Secretary of State for Wales, who is enabled rather than required to establish a GTC, Cyngor Addysgu Cyffredinol Cymru, and who may require it to promote teacher recruitment. It is intended that the Secretary of State's powers will transfer to the National Assembly for Wales.

Section 1 incorporates the principal aims of the Council:

(a) to contribute to improving the standards of teaching and the quality of learning;
(b) to maintain and improve standards of professional conduct among teachers, in the interests of the public.

The Council is to be composed of teachers; employers of teachers; providers of teacher training; persons concerned with teaching those with special educational needs; religious bodies involved in the provision of education; parents of pupils; commerce and industry, and the general public, together with such other interests as the opinion of the Secretary of State will enable the Council to carry out their functions more effectively. Regulations must provide for a majority of members of the Council to be registered teachers, either currently or recently employed as teachers.

Section 1 also governs the first schedule of the Act, the small print. It sets out the financial and employment powers of Council, enables regulations to provide for the appointment or election of one of the Council members to be chairman, and for the appointment or election and tenure of office of members of the Council, and provides for committees: some may be required by regulations for specific purposes; others may be for any purpose as decided by the Council. Regulations may also stipulate membership and procedures of the required committees. The Secretary of State may be represented on any committee by participant observers and has a right to documentation. The Council is required to make an annual report, which it may also publish, to the Secretary of State, who in turn is required to lay a copy before each House of Parliament. The Council accounts must also go to the Comptroller and Auditor General, whose report with the statement of accounts must also be laid before each House of Parliament. So there is regular opportunity for parliamentary scrutiny and attention.

Section 2 sets out the advisory functions of the GTC, which are, as they think fit or as the Secretary of State may require, to advise the Secretary of State and others he may designate or the Councils may choose, on standards of teaching, standards of conduct for teachers, the role of the teaching profession, training, career development and performance management of teachers, and medical fitness to teach, and on such other matters as the Secretary of State may require, which may include his powers to prohibit and exclude teachers from employment in any particular case. The advice the Councils choose to give is to be advice of a general nature, and it may publish its advice. These provisions also apply under Section 9 to the GTC for Wales, where in addition the Secretary of State may require the GTC to undertake or share activities designed to promote recruitment or continuing professional development.

Section 3 requires the Council to establish and maintain a register of teachers, sets out terms of eligibility for registration, including a reference to induction requirements (see Section 19 of the Act), and Section 4 provides for regulations to cover aspects of registration. Section 11 requires persons employed at schools covered by the 1988 Act c. 40 to be registered (these are all maintained schools and also independent special schools), and Section 12 deals with regulations for the payment and collection of registration fees. Section 5 enables regulations to authorize the Council to issue and revise a code laying down standards of expected professional conduct and practice, and to take proceedings against registered teachers failing to comply, whilst Section 6 covers a second schedule conferring disciplinary powers on the Council. This schedule provides for regulations for the Council to investigate alleged unacceptable professional conduct, 'serious professional incompetence', or previous conviction of a relevant offence, and, where there is a case to answer, to take proceedings and to take disciplinary measures which may include reprimand, conditional registration, suspension or prohibition from teaching. The schedule also sets out the right of appeal to the High Court.

Section 7 enables the Secretary of State by order to confer or impose additional functions on the Council, after appropriate consultation, to advise him whether a person is a qualified teacher, and to maintain records on categories of persons other than qualified teachers. Section 13 requires the Secretary of State to consult the GTC before making or varying regulations about the standards required for qualified teacher status, whilst Section 14 requires both the Secretary of State and the GTC to supply each other with 'such information as he considers it to be necessary or desirable for them to have' or 'such information as he may request' for their functions relating to teachers. It also usefully requires the GTCs for England and Wales to share information necessary or desirable for their work. Finally under this Chapter clauses are inserted into the Teaching Council (Scotland) Act, bringing the GTC for Scotland within the same duty to have regard to the requirements of disabled persons, and requiring the Secretary of State for Scotland to have regard when nominating to the desirability of the Council reflecting the interests of persons teaching those with special educational needs.

Chapter II (Section 18) enables the Secretary of State to make regulations which require headteachers in England and Wales to possess a professional headship qualification. Whilst this will not affect the GTC directly, it will be part of its duty to advise on the training of heads along with other teachers, and the qualifications being developed and the training for them, including the proposed new National College for School Leadership, can be expected to be under the advisory scrutiny of the GTC.

Similarly, the work of the GTC will be strongly affected by Chapter 3, 'Teacher Training', which makes two major provisions. The first in Section 19 is to enable regulations requiring an induction period for teachers 'at relevant schools'. Whilst the GTC has the duty to advise on induction, the procedures for induction will not be the responsibility of the GTC as they are in Scotland; instead, the regulations (not the Act itself) are introducing the GTC to be responsible as the place of final appeal. This is discussed in a later chapter of this book. The second provision on teacher training in this part of the Act (Section 20) is to enable the Chief Inspector to inspect and report on any initial and any in-service training of teachers or specialist teaching assistants for schools and, when asked, to advise the Secretary of State on such matters; and it enables the Chief Inspector to advise the GTC or a funding agency on such matters, and to report and publish as appropriate. Furthermore, Section 21 establishes the same powers on the Secretary of State for Scotland to inspect higher education teacher training, through HM Inspectors or other persons appointed for that purpose. Since in Scotland the GTC carries out visitations to accredit training institutions or programmes, a *modus vivendi* will have to be worked out there, whilst in England and Wales there will have to be accommodation of GTC and Chief Inspector advice.

Consultations before and after the passing of the Act, and resulting regulations and decisions are considered in later chapters, which will look to the future. This, however, has been the starting point from which the GTC must develop. There is, partly as a result of informed and timely parliamentary pressure, just enough there for the Council to begin and to become effective. There is scope and hope for the future, and that must be earned by the early Councils and pressed into the future legislation indicated in Ministerial assurances before Parliament.

To demonstrate that this can happen, the next section of this book traces from its origins how the GTC has come to this starting point. In the past are the seeds of the future. Growth will be in an uncharted environment; but it is the gap between those aspirations which have brought the Council to life, and its modest beginnings which will inform the journey still to come.

Part II: How the GTC Has Come About

Chapter 2

A Backcloth

BACKGROUNDS OF TEACHER TRAINING

The history of moves towards a GTC has to be seen in a context of what has been perceived to be a qualified teacher, teacher supply, and the tension between qualification and remuneration. It must also be understood in a uniquely British context of the growth of professional councils for other professions (the General Medical Council having been established in 1858), whereas in other European countries the licence to teach was derived from university and State. The story goes back to the Middle Ages, though here only briefly, to show that blend of qualities and qualifications which has ever since been sought in changing contexts.

The medieval Master's Degree in Grammar was in effect a licence to teach 'sound learning and good manners' and the Bachelor Degree a qualification as second master. God's Hall at Clare Hall Cambridge was established because of the acute shortage of masters to teach grammar outside the universities, and may be seen as the precursor of teacher training colleges in England. The seventeenth-century statutes for Chigwell School contain many of the elements translated into stages of nineteenth- and twentieth-century expectations: they specify that:

> The Latin schoolmaster be a Graduate of one of the Universities, not under Seven-and-twenty Years of Age, a Man skilful in the Greek and Latin tongues, a good Poet, of a sound religion, neither papist nor Puritan, of a grave Behaviour, of a sober and honest Conversation, no Tipler or Haunter of Alehouses, no Puffer of Tobacco; and above all that he be apt to teach and severe in his Government.

The 1662 Clarendon Code reasserting adherence to the 39 Articles of the Church of England was formally withdrawn as late as 1869.

Particularly in the nineteenth century, the debates about higher qualifications for teachers centred on whether this would attract higher quality or whether with higher qualifications graduates would prefer more highly remunerated employment than teaching. So the 1847 report of the Commissioners of Inquiry into the State of Education in Wales includes a member's view that:

No person, really qualified for the office of schoolmaster by moral character, mental energy, amiability of temper, and proficiency in all the elementary branches of education, together with aptitude in imparting knowledge, will doom himself to the worst paid labour and almost the least appreciated office to be met with in the country.

Were even the means of training schoolmasters as ample as they are defective, and were the number of men adequately trained to the work at hand, the generality of schools would be not one jot the better supplied, for such training would fit men for employment in other spheres, where they would realise four or five times the emolument and enjoy a much higher social position than they can hope for as schoolmasters in Wales under existing circumstances.

It is nearly 140 years since the first moves were made towards a General Teaching Council. The College of Preceptors first made a proposal for a 'scholastic council' in 1862. In 1879, Dr Playfair sponsored a Bill to Parliament, and in 1889 two Bills were drafted and considered by a Select Committee of the House of Commons, one for secondary teachers in England and Wales, the other for all schoolteachers in the United Kingdom. The 1899 Education Act made provision for setting up a register of teachers.

Teacher–State relations in the twentieth century were convincingly analysed by Gerald Grace (1987) as moving through four phases:

- confrontation (1900–20);
- political and union rather than professional identification and role (1920s–30s);
- partial social democratic and professional consensus (1940s–mid-1970s);
- the return of a politics of confrontation (1970s–80s).

The last-mentioned period may now be seen to have extended to the mid-1990s. Time and history will tell how this may now be evolving. I shall hope to show that a conceptual change is now possible, rather than a return to mere compromise, and that the GTC now sought could represent a key feature of that change.

The Board of Education Act of 1901 laid upon the Board the duty to establish a Teachers' Registration Council. However, this was a period of hostility between civil servants and elementary schoolteachers. Civil servants under Sir Robert Morant produced divisive proposals for legislation which could not survive (compulsory registration without fee for elementary schoolteachers, voluntary with fee for secondary), and the Council was abolished in 1906. The confrontation with schoolteachers in turn contributed to the enforced resignation of Morant in 1911, and in 1912 an acceptable voluntary Teachers' Registration Council was established by order of the Privy Council. Despite unproductive attempts in times of civil unrest to establish political control over teachers, whether by making them civil servants or by introducing a Seditious Teachings Bill or demands for enquiries into political indoctrination in schools, Lord Percy as President of the Board of Education persuaded fellow-Conservatives that greater State control could be turned against them by a future Labour government. Instead, he successfully encouraged teachers to be trusted not to mix with politics, e.g. the General Strike of 1926, and the elevation of the Registration Council in 1929 to become the Royal Society of Teachers may be seen in this context. Its statutory duty was to establish and maintain the standards of academic attainment and professional training among teachers, and it admitted to Registration as Associate Members those who had reached the required standard, and as full members (MRST) those who had then completed a period of approved teaching experience. This voluntary society was intended to precede registration for all practising teachers, but sadly the 1944 Education Act did not include the necessary legislation, and the Royal Society of Teachers was wound up by an Order in Council in 1949. However, what Grace identifies as an ethic of legitimated professionalism continued to be observed by NUT and Joint Four, until gradually undermined in the next two decades by declining salaries and the rise of more confrontational unions and NUT splinter-groups. This professional ethic and the conditions necessary for its exercise were moreover recognized by perhaps the most notable Permanent Secretary that the new Ministry of Education and the subsequent Departments of Education, Education and Science, or Education and Employment have seen. This was John Maud (perhaps best known for his later chairing as Lord Redcliff-Maud of the Royal Commission on Local Government which reported in 1969). 'Freedom', he was to write in 1952, 'is what the teacher needs more than anything . . . perhaps the most essential freedom of the teacher is to decide for himself [sic] what to teach and how to teach it' (Lawrence, 1992).

The McNair Committee in 1944 had meanwhile recommended a single scheme of remuneration for primary and secondary schoolteachers, area training boards and a Central Training Council, but its principles of professional status were largely ignored, and the subsequent National Advisory Council for the Supply and Training of Teachers can be seen to have heralded the divisive features of the Weaver Report in 1970. At least McNair ended the restrictions on marriage for teachers and led to a reconstituted Burnham Committee, now given statutory recognition by the 1944 Education Act, to recommend for the remuneration of teachers on the same basis across primary and secondary schools, and eventually to the phasing in of the same salary scales for men and women by the 1960s.

By 1957, renewed pressure began for a GTC, resisted in 1959 by David Eccles, and more disappointingly (as shown below) by Anthony Crosland in 1965–66. Meanwhile in Scotland the Committee chaired by Lord Wheatley recommended in 1963 (Scottish Office, 1963) 'that there should be established a General Teaching Council for Scotland broadly similar in scope, powers and functions to the Councils in other professions'. The Teaching Council (Scotland) Act ensued in 1965, the Council being established in the following year.

In 1968, the incoming Secretary of State for Education, Edward Short (now Lord Glenamara), announced his intention to establish a General Teaching Council and established a working party chaired by (later Sir) Toby Weaver, with all the teachers' unions and associations, universities and teacher-trainers, LEAs and the DES. There was much difference between the teachers and the civil servants. Although the Weaver Report in 1970 considered the case for a professional council already to have been accepted, and did much detailed groundwork which is still valid, it recommended a division of functions under two separate Councils, one for registration and discipline, the other for training. This division, together with the recommended composition of the 'rump' GTC, failed to command full professional support. Similarly, the 1972 James Committee's proposal for a National Council for Teacher Education and fifteen Regional Councils did not command support, and all that emerged from Weaver was the Advisory Committee on the Supply and Training of Teachers. For the next decade, successive governments were to declare themselves in favour of a GTC, provided teachers' associations could agree on its composition. By the time the associations appeared able to do so, government ministers had become divided on the issue, and were raising different questions in a changing context.

In 1978, on entering the discussions among associations to explore whether progress could be made on a GTC, I was able to catch the much more positive spirit of what had happened twenty years earlier, from a colleague, Leslie Scott, long-standing Head of City of Bath Boys School. One of the last letters he wrote is reproduced here partly to show the threads of professional and indeed personal continuity (Charles Thompson was my first head before I moved to a school in Bath and came to know the writer), partly to show how clear much the same issues and tensions were which had to be revisited in the 1970s, 1980s and 1990s.

Bath, 15.4.78

Dear John,

You know all about this – the modern campaign was inaugurated at the 1958 NAHT (May Conference on a proposal made by myself as chairman that year of the Bath Council of NAHT). The formula was worded by H. M. Porter, a Division IX HMA Council member. He and I on behalf of Division IX persuaded a rather reluctant HMA to accept the NUT desire for the definition of a 'qualified teacher' to include approved professional training (with special entry allowable for older graduates to satisfy the common practice of HMC schools).

This cleared the ground and a joint committee was formed with Ronald Gould (NUT) as chairman, F. L. Allan for HMC/HMA, a Headmistress (was it Diana Reader Harris?), Sheila Wood and Hutchings for Assistant Masters and Mistresses, and Terence Casey for NAS (NUT resisted recognition of NAS, but we got him in) and the then NAHT secretary (1964 or so). F. L. Allan died in the first few months and HMA put me on in his place, as the chief advocate of the idea in HMA Council. Several very good meetings were held – and NAS became very keen, even claiming it as their own idea!

I remember Gould telling me privately that he doubted the ability (and quality) of his own council to carry such a degree of professional responsibility, as they had too often been too soft with professional misconduct.

With the graduates reconciled to the diploma for graduates requirement, we approached Crosland in 1966(?), through Derek Morrell, for his approval and support. Morrell, the best civil servant the Department of Education ever had, was already launching the Schools Council as a means of helping teachers towards accepting and being ready (in all senses) to carry the burdens of the responsibility of self-government. Crosland listened, said he would consider it, then fobbed us off. But his successor, Edward Short, ex-member of NAHT, promised (I think indeed 'pledged') his support.

Meanwhile the NUT insisted on a built-in NUT majority on the Schools Council, and took the same line on TGC proposals – and the 'movement' came to a standstill. The NAHT has continued since 1959 annually to reassert its belief that a TGC is a top priority. I doubt whether HMA maintained its full-hearted support after I retired from Council. But a first-class HMA report on Teacher Training by a working party under S. C. Thompson of Brockenhurst GS [in fact Itchen GS] was adopted, which I'm sure would still read well. It asked for a far higher element of school participation in training, and full movement between school and college staffs. (The separate Lecturer scale was always a barrier to free two-way flow. It should be incorporated in Burnham.)

The Scottish (all-graduate) experience of their Teachers Council showed up some difficulties, but I'm sure the idea is still sound – and its hour may at last have come. The heart of the matter is RESPONSIBILITY FOR . . . on which real stature and full involvement (commitment) ultimately depends.

Cross's *Observer* article over-emphasises the dismissal element. But in 1958–59 I made very effective use of the fact that the Fascist Colin Jordan could only be dismissed, disqualified, by his employers, Coventry LEA, whereas a doctor or lawyer would be disqualified by his fellows.

Your move!

Sincerely

Leslie Scott

This highly personal account reflects well the impact on teachers of policy deliberations often recorded more cautiously. Crosland could not agree to relinquish control of entry to the profession at a time of teacher shortage or 'a transfer of controls over the fundamental matters of teacher recruitment from the Government to the proposed Council' (*The Head Teachers Review*, July 1966), and had obviously not been advised of the reserve powers in the Act which had created a General Teaching Council for Scotland in the same session of Parliament. 'Fobbed off' is not far from the facts.

The reference to Colin Jordan raises questions which have not been addressed since. At the time, however, much as after World War I, the political safety of children was a commonly voiced concern, and from the 1950s, equivalents of McCarthyism or *Berufsverbot* were being exercised or proposed in a policy vacuum.

The reluctance of NUT to sit round the same tables as the new NAS in the 1960s was to be mirrored in the 1980s by NAS/UWT's difficulty in recognizing the PAT, newly recognized by Mark Carlisle. It may be worth noting, however, that teacher disunity in the 1960s did not prevent the creation of the Schools Council, and has been too easily seen as the stumbling block for a GTC, dire though inter-association meetings certainly continued to be.

1978–79 EXPLORATIONS

Of the meetings for a GTC held in 1978, the October gathering of twenty representatives from NUT, SHA, AMMA, NAS/UWT and NAHT brings out all the inter-union problems. For some, Weaver was dead; for others it was still a deal. A NAHT member Matt Camish 'ruefully reflected that in the late 1960s the battle had been with Mr Weaver and his colleagues but recent events had engendered a state of affairs where the teachers' associations were fighting amongst themselves', and that is reflected in the record. It was indeed surprising that this vitriolic meeting decided one more attempt would be made to see whether progress could after all be achieved.

A meeting of 11 June 1979 was of a smaller group, itself an advantage. It was not so acrimonious. There was careful discussion of the involvement of NATFHE and the FE sector. In one respect, the meeting marked a breakthrough when Alan Evans of NUT indicated that his union might consider moving from its insistence on an overall majority and accept a measure of direct election; the meeting was closed by the chair when it became clear that NAS would not countenance the NUT suggestion; but having foreclosed, discussion continued, and it was suggested that associations put written responses to the new proposal (which had taken everyone by surprise) and any of their own, so that the joint hosts, NUT and Joint Four, could decide whether it would be productive to convene again. Of the responses made, that from NAHT (with which SHA was able to indicate broad agreement) was particularly interesting in its formula of weighted representation, and may be seen to have informed the proposal put later to the UCET-hosted initiative and adopted by GTC (England and Wales), both in its own constitution and in its outline for a statutory council.

1979 saw a change of government. Shirley Williams as Secretary of State had been positive and encouraging about a GTC, provided teachers could agree among themselves, and indeed she was to remain so in the House of Lords. The new Secretary of State, Mark Carlisle, was an unknown quantity, and was charged with an immediate Bill to introduce policy changes. However, a barrister himself, he was equally supportive of a professional council, and in a speech in the summer of 1980 he declared:

> I will give all the help and encouragement I can to the establishment of such a Council, but I must emphasize that it would defeat the whole object of the exercise if Government itself set up such a Council. Such a Council, as with the Law Society, should be independent of Government, a separate, self-regulating disciplinary body for the teaching profession. Here too is another way in which teachers can enhance and strengthen their profession, and I would welcome it.

Unfortunately, he chose the NUT annual conference to announce this view, but was greeted by booing, not for this part of his speech, but for being there as a Conservative Secretary of State at all. His later account (Ribbins and Sherratt, 1997) confirms his continuing support despite what he took to be negative union views. For the record, it is worth noting that his address and responses to questions on a GTC when invited to the Council of SHA over which I was presiding at the time were very strongly applauded; no wonder Edward Simpson, the Deputy Secretary accompanying him, remarked to me on the way out that such a reception had done a power of good.

There may have been another reason too: the government needed help. A letter I wrote to *The Times* in the same week 'from the President of the Secondary Heads Association and others' was to be echoed in 1990 by the House of Commons Committee on Science Education and the Arts, and could be written again today:

From government sources, from committees of inquiry, from professional surveys, and from the frightening shortages in individual schools, there is now incontrovertible evidence of the protracted and worsening shortage . . . of well-qualified specialist teachers in the very subjects which have been identified as essential to the nation's economic recovery: mathematics, physical science, technical subjects and foreign languages.

This fundamental difficulty will not be resolved by mere wishing. It grows steadily worse, despite government awareness and a national will to extend the teaching of these subjects in all schools. There is either less time given to these key subjects in the hands of expert practitioners, or an increasing proportion undertaken by others. Whichever happens, the problem is compounded.

A massive drive is now urgently required to bring many thousands of well-qualified and well-motivated teachers of these specialisms into the nation's schools. It must be concerted: the Government has somehow, despite and because of the economy's frailty, to invest in a programme to recruit, train and retrieve the numbers needed.

The reconstituted Advisory Committee on the Supply and Education of Teachers must be asked to give this matter the highest priority both for initial and in-service education. It is our plea that there should be more planned and deliberate interaction between all kinds of establishments for higher education, the schools and other places of work. Acceptance of the Clegg commission's findings will have gone some way in helping to restore confidence among potential teachers that a career will be offered to them which is not only eminently worthwhile, but may bring with it a salary no longer seriously out of line with that which they could expect in other employment.

We urge our colleagues in schools, colleges, polytechnics and universities to work together to improve young people's understanding of teaching as a profession, and to help them identify these areas of grave shortage. We would like young people to register the view that schoolteaching is a profession of vital importance to the health and prosperity of this country, worthy of consideration by those having the highest ideals and most able minds in all disciplines. (*The Times*, 20 June 1980)

The letter, co-signed by the Chairs or President of HMC, GSA and the Committee of Directors of Polytechnics, illustrates also the importance attached at that time to concerted action across all sectors of education, as reflected strongly in the GTC proposals to be made in the next decade. It contrasts with the initially limited scope of the General Teaching Councils now emerging.

CATEC

The Campaign for a General Teaching Council (CATEC) was instigated by (now Sir) Robert Balchin in 1980, supported by the College of Preceptors of which he was Treasurer. There were encouraging noises from the Minister of State Baroness Young and from Lord Glenamara (Ted Short). CATEC came close to succeeding, and in the attempt served to restore the issue to public and professional attention. It published a News Sheet, organized discussions and a day conference in May 1981. Bob's tireless visits to teacher associations brought him to a formula of composition on which he considered they might agree, and after a year he was ready to approach the Secretary of State. Himself a Conservative County Councillor in Surrey (though scrupulous to ensure that CATEC was cross-party), he hoped to make that approach as an insider.

By this time, however, Mark Carlisle had been succeeded as Secretary of State by Sir Keith Joseph, who was not amenable to even discussing the proposal. As Bob Balchin was to record ruefully two years later:

> If only I could get some sense into Sir Keith Joseph! Unfortunately he remains totally unconvinced about the prospective efficacy of a General Teaching Council and so, all the while that he remains Secretary of State, there is no chance that CATEC can push its recommendations any further . . . We have decided, therefore to put the Campaign into the deep freeze for a while but it will certainly be thawed and resuscitated as soon as there is a political change at the Department of Education and Science . . . Sir Keith Joseph finds himself totally out of sympathy with the kind of professionalism for teachers we support. I have talked to him reasonably about many other things, but this one he shies away from . . .

It should be recorded as a strand of continuity that Bob Balchin was to become a member of the working party for the later UCET-hosted initiative, and that the princely residual funds of £56 were donated to the working party from CATEC when it wound up. This was to be the only formal funding for the UCET-hosted initiative throughout the 1980s.

THE JOINT COUNCIL OF HEADS APPROACH

The Joint Council of Heads was a consultative body across NAHT, SHA, and the independent heads' associations. It met regularly but inconspicuously through the 1970s. In 1978, NAHT had initiated discussion of a professional code of conduct for the teaching profession, and had hoped this could be a way forward, despite the impasse over composition, to the 'Teachers' General Council', as it was still being called. In 1981, when I was chairing JCH, the proposed code was adopted with minor amendment by that body and commended to all its associations. This also gave us a cause to seek a meeting in 1982 with Ministers, with something positive to offer towards re-opening discussion of a GTC.

The JCH found junior ministers sympathetic, particularly Rhodes Boyson and later the perennial Bob Dunn, but at the DES meeting with Rhodes Boyson there were two reactions: the first was to confirm his own interest (which he was to maintain throughout his parliamentary career) but to point through the ceiling without words that Sir Keith Joseph would not be moved; the second was to comment that a Council would have to be elected by direct franchise. When told that the National Union of Teachers had already abandoned its insistence on a majority and had mooted direct elections as a means to resolve the differences among teacher associations, he was so surprised to be in the same camp that he swivelled right round in his chair, arms aloft in mock horror. But at least the approach in 1982 drew from Sir Keith Joseph, in addition to the customary response that the government would first require broad agreement among teacher associations, the written comment that he would also have to be satisfied that the public interest was adequately represented. Those representing

JCH, including David Hart of NAHT and myself as JCH chair, were able to note this as a point of view which could be shared, now that teachers had adjusted positively to the Taylor Committee and to the consensus on partnership in school governing bodies.

The NAHT/JCH example of a code of conduct is published, together with other teacher associations having a variety of codes and rules of conduct (Harris, 1996) and this essential question as groundwork for a GTC was to be addressed by GTC (England and Wales) and in particular by Meryl Thompson in the 1990s.

TEACHING AS A PROFESSION

Overshadowed perhaps by the 'Great Debate', but in many ways more productive at this time was a new scrutiny of teaching as a profession. Through the 1970s and into the 1980s, major studies of the professions were to filter into policy rhetoric if not yet into policy deliberation. It was an area of intellectual controversy, particularly among sociologists. From Millerson's definitive work in 1964 (which did not include teacher associations in its qualifying list) through to Peter Gosden's study of the evolution of school teaching as a profession (Gosden, 1972), to the challenge of Jenny Ozga and Martin Lawn (1981) there is a rich debate, with major contributions by Eric Hoyle from 1969 and Hugh Sockett from 1976. The ground was being well prepared, and the issues being addressed were those which were to inform debate twenty years later. Indeed, two of the major sources of thinking on this topic, Eric Hoyle and Peter Gosden, were to continue to play an active role in bringing about a GTC.

Chapter 3

The UCET-hosted Initiative 1983–90

DEVELOPMENT WORK IN ENGLAND AND WALES FOR A GTC

The attempts by CATEC in 1980–81 and by the Joint Council of Heads in 1982 to persuade the government had been unsuccessful; but even more seriously, the teachers' associations were no closer to agreement, whilst continuing to confirm that in principle they would support a GTC.

The breakthrough came in November 1983. Representatives of the teacher associations while guests at the annual conference of the Universities Council for the Education of Teachers (UCET), responded to the lead given by a discussion paper from Ian Morgan, President of NUT:

> Although problems about composition remain apparently intractable, the teachers' associations have an obligation to respond to the White Paper 'Teaching Quality' by convening yet again meetings to explore the possibility of a Teaching Council. The teaching profession has never been offered an organ of self-government and has not been able to achieve it through its own endeavours. There is nothing on offer at the present time, and any consensus that the teaching profession can trawl from its collective disarray will be difficult to deliver. The effort must be made, however. (personal paper, 19 September 1983)

The associations asked UCET, as the least threatening and most impartial body in sight, to host an attempt to reach the agreement they all desired but had failed to find among themselves. The UCET chair that year was occupied by Professor Alec Ross, and the response was encouraging.

By this time, another change was approaching in the political–professional context. The last major representative advisory council, the Advisory Council on the Supply and Education of Teachers, was coming to the end of its five-year tenure, and most of us were aware that it was unlikely to be renewed, despite very active and productive work since 1980. ACSET had established new criteria for teacher education and training, including far-reaching recommendations related to special educational needs and ethnic minorities, and had consented uneasily to the establishment of a new government body proposed from the DES, the Council for the Accreditation of Teacher Education. Some of us had hoped that ACSET would continue to be the representative body advising on the criteria to be applied by CATE; but the announcement in 1983 that ACSET would not be renewed in 1995 made it clear that professional judgements were to be firmly controlled by government. ACSET was of course the successor to the Advisory Committee on the Supply and Training of Teachers (ACSTT), which had been the outcome of the 1970 Weaver Report and had taken forward the James Committee recommendations. So now teacher educators were to lose their representative advisory body too, and Alec Ross was supported in responding positively to the GTC approach, provided a consensus could be found.

A large representative but informal meeting of sixteen associations was convened by UCET on 26 April 1984. A consensus was registered for pursuing the proposal of UCET-convened meetings, and a first conference of associations was agreed for 3 October 1984, to be informed by conference working papers from associations. The UCET record of that conference shows that the main questions to be addressed in the next two decades were in mind; it also shows very clearly that the imminence of CATE was an additional spur towards a GTC. 'All felt that the existence of a GTC would obviate the need for a Council for the Accreditation of Teacher Education' (Minute 3 a iii) and 'Universities were likely to be happier with a relationship with GTC than with CATE, a government body' (Minute 3 f). An amendment to the minute which registered that 'the private sector could also eventually be involved' reads 'registration would be a requirement for practice in the profession, from both the private and the public sector' (Minute 3 d). The initial focus was to be on primary and secondary schoolteachers, but a formula was sought which did not exclude those working in other sectors, and questions relating to further education could be addressed at a later stage. It was acknowledged that local authorities would need to be involved and the place of voluntary associations also considered.

A working party was established to draw together the conference papers and discussion to produce a document on the roles and functions of the GTC, and how a suitable climate of opinion might be generated, by the following spring. Seven individuals were nominated, not as representatives of their associations, but in fact drawn from SHA, NAHT, SCETT/PCET, NUT, NAS/UWT, AMMA, and CATEC/CP, with myself to chair. The conference was confident enough to issue a press release announcing the working group; looking back, it is possible to relish the words: 'The aims of the group are long term rather than short term'.

The working group held three meetings between October and January, followed by three drafts of the paper to the conference of March 1985. Its papers on roles and functions, finance and organization and on GTC composition already represent a blueprint for what was to be proposed and much of what was to be adopted through the 1980s and 1990s. However, it invited the second conference of associations not yet to endorse its papers as recommendations, but to address the issues raised so that the working party could work further on them.

The record of this second conference shows even more clearly the impetus of other developments: the announced future demise of ACSET and the start of CATE.

It was pointed out that when CATE was set up ACSET existed as a representative body recommending criteria by which CATE was to operate. Any review of criteria was to go back to ACSET. CATE was a nominated, not a representative body, and this would have been objected to more strongly if it had been realized that there would be no representative body like ACSET to refer back to. (Minute 2 b)

The question is similar to that which was later to arise in the relationship of GTC and TTA, and which has still to be satisfactorily clarified.

The conference of associations was positive, productive, and encouraging. It agreed that the working party chair should revise the proposals, have them scrutinized by member associations, and invite specific questions on size and representation. The working party would address promotional strategies. The conference would be reconvened in September 1985. Again, the transactions were accompanied by a press release. A small group of journalists – George Low of *Education*, Bert Lodge of *TES*, Lucy Hodges of *The Times*, were by now making regular comment and probing ministerial intentions.

Parliamentary questions were continuing to draw Sir Keith Joseph, but without modifying his response. On 23 July 1985 he was asked by Edward Leigh what representations he had received towards the establishment of a General Teachers' [*sic*] Council, and replied:

> In 1982 I received requests from the Campaign for a General Teaching Council, the Joint Council of Heads and the Professional Association of Teachers for an enquiry into the possible establishment of a Council. Rt Hon and Hon Members and others have enquired from time to time about my views on the case for a Council. I have replied that I would need to be convinced that such proposals commanded wide support and safeguarded the interests of producers and consumers alike, before the Government could consider whether to support the establishment of a Council. (*Hansard*, 23 July 1985)

The GTC technical working party was having to come to terms with the 'producer-consumer' language without adopting it. It was to be the language of successive Secretaries of State for the next decade. Contact with DES officials to keep them informed of progress and to gauge likely responses was more helpful. Hilary Douglas, for some years the only woman in a recognizable position of the DES hierarchy, and one who had shown outstanding ability in her work with ACSET, summarized the position in a letter of 26 July 1985:

> As you imply, there is still some way to go before the teachers' associations collectively are ready to put agreed proposals to the Secretary of State, and it is therefore difficult for me to anticipate the reaction which they might receive. One, perhaps self-evident, observation is that he would be unlikely to be prepared to relinquish control over the criteria for initial teacher training and the conferment of qualified teacher status unless he were satisfied that appropriate arrangements would exist for the setting and safeguarding of standards. He would also need to be satisfied that the body would act positively within its powers, in collaboration with employers and other interested parties, to promote teaching quality. A closely related theme is, of course, the safeguarding of the consumer interest, which the Secretary of State has not attempted to expound in detail in this context, but which would certainly include appropriate provision within the membership for what you have termed the 'client interests'.

Such comments certainly helped the working party in its drafting. The revised document and specific questions were circulated in May; available responses (eleven) were to be collated by the working party in July in readiness for the third conference of what would, after delicate negotiation, become seventeen associations to include PAT; and a three-year action plan for promotion and implementation was proposed. This was a meeting demanding and receiving all the mediating and conciliatory skills of Alec Ross as Chair, but it led to further stages, more technical exploration for the working party, full space for each association to provide a considered response, and a fourth meeting of associations to be held in March 1986. By this time, the national media had become more aware of the initiative, and an excellent article appeared in the *Times Educational Supplement* ('Softly, softly for 100 years', by Carolyn Dempster, 3 January 1986).

It had become evident that a very clear distinction would have to be drawn between GTC functions and matters of employment and conditions of service, to be seen as negotiated between government, employers and unions.

In the working party note to the March meeting, I was recording that: 'during a period of great difficulty, it has been a pleasure to be part of a working group which has been committed to a task beyond any one interest, and has somehow found time to meet and communicate regularly' (10 March 1986).

The working party had indeed achieved a unity of purpose and was identifying the danger that it would go beyond its brief, which was not to become the promotion group. Having provided an outline as requested for a development action plan, it also invited the meeting to consider what kind of steering group should direct the task of promotion.

However, this was an even more difficult meeting and it required all the goodwill on most sides and chairing skill to make progress without division. The stage had been reached when associations had scrutinized in detail, and there were some challenging and therefore eventually very useful disagreements. There was not yet a consensus on whether the GTC should limit itself to schoolteachers or should seek to embrace the whole educating profession and its constituencies. One large school association asserted that a GTC for schoolteachers only was unacceptable, whilst NATFHE and AUT at that time were hesitant about involving members other than teacher-educators. There was difficulty in addressing the setting-up stage, and how far the eventual composition and functions of a GTC should be predetermined before further approaches to the government, or how far left to the initial and transitional body to shape. On the whole a short transitional period was favoured whilst compiling a register, to be followed by a previously agreed and legislated composition.

The gathering was still far from the consensus required to contemplate action, but as one association recorded to its members: 'however, contrary to everyone's predictions, the show has remained on the road' (NATFHE, 25 April 1986). Two sub-groups of the working party were set up to resolve issues related to further education and among teacher-educators, for the working party to incorporate and report to a further meeting in September 1986.

This was yet another difficult and testing meeting. At the time it was exasperating to working party members, and revolved round many of the same issues. It had however succeeded in clarifying thinking about further and higher education, and about teacher-educator views (despite one acrimonious exchange of correspondence on whether or not minutes should include professorial title!). In retrospect it is worth recording that it introduced John Tomlinson (see Chapter 4) to these meetings for the first time, and the record shows already how his careful and informed comments during this baptism of fire would help resolve issues through the 1990s. Finally, it was agreed that members should take the consultative document to their Executives with the composition attached as a feasibility example, and that the constitution of the Council would be the sole agenda for a full meeting in December 1986, prior to what it was hoped would be an adoption meeting in February 1987. No approach would be made meanwhile to the government until 'further consensus' had been reached.

It should be remembered that this was the period in which it was becoming clear that Sir Keith Joseph would not long remain Secretary of State, when the 1986 legislation was being enacted and when the government was in effect securing control of public examinations while adopting the GCSE proposals. The government had rid itself of the Schools Council for Curriculum and Examinations, despite a positive independent review, and had put to sleep the Advisory Committee for the Supply and Education of Teachers, the last representative advisory body. Relations with government in general continued to worsen. Even as late as 1985, surveys had shown a majority of teachers would vote for the government party; that support was very soon to be lost.

There were moments of surprise; during his short stay as Minister of State for Education, Chris Patten was to voice not only general support for a GTC but to make the unlikely suggestion to a PAT conference (July 1986) that if the teachers could not soon agree, the government would have to intervene and impose one. At least that demonstrated that the government did not know how close teachers were to agreement. However, the associations were not yet ready for my suggestion that we seek a conversation even with Chris Patten, let alone Kenneth Baker, whose actions in the next two years were to make discussion mutually unacceptable.

Other voices were being raised more publicly. Mary Warnock in the Dimbleby Lecture of 1986 spoke out very strongly in favour of a GTC. It was perhaps unfortunate that she at that time suggested such a body would also be involved in salary matters, and this inhibited expressions of support for her general proposal. Baroness Warnock was later to become a valuable protagonist in her writings and in the House of Lords. Another awkwardness arose later in the 1980s through the splendidly energetic initiative of Gerald Smith, head of St Peter's Independent School in Northampton, who for five years used all his dramatic verve and flair to summon together the great and the good to promote a GTC with maximum publicity, being viewed – he would probably agree – as something of a knight errant. Both these very different public expressions of support for a GTC caused some difficulty in the quieter coaxing which was being led by Alec Ross; but importantly they helped keep the question in the public eye at a time when the associations were not ready to do so.

So on to the sixth meeting of associations in December 1986. The larger associations wished to ensure a clear elected schoolteacher majority, and presented without notice an alternative proposal to that effect, whilst most smaller associations favoured the working party proposal as a basis for further discussion, since it allowed for an eventual coverage of the whole profession.

It became evident at the meeting of 17 February 1987 that the association most reluctant to move ahead was more affected by the external climate of current hostility with the government than with the proposals themselves. Alec Ross proposed from the chair 'that the meeting would commend the paper as a model of a GTC on which they would like to have the views of the associations represented, recognizing that not all the details would be acceptable to all the members, but hoping that the broad principles would'. This was accepted, but of course it was far from the agreement needed to proceed further. There was considerable bitterness expressed after the meeting at what appeared to be the blockage by one association of an aspiration so nearly realized. It could be seen, however, that the association in mind had been consistent with its declared policy. There was rumour in the press that it would withdraw from the initiative and thereby destroy any hope of consensus, but this proved ill-founded. The working party, which had already developed a promotion campaign proposal needing £300,000 over three years, seemed to be back at the drawing board. In the event, however, once the larger associations recognized that they would not have the support of the majority, the working party suggestion for composition of the Council was accepted *nem con.* as a basis on which to proceed. It should be emphasized that it was for a proposed initial period, during which the GTC would recommend modification within the general principles agreed.

The remaining problem was what to do about it, and by 1987 there was no mood to approach the government. The new Secretary of State, Kenneth Baker, was either not talking to teachers or teachers were not talking to him. An introductory personal letter from the UCET initiative was barely acknowledged by a civil servant. Eventually, Kenneth Baker curtly declined to meet to discuss the proposal. This was to prove typical. It did not require post-modernist deconstruction for the new incumbent to start from scratch without reference to the 'educational establishment'. No sooner had teachers agreed on a newly piloted approach to conditions of service and appraisal than the agreement was swept aside and virtually the same elements imposed instead, it seemed, as a matter of principle. The Burnham Committee on Salaries and Conditions of Service was abolished. The 1988 Education Reform Act completed the task of securing central government power over schools, at the expense of local authorities. Nothing would be countenanced unless it was part of the government agenda. The junior minister Michael Fallon was the most inclined towards a GTC but was not available as a discussant. However, the UCET-hosted meeting of 7 November 1988 sought another route, and passed a series of resolutions not only for its member associations, but to the House of Commons Select Committee on Education, Science and the Arts, currently examining teacher supply.

This meeting:
– conscious of the evident need for the morale of the whole teaching profession to be raised and, incidentally thereto, to make teaching more attractive to the well-qualified entrants needed to ensure that the national curriculum is fully implemented for every child and,
– whilst acknowledging that under present arrangements real progress towards the creation of a General Teaching Council for England and Wales will be possible only with the co-operation of the Secretary of State,
– declares that it is unwise for the present system of detailed control by the Secretary of State over a profession such as teaching to be continued indefinitely and therefore

– calls upon the Secretary of State to arrange a round-table conference to examine the arguments for providing the teachers of England and Wales with such a body. (Issued 9 November 1988)

Alec Ross informed the Secretary of State of progress made and expressed willingness to be approached; an equally civil and distant response was received in January 1989, asking to be kept informed.

The working party had argued that the time to raise the profile was at least three years before expecting progress towards legislation, and wished to work in anticipation of a window of opportunity rather than wait for it. From 1987 to February 1988 I was taking informal soundings on ways forward. There were also encouraging off-the-record discussions with Jack Straw as Shadow Secretary of State, and with the Liberal Democrat spokesman. When I proposed publication of the document and wider discussion through a series of regional seminars, there was polite permission but no financial support. So the agreement was published at personal expense within a monograph, *Towards the General Teaching Council,* in advance of a series of seminars early in 1989, in Manchester, Warwick, Salisbury, Huddersfield, and Swansea (one in London having to be cancelled), publicized through the press and through local leafleting. Invited speakers included Ian Morgan (a reminder of 1983), John Tomlinson, who was soon to take the central role, Gordon Kirk from the GTC for Scotland, the Chair of NCPTA, and Kenneth Miller, founder Secretary of the Engineering Council. The seminars were not a success in terms of dissemination, but the document was soon to play a fuller role. Subsequent revisions were simply to add to the numbers of associations in agreement and membership, and to modify terms such as 'licensed teacher' which were to acquire a different connotation.

The publication proved to have been timely. On 5 April 1989, Lord Glenamara (former Secretary of State Ted Short) initiated a debate in the House of Lords to ask the government to establish a General Teaching Council. He was able to refer to the UCET-hosted initiative, to the regional seminars and to the published document, which was extensively used in the debate. There was informed and persuasive support from Lords Beloff, McNair, Taylor, Dormand, and Baroness David. Despite the negative tone of the government spokesman, Lord Henley (a former Chief Education Officer for Berkshire), the only speaker who seemed not to have read the document and who was raising questions already answered in it, this debate can be seen as a turning point from the 1980s, and the opportunity for political progress to be made.

The July conference was faced with alternative ways forward. The Select Committee was inviting evidence on the Supply of Teachers, an issue which as we have seen penetrates as a political crisis in each decade. The government was imposing the 'licensed teacher' scheme, which was to prove both expensive and unproductive, whilst in Scotland a GTC could state that it would be unacceptable and was able to agree with the Scottish Office a professionally respectable 'wider access' scheme instead. New proposals to consolidate CATE, and a network of regional boards for teacher education, were on the table. The House of Lords question and debate on a GTC proposal had put the issue back on the political map. Other associations were showing interest in becoming involved. Lay interest was being shown: an encouraging letter to *The Times* by Peggy Pyke-Lees, whose husband had been a long-standing registrar of the GMC, led to welcome pressure on the government from her network; but the meeting of associations needed to decide how to involve such supporters. These questions were referred to associations, to prepare for debate in October.

The conference could organize itself to choose the right moment for a renewed approach to government; it could broaden and strengthen the base of associations involved; it could decide to improve its dissemination of information; it could update and develop the agreed consultative document; it could make common cause on single issues related to a GTC; and it could make a start by setting up a non-statutory body.

The October 1989 meeting showed that whilst the consultative document had been agreed, there was still disagreement about acting on it. One association suggested that the timing was not right, and it should be left for some years; this was a scarcely veiled reference to the expected span of the current government, with which dialogue was not considered possible. There was disagreement about extending the membership of the invited conference, especially from those anxious to ensure a majority of teachers (however defined). The disagreement extended to the membership of the proposed company, for which articles and memoranda were tabled. So the technical working party was asked to reconvene and negotiate an extended document for full meetings in November and the following February, the latter to be the formal AGM of the still-dormant new company, and then to have a separate session for the 'wider group' of supporters.

Two surveys had meanwhile shown a high level of support among teachers for a GTC. A Gallup Poll conducted by the *Daily Telegraph* showed 80 per cent of teachers wanted a GTC, a higher percentage than shown for any of the reforms under way. A much fuller and more detailed survey by the College of Preceptors of over half its membership (which it pointed out tended to be in senior school positions, as well as a minority from higher education and local authority advisers) showed 94 per cent in favour, with a range of preferences about composition and modes of election. It was interesting to note from the preliminary analysis made available in confidence that a small majority favoured parental involvement, a large majority inspectors and advisers, but only a small minority at that time favoured involvement of governors. There was a very strong majority for a binding code of conduct, but a range of views on what it should include. An even stronger majority from all sectors of the education service considered there are identifiable skills and knowledge which all teachers and educators should possess, but again with differing views on what these are. The survey was valuable in identifying many of the issues which would have to be addressed both in preparing to set up a GTC and in its work once established.

By the meeting of 6 February 1990, most of the issues had been resolved. Five more associations had been invited in to what was now described as the Forum; other supporters were drawn into the extended forum. Two other factors were at play: first, a new Secretary of State was replacing Kenneth Baker, and it was agreed that Alec Ross would write (though as an individual) to explore the possibility of a meeting; and second, it was realized that a GTC proposal might play a part in the run-up to a General Election, especially if the Select Committee as hoped were to pronounce in favour. This and the following meeting on 30 April made real progress in organizing for the future. The Royal Society of Arts had sponsored a meeting on 20 February, at which eight of the nine speakers (including Jack Straw as Shadow Secretary of State) had spoken strongly in favour of a GTC, whilst the ninth had confessed afterwards not to have been aware of the new nature of the proposals. The HMI for teacher training was by now involved as an observer. The Association of Metropolitan Authorities seemed to be turning towards a more favourable stance. The directors and secretary of the company were elected harmoniously, with one place left for co-option. After six years of intensive work, there was a mood to make progress together.

Two further related events were to crown the efforts made in the UCET-hosted initiative. First, the publication of the Education, Science and Arts Committee Report on the Supply of Teachers for the 1990s, which made clear recommendations (§§ 23, 25 and 26) for a General Teaching Council, quoting the discussion document in doing so.

> 23. We consider that a forum in which new ideas can be discussed is vital to developing partnership and improving the morale of the profession. We therefore **recommend that an advisory body, on which teachers are represented, should be established. Projections and action on teacher supply should be among the major topics for discussion by such a body. We believe a General Teaching Council (see paragraph 26 below) would be a suitable body to undertake this task.**

> 25. *Involvement in the running of the profession:* In discussing a possible national advisory body, the AMMA in their evidence to us suggested this might be 'a helpful precursor to an independent General Teaching Council'. We have been extremely interested by the idea of such a professional body. Three important functions for such a body might be regulating methods of training, developing professional standards, and monitoring professional conduct. It could also act as a forum for views on topics in education, e.g. teacher supply.

> 26. The General Teaching Council is not a new idea: there has already been 'a century of aspiration followed by a generation of disappointed initiatives' as a discussion document on a GTC put it. We recognise that establishing a GTC would involve reconsideration of other policies and bodies, including as further review of the role of CATE. However, we believe that the positive effect on morale from a properly constituted and effective council warrant such effort. To move forward on this, we consider that a lead from central government is essential and we therefore **recommend that the Government create a General Teaching Council to work for the enhancement of the profession.** (ESAC, 1990)

Second, related to this, the meeting took place on 5 June of Alec Ross, Mary Russell and myself with the new Secretary of State, John MacGregor. We recognized, and indeed Clive Saville, the under-secretary for teacher training was at pains to brief us, that the aim in current contexts must be not to secure a commitment but to re-open or prevent closure of the very possibility of a GTC. John MacGregor, a lawyer like Mark Carlisle and also a listener, could accept that the teaching profession would wish to have some responsibility for exits and entrances. The meeting also resulted in a named contact from the Department, Stephen Mellor, becoming involved in GTC deliberations. However, there was no prospect that John MacGregor could persuade the cabinet of Mrs Thatcher, including his predecessor; in the event, his response, that the government would not accept the Select Committee recommendation *in the near future* (Command Paper 1148, 1990) was the most that could have been hoped for. It was the only major recommendation in the ESAC report which was not acceptable to the government. Like one of his predecessors, Timothy Raison, the Conservative Chair of the Select Committee, Malcolm Thornton was to continue to be a strong supporter of the GTC proposals, as will be seen.

UCET had by now played its part. The servicing and hosting of the GTC initiative was a very considerable additional undertaking for the administrative secretary Mary Russell. Alec Ross had offered and given six unstinting years and had achieved all that could have been hoped for. His memorandum to associations in October 1986 had already set out options for the future and anticipated a stage beyond UCET's 'neutral territory'. The document on roles and functions had been endorsed in 1987, together with the suggested composition commended as a basis for discussion, the associations having eventually agreed they could all 'live with it'. In October 1989, UCET reminded the associations that its time as host was up, and it would become just one of the seventeen associations. However, Alec Ross and Mary Russell agreed to continue until the new company had been set up, and were indeed to continue to play key roles; this was to be acknowledged in gratitude in June 1990, when they judged it timely for the initiative to organize itself for the future. Without Alec Ross, it is difficult to imagine the level of agreement which had been reached, and the tributes paid to him in the House of Lords debates echoed the feelings of all who had been involved in a painful but most productive process informed by his patient vision. The UCET-hosted GTC initiative was the only example in the 1980s of the education profession coming and staying together, acknowledging and resolving differences, preparing to work as a GTC would have to work. It was the one meeting place for the profession and its constituencies, in most other matters torn apart in reactions to a hostile government. And it worked, forming the basis for that continuing and expanding forum to take positive action through the 1990s.

Chapter 4

GTC (England and Wales):
From Agreement to Activity 1990–91

By 1990, a working agreement had been reached across the teaching associations. Of course within that agreement or accommodation, there were variations of enthusiasm or priority, but there was no longer resistance to action towards a General Teaching Council. While maintaining a clear majority of teachers, the agreement had moved beyond the Burnham Committee basis of schoolteacher representation, even before that Committee for negotiating salaries of schoolteachers was abolished by a non-negotiating government. The scope was extended to teachers in other sectors of education, teacher-trainers, further and higher education, advisers, education officers, educational psychologists; the public interest as represented by parents, governors, the world of work; and providers of schools and training institutions, including local authorities, churches and higher education managers.

There are two vital elements in this extension, marking a clear change from the past. The first is the recognition that schoolteaching by itself, whilst the most important part of the teaching profession, does not constitute a profession in the full sense. The second is the involvement of the public interest, since the very basis of a professional council is its duty to the public. Given the moves since the 1970s in particular towards the involvement of parents as co-educators, the growing importance of governing bodies, and the development in some areas of community schools and colleges, what was emerging was a new form of professionality: what I tried to describe as 'open professionality'. Ironically, this new partnership may be seen to have been furthered by common cause made by teachers, parents and governors in opposing the actions of a government which did not wish to be in touch with teachers, and had wrongly assumed that parent and governor power would be a conduit for government programmes.

GTC (ENGLAND AND WALES)

Another quiet initiative in March 1988 was to form a registered company, GTC (England and Wales) in order to ensure that there was a recognizable entity to take over from the UCET-hosted initiative once the associations were ready to make further moves, and to create a body which could receive and generate funds for development. Incorporated in August 1988, the first directors were Mary Russell and myself, but we kept the company quiet, indeed dormant, for a year. It was to be the link between the 1983 initiative and the work of the 1990s. It was offered to the invitational review conference, an extended gathering, on 3 July 1989, and those associations were invited to take up membership which agreed with its principles and which were being proposed as members of the eventual statutory Council. Its memorandum and articles of government were a direct translation into company terms of the agreed roles and functions for a GTC, to which was added the purpose of acting to secure a GTC.

(a) to promote the establishment of a statutory General Teaching Council for England and Wales, which will serve the following purposes:

i.   to advise the Secretaries of State on matters (other than remuneration and conditions of service) relating to the supply and education of teachers;
ii.   to determine minimum qualifications for entry to initial training, the length of initial training, and general criteria for its nature, coverage and quality;
iii. to accredit existing and proposed courses of initial training in England and Wales, and to decide on the acceptability of training and qualifications obtained elsewhere;
iv.   to be solely responsible for conferring eligibility to teach by registration with the Council, and to maintain the register of all persons eligible to teach in England and Wales;
v.   to maintain professional standards of conduct in the education service, and to determine whether in any particular case registration is to be withdrawn, refused or reinstated;
vi.   to advise employers and the Secretaries of State on the continuing training and development of teachers throughout their professional careers in the education service, and to recommend an accreditation of existing and proposed courses of in-service education and training designed to permit access to designated areas of the teaching profession;
vii. to recommend good practice for the induction of teachers to first posts and to posts with significant change of responsibility;
viii. to advise the Secretaries of State and employers on targets for numbers to be drawn back to teaching from other careers or breaks in career, and on appropriate provision of courses and other support for successful re-entry or change of direction in the education service;
ix.   to promote research and enquiry in fields closely related to the Council's functions;
x.   to disseminate information and advice about the profession and to make representations to government and other agencies on matters within its remit.

(b) In furtherance of the foregoing object to liaise with the teaching profession and its representative associations, with statutory and non-statutory educational bodies, and with others representing key public interests.

The transition from the UCET-hosted initiative to a self-sustaining organization, the company registered as GTC (England and Wales) in the previous year and left dormant until adopted, was agreed on 6 February 1990, at the thirteenth meeting of the Forum of Associations, now extending to 22 major associations. Full membership was reserved for associations which accepted the general principles of the agreed document and which were included in the proposed constitution of the future statutory Council. A 'wider forum' now included other bodies and individuals which had declared their support.

The next meeting in April 1990 elected eight Honorary Directors and an Honorary Secretary. Whilst it was emphasized that once elected they represented the whole body of associations and not just their own, the election showed an awareness of the value of drawing on and including the major associations. Directors were elected from all six school associations together with the College of Preceptors and the independent schools. I became the Honorary Secretary. There was a high level of continuity from the UCET technical working party. One vacancy was left open. The constitution allowed for Directors to select their own chair, and to co-opt.

By the summer of 1990, I was able to record both for members and for the public the stage reached, for example in the following paper to the Labour Front Bench team, while awaiting a government response to the ESAC recommendations. The Labour team at that time was particularly strong: with Jack Straw were such people as Hilary Armstrong, Derek Fatchett, Andrew Smith, and also there was Tessa Blackstone, who was to introduce legislation eight years later.

THE GENERAL TEACHING COUNCIL PROPOSALS

This paper invites discussion of the recent moves towards establishing a General Teaching Council for England and Wales. It introduces the concept of 'open professionality' on which the proposals are based. It refers to some of the attempts made in the last twenty years to establish a GTC. It outlines government-related responses. It describes the nature of the proposals which now form the basis of agreement in principle across 23 major associations of teachers, parents, governors and teacher-trainers. It looks ahead at some of the issues still to be addressed.

The Select Committee on the Supply of Teachers has now given a strong recommendation to a lead from Government in creating a General Teaching Council, as the appropriate advisory body on teacher supply, as the professional body to regulate training and professional standards, and as a key to improved morale.

THE GENERAL TEACHING COUNCIL PROPOSALS

Introduction

Teachers carry out an essential service in the public interest and according to the public will. They have the ingredients of a profession, without the hallmarks. In a recognisable profession, its members would subscribe to a professional ethic. It would take a large measure of responsibility for the way it works. Its activity would be founded on a distinctive body of knowledge and substantial research. It would require intensive initial training updated and improved by professional development. All those elements are around, but by such measures, no one branch of the education service, such as schoolteachers alone, would be described as a profession in the full sense. Put together, the education service certainly could be. Education is lifelong and lifewide, but historical accident has trapped teachers in separate public or private sectors and hierarchies, all with their separate national and local organizations, and most with their own career routes. There is no vehicle for the whole profession to match the wholeness of learning and to serve a whole educative society.

Most teachers have a sense of their shared professional purpose not being articulated, and whether through their separate associations or through Gallup Poll and other surveys have shown very clear support for the creation of a General Teaching Council for England and Wales. But educators are also looking ahead, and are re-interpreting what a general council for a professional public service should and should not be.

It should reflect the professionality of the whole service. To express the measure of responsibility for the development and discipline of their profession, trained, registered teachers (in the broad sense of teaching) are a majority in shaping policy. That professionality is not, however, a private domain. A full profession has to have a public identity, over and above the protection of special interests. Education is public business, not because a government may say so but because learning goes beyond the institutions and is the job first of parents and then of everyone else to take on from childhood. Parents, governors, other areas of employment, local and central government and other employers of teachers are inside a GTC, sharing and informing the professional responsibility. Jibes about cartels or mediaeval structures are simply ill-informed and themselves out of date.

Previous initiatives

The teacher unions tried and failed through the 1970s to reach agreement on seats round the GTC half-table suggested by the Weaver Committee (DES, 1970). The College of Preceptors attempted a campaign in the early 1980s, combining insider knowledge of the ruling party with honest broker negotiation across the associations, but the insider trading broke down as soon as the brokerage looked productive. The Joint Council of Heads tried again in 1982. The present initiative dates from November 1983, when some of the teacher association guests at the Universities Council for the Education of Teachers (UCET) annual conference asked that most unthreatening of bodies to host another attempt to reach agreement. Perhaps the imposition as a government-nominated body of the Council for the Accreditation of Teacher Education (CATE) gave added motivation to UCET to accept the invitation. It is remarkable that through all the bitterness and division of the years 1984–89 the forum of associations remained together on this one issue of a GTC, and have this year moved beyond the need for UCET's mediation.

Twenty-three major associations have agreed in principle the text of a proposal for the General Teaching Council. They include all the unions and associations for teachers in maintained and independent schools, further and higher education, advisers and officers, bodies for the education and training of teachers, parents, and governors. Employers are involved in consultations, and would be involved in a statutory GTC, but will properly remain neutral in any campaign on the way. The Forum of 23 Associations also has the support of several other major groups such as the Campaign for the Advancement of State Education (CASE), the National Association for Primary Education (NAPE), or the Association of Principals of Sixth Form Colleges (APVIC), which would doubtless have a strong input to particular aspects of a GTC.

The forum of associations has now expressed its unity of purpose by setting up a legally recognisable body to promote these aims, a company limited by guarantee, GTC (England and Wales). So there is now a single body through which to negotiate details within a text of agreed principles to which member associations agree.

Recent government-related moves

The Scots have had their GTC established by statute for a quarter of a century now. South of the Border, a GTC was at the same time recommended and frustrated by the Weaver Committee. What Weaver (DES, 1970) proposed was a half-GTC, for registration and discipline, with a composition to which nobody could properly have agreed, alongside a separate advisory half-body on supply and training of teachers, born as the Advisory Committee on the Supply and Training of Teachers (ACSTT), reincarnate as ACSET, r.i.p. 1985.

From the mid-1960s to the mid-1980s, successive Secretaries and Ministers of State, and opposition spokespeople, declared themselves in favour of a GTC provided the teachers could agree what they wanted. Keith Joseph was less positive than predecessors or than his junior ministers, wanting (quite properly) to ensure that the public interest would be served. His successor, more interested in power to the DES while he was there, was unresponsive. However, elsewhere in the same régime, there has been massive government support for the creation of the Engineering Council. Even more interestingly, this government established the English National Board, bringing into one professional council three professional branches of the Health Service. The government recently briefed Peat Marwick to conduct an efficiency review of this new professional council, with a specific instruction not to address the issue of whether or not the Council should exist. The Peat Marwick report nevertheless came out very positively indeed, not only in terms of the Council's effectiveness but in terms of its value to professional confidence, responsibility, morale and motivation. Last year, the April debate in the House of Lords showed clear support on all sides for a General Teaching Council.

Relevant extracts from this year's report from the House of Commons Select Committee on the Supply of Teachers show strongly in favour of a GTC, as a central recommendation.

The Secretary of State will have made a response by about the time of the Labour Front Bench conference on teacher training. The Select Committee findings are clear on two counts: first for the GTC as a suitable body to take on advice on supply and training to fill the gap left after ACSET; but even more strongly on general professional grounds. There would seem to be political mileage in taking on the initiative or giving it sufficient encouragement for future credit.

The nature of the Forum's agreed proposals

The GTC would, as now conceived by the Forum of Associations, be the overarching professional body to determine or advise on the necessary standards of training, qualifications and conduct appropriate for public recognition as a teacher entrusted with helping to educate future generations, or for an initial trainer of teachers. Part of its function would be to give or withhold recognition for qualifications and training in Scotland, the EC, and abroad. The GTC would maintain the register of those so recognized and entitled to teach, in the first instance in schools and professional aspects of initial teacher training, and would determine whether a registered teacher should have that recognition withdrawn. It would be the body to advise on the supply of teachers, on their initial training and professional development, on re-training, on good practice in induction and supervision of probation. It would absorb CATE and replace ACSET. It would promote research and enquiry related to these purposes, and be concerned with giving responsible information and advice about the profession.

The GTC would not be involved with salaries, pension or conditions of service, which are matters for employing authorities and unions. It would not be directly involved in negotiating curriculum and examinations, other than for the education of teachers.

The next steps
It will take time for primary legislation to see a GTC on to the statute books. Before that process begins and while it is progressing, there are a range of questions and issues requiring work.

1. A series of feasibility exercises is needed, to prepare for political decision-making. They will include analysis of current DES functions which would become the responsibility of the GTC; taking on board present positions, such as that of CATE or of government teacher recruiting schemes; and estimating costings for each of a GTC's areas of activity, through which to negotiate start-up costs and support needed, and the level of required subscription for registration as a teacher.
2. The options for a GTC infra-structure have to be worked out in advance, bearing in mind the need for teachers in particular to be and to feel involved in and responsible for their professional council. These are not matters which ought to be decided for a GTC; once established, it will make its own decisions within the basic principles previously established. However, a GTC cannot spend its crucial initial period pottering about with details of its own infra-structure, if it is to play the major rôle envisaged in giving sense and purpose to the service. The groundwork of alternatives has to be completed beforehand.
3. Whilst the associations have a suggested composition for the initial governing council with which they could all live for the time being, this will have to be reviewed and doubtless modified by the GTC itself once established. One question will undoubtedly be about the mode of election. It might initially be largely through the good offices of the associations, but it would be for the GTC, once it has teachers registered, to decide what would be best thereafter. In the suggested starting composition, there is already space for a measure of direct election, but the GTC has to exist first with its own register and organization to contemplate that route. What should be the balance between representation through associations and direct election? How, if numbers are not channelled through associations, can there be members from all the significant areas of the service, whatever their numbers? How, if all elections were direct, could the basic principle be upheld that no one organized body should have a majority?
   These are questions which cannot properly be pursued by any body other than the GTC itself. What has been proposed is a set of basic principles, and an initial composition with which the key constituencies acknowledge they could live whilst registering teachers and then working out with those on the register how best to conduct the Council's activities in the future.
4. Whatever the mode of election, a GTC will be felt to belong to its members only if it

has a local dimension to which they can relate, and from which they can contribute members for the central council. Had the ACSET proposals for regional or area councils for professional development been accepted, they would also have provided an obvious and uncontroversial local framework for a GTC. This is an aspect of development which I am engaged in at the moment. The last thing wanted would be yet another area or regional structure. Teachers, wherever they may be, have to relate to scores of different geographical systems already. Part of the exploration has to be the future local and regional structures for the education service as a whole. How far will the service as a whole modify its all too varied local and regional structures, for example if a future government distributes to regions some of the functions now centralised, or if a significant move were made towards the regionalisation of higher education across the binary divide?

5. The concept of 'open professionality' which underpins these proposals constitutes a new form of partnership, finding a way between the extremes of the professional cartel objecting to a busybody's charter and the notion of education being too important to leave to the teachers. The consequences of that concept have been agreed in principle. To sustain and extend the measure of agreement reached, and to give priority to translating it into practice, there is much to be done across the education service to strengthen the new foundations, and to enable central and local government to identify with them.

Conclusion

In adopting the proposals worked out in detail by teachers, and agreed by parents and governors, a new government would depart from the unacceptable imposition of structures which has been the feature of recent years and would give a clear signal for future partnership. This in itself would provide a framework for restoring morale and energising the service.

Within the broad principles already agreed and ready for legislation, a GTC will itself be capable of sorting out modes of election. That need not be and ought not to be a matter for political dispute. A GTC could start with the composition suggested, for a three-year initial period, whilst establishing its register and working out its modes of election. For most practical purposes, the government would be dealing with the small GTC Executive Committee, or small specialised sub-committees, who from the outset would be there to represent the whole range of the governing council and not be directly representing any one association.

An initial setting-up government grant should be anticipated, and some continuing grant for work which the DES will have relinquished, and for the involvement of public interests. However, beyond the start-up period, the main income will be from GTC members themselves.

John Sayer
July 1990

Jack Straw, with whom we had had discussions since March 1988, became and continued to be a strong advocate of a GTC, seeking to build on the UCET-hosted initiative, but also favouring directly elected teacher representation, and, interestingly for future comparison, regional constituencies. He wanted a small body to deal with, alongside a small Education Standards Commission (not confused with it as suggested by Lawrence (1992)) but seemed satisfied that a GTC Council Executive on the model already operating could work. Liberal Democrats were meanwhile firmly and consistently in favour of a GTC, and there was significant Conservative support outside government.

The executive committee of GTC (England and Wales) Directors was for the next nine years to meet one month before and after each of the termly Forum meetings. It would follow the instructions of the now rapidly expanding Forum, and would prompt and prepare agendas. Its first pleasure was to prepare in June for Forum XV, the meeting which both paid homage to Alec Ross and Mary Russell and gave them the assurance of the real drive now being mounted for which they had patiently prepared us. The record of its earliest meetings shows a determination to create an effective organization, to identify and seek necessary premises, services and funding, to make political overtures and responses across the spectrum, to draw in key speakers and engage the media – in fact all the actions which had been constrained until 1989. A co-option was made from NATFHE to ensure the inclusion of further education; an arrangement was made with SCETT, subject to funding, to share administrative services. After an initial rotation of the Chair, Directors were soon, in November 1990, to decide not to appoint from their own number, but to approach a person of public standing and sympathy with the GTC cause, and one who was known as an accomplished Chair, this last being a rarity in the education world. Of three excellent names considered, it was agreed to approach the first choice informally.

This was John Tomlinson. Formerly Director of Education for Cheshire, Chair of the Schools Council during those critical years 1978–81, Chair of the Society of Education Officers in 1982, a member of the Advisory Committee for the Supply and Training (later Education) of Teachers until 1982, he had made the transition to becoming Director of the Institute of Education in Warwick University in 1985, and had immediately become visible as a UCET representative in the GTC initiative, which he was further to support in the 1989 series of seminars. John was known for his work across an extraordinary range of education-related concerns – child care, community service, further and continuing education, nurse education, education for the arts, education and business, the Royal Society of Arts, the Schools Curriculum Award, most indeed of the worthwhile education initiatives which had developed alongside and beyond ever-growing government control. John was properly cautious in allowing his name to go forward as a GTC Director (and intended Chair) for the February AGM. He wished to ensure that this was now an organization which could work and to which he could contribute successfully. From the moment when he agreed, he was to work tirelessly through the 1990s, continuing to keep the GTC proposal in the public domain, and to keep associations together in persuading the public and the bodies politic of the GTC case.

In readiness for the February 1991 AGM, Directors had agreed a funding basis which was to be accepted and to remain intact through the 1990s. The proposed sliding scale for contributions was for guidance only, leaving associations to interpret the contribution they could properly make, and yielding an annual income of about £10,000, sufficient to cover basic administration and meetings, although the real annual costs, including voluntary contribution by individuals and associations, was about £50,000. It says much for the spirit of the Forum members that this voluntary basis was not once abused in the next ten years. A generous offer of a London base was made by NATFHE in association with a shared part-time secretariat with SCETT. 27 Britannia Street was to be the GTC (England and Wales) address and meeting place for the next decade.

This change to action was to prove timely; in the run-up to a general election other voices were being raised, and the GTC movement was able to prompt, support and sometimes influence them. In the House of Lords, every opportunity was being taken by peers of different or no party allegiance to echo the support for a GTC, as in the debate in May 1991 led by Lord Butterfield; and Lord Glenamara, who as Ted Short had pledged himself to introduce a GTC, was offering to host a reception to bring together both Houses, an offer accepted gladly by GTC Directors and to be fulfilled in 1992. A new public initiative was the Institute for Public Policy Research (IPPR), established in 1988 with Baroness Blackstone to Chair, as a think-tank to counterbalance the activities of Sir Keith Joseph's Centre for Policy Studies or the Institute for Economic Affairs and its several variant headed notepapers. In 1991, the IPPR commissioned further papers related to a GTC; its Education and Training Paper No. 7, co-authored by Alec Ross, summarized the GTC case. Another strong voice raised in support was that of Sir Claus Moser, Warden of Wadham College, Oxford, distinguished economist and for many years Director of the Central Statistics Office and Head of the Government Statistics Service. From his presidential address to the British Association for the Advancement of Science, which headlined the case for the GTC, was to come the notable initiative to establish the National Commission on Education (NCE).

Despite the non-co-operation of the government, the NCE was to draw on a remarkable range of penetrating studies and insights, supported by the Hamlyn Foundation. (Ironically for the GTC movement, this massive commitment superseded what seemed likely to be direct support for GTC dissemination and regional studies proposed to Paul Hamlyn in 1990, but we were acceding to the greater good, and were also later to have welcome direct support from the same source.) In the Chair of the National Commission was to be the cross-bench peer Lord Walton of Detchant, Warden of Green College, Oxford, the distinguished President until 1989 of the General Medical Council and to become a strong personal exponent, supporter and adviser to those of us who were working for the GTC. The NCE was in 1992 to commission a paper on the GTC by one who could have been described as a sceptic, Stuart Maclure, for twenty years until 1989 Editor of the *Times Educational Supplement*. He looked at the evidence, by then including the full GTC proposals (1992) and came round in favour of them. This was then to be reflected even more strongly in the full NCE report published in 1993. The local authority associations, also, were moving towards support, from previous suspicion.

All this was already in the air in 1991; there was public, professional and political support for a GTC and increasing dismay at the contrary directions being pursued by the apparently fading government. John Major's November 1990 entry to 10 Downing Street was accompanied by a pledge to raise the morale and status of the teaching profession, but this had so far amounted to no more than a pay review board under the ex-Chief Executive of the stricken Rover car company, Sir Graham Day. The GTC press release of 16 July encapsulates the different languages being used about status.

A public statement from GTC (England and Wales), the combined Forum of 31 major associations across the education service and its public, working towards a full statutory General Teaching Council.

16 July 1991

A TEACHERS' PAY REVIEW BODY IS NOT ENOUGH

Summary

Recent government statements still confuse status measured by salary and material conditions for schoolteachers, and proper responsibility by the teaching profession for the development of its service to the public. A Pay Review Body is not the same as a General Teaching Council. Their purposes and functions are quite separate and must be kept distinct.

The finest people will be attracted into teaching not just by recruitment commercials in cinemas, but by seeing a future for well-trained people to take back responsibility for the professional development of teachers, which politicians and bureaucrats should not and cannot properly exercise.

Background

In a statement of 12 May 1991, Directors of GTC (England and Wales) alerted the government and the public to the danger of confusion between the intended recognition of professional status which the government believes it is reflecting in its new review body for the salary and conditions of service for schoolteachers, and the full recognition of teaching as a profession which is at the heart of the proposed General Teaching Council. This confusion still exists in the most recent statement from the DES to us, dated 17 June, which is being repeated to others even after we have warned of its inaccuracies.

Re-statement

Directors of GTC (England and Wales) must again make it clear that agreement on a salary review body for schoolteachers, however welcome in its own right, is only one part of recognition of professional standing. It does not provide a framework in which to protect the public interest in a first-class service and to develop full professional responsibility in all sectors of education. The teaching profession requires a proper measure of recognised responsibility for standards of entry, initial training, induction and development; for ethical standards in the public service; for research into professional matters; and for reliable public communication to the public about these. This is how a charter between professional educators and other citizens can best be achieved.

There should be the clearest distinction between these proposals and questions of remuneration or conditions of service, which are for government to agree with employers and teacher-associations.

The proposals we have made to Government for the General Teaching Council to be established by statute in England and Wales, building on the well-established precedent of the GTC for Scotland, will provide a framework for a forward-looking profession in partnership with its public. This has been strongly recommended by the cross-party House of Commons Select Committee for Education, Science and the Arts. It has been recommended repeatedly in the Lords. It is not the body of the Conservative Party which is resisting this vital reform, but apparently those advising current Ministers.

The time is right for a government of vision to give its support to the emergent General Teaching Council, so recognizing that further dimension of professionality which will ensure the future quality of dedicated service to the public by committed and well-motivated teachers.

Kenneth Clarke in his short sojourn as Secretary of State (November 1990 to April 1992) was to sweep away the teacher's probationary year in England whilst the Scots were extending the probation period supervised by the GTC to two years. Although our inside information was that he could be convinced of the GTC case, and his junior minister was in support, the Secretary of State replied after five months to the renewed GTC offer, which was merely to be ready to help should the government wish to initiate discussion on a statutory GTC, with a clear refusal: 'I do not think that the Government or Parliament could surrender control of teacher training and recruitment and dismissal of teachers to a body elected by the profession' (17 June 1991).

This was accompanied by a throw-away remark that the 'other objectives' of proposals studied so far seemed 'very vague'. When he was asked (21 June) to indicate what elements he was referring to, the task was left to Stephen Mellor, a civil servant in the Teacher Supply section, who produced six questions, here summarized, since they represent well the bundle of anxieties, misunderstandings and evasions of the time:

- How are consumer interests to be protected?
- How would a GTC coexist with CATE and funding councils, and what would it add to discussion on teacher supply and quality?
- What would a GTC add to present arrangements for consultation?
- How would a GTC prevent itself becoming a 'megalithic lobby' of teacher unions?
- How would a GTC avoid the restrictive practices of other professional bodies? Scotland is different – how would the separate interests of Wales be protected? (24 September 1991)

These were answered very fully, and apparently to the satisfaction of the civil servants who had produced the questions.

Kenneth Clarke brushed us aside in a few lines by saying the response had done nothing more to convince him and that nothing would be gained by a meeting at this time (13 December 1991). Yet Conservative Central Office was issuing the much more positive response from Chris Patten, Party Chairman, that the government had 'never opposed the principle of a General Teaching Council, but it must be one wanted by the profession and not imposed by government'. If we ask why this dismissive stance was adopted, the answers may be, first, that this was the style expected of Kenneth Clarke first as Secretary of State for Health and then of Education, to be bullish, blunt and uncompromising in controlling spending services; second, that he will have had conflicting advice from his civil servants, John Wiggins being opposed, whilst Clive Saville was more open, and soon to be banished to international work for speaking up against the savaging of teacher training; third, however, that he had no lead from the new Prime Minister of whom more had been hoped, and as Gillian Shephard was later to find, no hope of persuading Downing Street or the cabinet.

However interpreted, these confused messages had two effects: first, the lack of response from government was by now fuelling professional and public support; and second, it gave a spur to the work already started in 1990 and going through drafts to GTC Directors on a much more detailed set of GTC proposals.

When John Tomlinson, after chairing two preparatory Directors' meetings, made his introductory Chairman's remarks as a paper to the June 1991 GTC Forum, it was in a climate of anticipation that change could be achieved. However, not satisfied with surfing, he chose to bring depth and direction to the debate, and his paper, echoed in journal articles at the same time, still stands as a challenge to the future. It explores the consumer/customer language of the day, and centres on the client interest.

> The fundamental purpose of the teacher is to divine and serve the interests of his or her pupils and to do it within the entitlement to education afforded by the laws of the day in the public interest . . . a GTC must reflect such a view of professionalism . . . there arises an absolute need for a professional ethic and code of conduct. A professional is one so trained and disposed that he or she acts in the best interests of the client rather than in his or her own interests.

The paper proposes a triangle of relationships between State, profession and parents/pupils/students, in contrast to the present situation of State control or monopsony. The teachers' responsibility is 'quality' rather than standards.

> It is the teacher, ultimately, who must be responsible and stand accountable. And unless that accountability is as much to his or her own conscience as to public 'performance indicators' – whatever they may be – nothing of value will be achieved. A General Teaching Council would be about the public, visible and corporate means of creating the conditions in which that conscience could be nurtured, would be transmitted to each new generation of teachers, and would be made explicit so as to build public understanding and support for the values it promoted.

From this new balance within the nation-state, the argument should then extend to society as a whole; inter-state professional mobility; regional and communal organization, and the global society.

Accompanying this starting position was a checklist for action agreed by Directors.

- To behave as an emergent General Teaching Council;
- to programme publicity with clear targets;
- to widen the basis of professional understanding and support;
- to project to those with whom a GTC must work, e.g. CATE;
- to be in constant touch with politicians;
- to argue the public case with examples, e.g. nursing;
- to engage in fundraising;
- to make a start on, e.g., good practice for induction.

The statement concludes:

We must keep up the momentum. We must seize every opportunity. We must keep our heads. We must go on making friends.

That, in a nutshell, is what the GTC movement was to take as its guiding principles over the next decade.

Chapter 5

Foreshadowing the Statutory GTC

THE GTC (ENGLAND AND WALES) TRUST

In addition to promoting legislation for a statutory Council, the obligation was now accepted to behave as such a Council should be expected to conduct itself, and therefore to be proactive in advising the Government and others on professional matters. In the years 1991–94, GTC (England and Wales) was able to issue significant publications and responses on the key issues of teacher induction, initial teacher education and training, and continuing professional development. It was able to use the experience of the councils of other professions and of the GTC for Scotland. It was only partly successful however in promoting debate on professional ethics, and the reasons for this will be explored later. These issues are recorded here and the treatment of one of them recorded in more detail because they would reappear in the different context of 1998–2000 as central to the future of the statutory GTC.

Alongside the company limited by guarantee, which could not be registered as a charity because it was deemed quite correctly to have a political aim, i.e. legislation for a statutory council, the parallel GTC (England and Wales) Trust was created, became a registered educational charity in November 1992, and served as the vehicle for deliberations on professional matters. It also released funds from other charities, and in addition to the basic administration supported by member associations, it became possible to accept funding from, among others, the Paul Hamlyn Foundation, NATFHE Educational Trust, the Association of Education Committees Trust, the Comino Foundation, and Commercial Union, for non-political activity.

LEARNING FROM THE SCOTTISH EXPERIENCE

The General Teaching Council for Scotland was established in 1966 following the Teaching Council (Scotland) Act 1965. This early legislation was more limited than that which we proposed for England and Wales, but it did include, in addition to registration, probation and professional discipline, the responsibility to keep under review and recommend the standards of education, training and fitness to teach appropriate to those entering the teaching profession, and to consider and recommend on matters (other than pay and conditions of service) relating to the supply of teachers. It also had a unit to provide information to enquirers interested in being trained for teaching.

The Scottish precedent was of course in mind throughout the quest for a GTC south of the Border: it had been used by CATEC in 1981. In the 1989 regional seminars, Gordon Kirk, Principal of Moray House, had been one of the invited speakers, and again in the GTC Forum in 1991. I became a regular visitor to Edinburgh, and the Registrar, Ivor Sutherland, has continued to share and help our thinking throughout the development years.

In the early 1990s, the Scottish Council was not seen as a model. We were trying to propose not the legislation of 1965, but statutes of the kind which the Scots in retrospect would have wished to enact. In particular, we noted its still frustrated wish to relate its powerful role in initial teacher training and probation to a similar responsibility for continuing professional development, and the hope that the requirement of registration should extend to teachers in further education. We were also looking for a more integral involvement of parent and other lay representatives, rather than have them dependent on the gift of nomination by the Secretary of State. We were shown the different relationship with teachers' associations, since in Scotland the EIS was dominant, and most elected GTC Council members were in fact EIS members too.

GTC for Scotland had a Supply Committee formulating responses to queries to the Scottish Office Education Department. If it had not always been the most satisfactory committee in reaching a consensus between 'providers' of training and the employing regions, this could be attributed to three major causes: first, the Council had not developed its full capacity to develop criteria for staffing and being proactive in its deliberations; second, the composition of the Council was not yet sufficiently spread across all contributors to policy-making; third, the Supply Committee had been separate from the Council's Education Committee, which could be seen to jeopardize one of the main potential advantages of having the Council's advice, namely to relate professional education to supply, both in the deliberations on these matters and in the commitment of all those who will have to make resulting policy work.

This was well recognized by the Scottish Office in its 1992–93 Policy Review of the Council, in which it recommended a merger of Education and Supply Committees. 'This would integrate consideration of teacher supply issues more closely within the wider spectrum of developments in the structure of teacher training and the means by which that structure can respond to supply indicators.' Although the Council was not yet minded to accept this structural suggestion, the principle behind it was sound enough, and would be pursued in other ways. The general conclusions of the Scottish Office were also relevant to qualitative questions of appropriate supply. Indeed, its report was the strongest condemnation from official sources of the absence of such a Council South of the border.

> The close match between the qualifications of Scottish teachers and the subjects they are required to teach stands in sharp contrast to the position in England and Wales where there is no equivalent of the General Teaching Council. This impressive correlation between qualifications held and tuition given is due in no small part to the Council's

influence. It must be recognized that, were there is no such body, the retention of this level of control would be extremely difficult and standards in Scottish education would be at risk.

This conclusion was coupled with a more general view from the Scottish Office which again by implication is condemnatory of the lack of similar arrangements in England and Wales:

> The Council exercises guardianship of professional standards. As a professional body which is largely self-regulating, it is able to achieve this from within: its objectives are formulated by agreement between representatives of serving teachers, of their employers, of teacher trainers and of the wider educational community. Thus any developments proposed are discussed in a collaborative environment and are likely to receive a more positive reception than would be the case were a Government department seeking to impose top-down changes.

THE ISSUE OF SCHOOLTEACHER PROBATION AND INDUCTION

The first opportunity for GTC (England and Wales) to foreshadow the responsibility of a statutory professional council came with the Secretary of State's proposal to end schoolteacher probation in England and Wales, revoking regulations updated as recently as 1989. His reasons for announcing this intention (for by this time DES consultations had become a necessary convention rather than a serious dialogue) are not difficult to see. Successive HMI documents (HMI 1982, 1988, 1992) were highlighting the gaps between recommended practice and local variations, without there being signs of improvement. The probation of schoolteachers could be seen, to use one of Kenneth Clarke's favourite expressions, as a complete Horlicks. It was, moreover, a responsibility of LEAs, and the removal of yet another LEA power would not be displeasing politically. Pressure was building from independent schools, where (outside Scotland) teaching service was not recognized for probation and who saw themselves diminished. The same problem applied to service in further education colleges, whereas teaching in their rival sixth-form colleges qualified, until both groups were shortly afterwards to be removed from the LEAs altogether. Those of us who had been running schools, and who in practice undertook the responsibility for recommending successful completion, to be endorsed by the employing authority, could cite extreme examples of anomalies. What of a new head of a comprehensive school, appointed from local authority administrative work after teaching in the private sector, who had to supervise his own probation as well as that of new teachers? It should have come as no surprise that Kenneth Clarke, a person to get things done quickly, should propose, instead of improving the system, to set it aside completely; or to be more precise, to build it into the still undeveloped arrangements for schoolteacher appraisal, which had never been intended for new teachers. Politically, it was an astute decision; professionally, it was not likely to improve teaching quality. But it was going to happen anyway.

GTC (England and Wales) now had 30 member associations, all with particular viewpoints and including, for example, associations of independent schools, further education colleges, and local authorities. How, in the short time available, could a response be formulated which represented the whole profession? It will continue to be a vital question for the statutory GTC, with the balance of democracy and decisiveness even more a challenge to its individual elected representatives, and for that reason also is worth recording. It required confidence and trust for member associations to share their own draft responses with GTC Directors, for a GTC draft to be agreed by Directors and circulated to the 30 bodies prior to a full debate and approval. It also involved consultation with the GTC for Scotland, with whom very fruitful contacts had been developing over the previous four years, and which offered a much more fully developed perspective on teacher induction (GTC for Scotland, 1990) than anything south of the Border. But the exercise was carried through, and for the first time GTC (England and Wales) was able within the two months available from September 1991 to give evidence on behalf of the whole membership, as follows – seeking to make positive comments, but moving beyond mere datelined reaction to a government proposal to announce a thorough and professional reconsideration.

I have been asked to respond to the letter of 17 September, seeking views on the Secretary of State's proposal to end statutory arrangements for the probation of schoolteachers.

GTC (England and Wales) has sought evidence from its 30 major associations, from abroad and from other professions. A full and considered document on good practice for induction will be prepared in the course of the coming year. This statement, therefore, is little more than an initial response to the particular queries and views of the letter of 17 September.

The background
The expressed wish to develop continuity across initial training, induction and career-long professional development is welcomed, as are initial measures announced to encourage good practice and partnership in induction. (Paras 2 & 5)

It is recognised that the introduction of formal statutory appraisal, together with the delegation of powers to individual schools, have a direct bearing on existing arrangements for probation. (Paras 5 & 6)

The quality of existing arrangements for probation in England and Wales under existing regulations depends much on the priorities of individual schools and local authorities, and the time and training given to probationary teachers and those who supervise them. It is perceived to be variable. Recognition of experience in further education, overseas, and outside the maintained sector of schools is still an area of uncertainty.

Only in Scotland is probation systematised across institutions and regions through the General Teaching Council. We note the Government's further development grant for good practice in probation in Scotland. It may be that the apparent anomaly in government intentions north and south of the Border is more of nomenclature than of substance. The longer, two-year period of probation in Scotland, also permissible in non-maintained schools, should however be noted in the formulation of new proposals for England and Wales.

Such considerations add to the need for non-statutory guidance (Para 7), whether or not the Secretaries of State decide to revoke regulations for statutory probation. GTC

(England and Wales) will be happy to assist in the drafting of such guidance, and a future General Teaching Council will be expected to develop it. At this stage, parallel DES guidances, e.g. on the authorisation of overseas-trained teachers (Statutory Instrument 1991 No. 1134) should be borne in mind. In particular, attention is drawn to references there to designated mentors. Mentorship has to be systematically planned, with structure and prior training.

The proposals
Attention is drawn to the proper concern that guidance, designated mentorship, appraisal schedules and planned induction programmes should be in place before the date chosen (Para 8) for revoking regulations for statutory probation.

A decision announced before the summer of 1992 but with effect from September 1993 would largely remove the need for transitional provisions (Para 9) and go some way to meeting the concerns recorded above.

The desire (Para 10) for more systematic and effective induction of new teachers and identification of their needs is welcome. An extension of appraisal to new teachers could be the 'springboard'. How that metaphor is extended depends on guidance and preparation. The aims of appraisal as formulated in Statutory Instrument 1991 No. 1511, Education (School Teacher Appraisal) Regulations 1991, are seen as consistent though not identical with effective induction.

However, should the Secretaries of State extend appraisal to those in their first years of teaching (Para 10), the special nature of that induction period must be fully recognized as a significant *extension* of the appraisal scheme now being introduced, in which the distinctive purposes of probation are incorporated.

The special responsibility for induction would remain, whatever future changes were made to appraisal regulations in the light of experience. That special responsibility could be discharged effectively and systematically within an appraisal framework only if appropriately modified appraisal involved all new teachers in their first year of teaching. This would again indicate a starting date of 1 September 1993, making unnecessary the choice between options (i) and (iii) of Para 11.

It should be noted that formal appraisal is mandatory only in maintained schools (Para 5). A future General Teaching Council will be concerned with good practice in induction across the whole service.

Whilst a link between induction and appraisal may make for progression and continuity once teachers are appointed, much has still to be done to develop the continuum from the initial education and training of teachers. It is noted that the new specific grant for induction training will involve collaboration between LEAs, schools and teacher-training institutions. A General Teaching Council will be concerned to develop good practice in progression and continuity across the initial and continuing education of teachers.

GTC (England and Wales) is available to the Department of Education and Science for such further consultation as may be helpful on any of the above matters.

At the same time, aware that the decision was a foregone conclusion, Directors were setting in motion the announced 'full and considered document on good practice', and on 29 October 1991, in addition to debating its consultation response, sought the agreement of the Forum of Associations to the wider study.

This was modified in debate, and Directors were able at their next meeting to agree a more focused proposal on the induction of newly appointed teachers, to secure through the Chair financial and editorial support from AEC and NFER respectively, to identify a leading field exponent together with a leading thinker on teacher education to be commissioned for major contributions to the document, which would conclude with recommendations from GTC (England and Wales). Having secured their agreement in principle, the Chairman and Secretary met the two lead writers, John Lambert and James Calderhead, to develop and clarify the brief and the balance between them, and the document was written and published within six months (GTC, 1992) to coincide with the ending of statutory probation announced in March as 'the abolition of the pointless probationary year' and taking effect from 1 September. The GTC document had filled a vacuum, was in great demand and was rapidly reprinted. Moreover, it had demonstrated that a body representing 30 very distinctive organizations was capable, despite having no resources of its own, to respond at speed and to go beyond response to set down markers for future good practice. For those who were anxious that a future statutory GTC might become a mere talkshop, and possibly a negative one at that, it was a necessary example of what could be done given the will to do it. It became the springboard, to use the DfE metaphor, for GTC work through its original company on a rapid succession of invited responses 'by yesterday' to government, and subsequently through its charitable Trust in 1992–93 on initial education and training of primary schoolteachers. The resulting evidence to the DfE and publication in 1993 of the GTC Trust document on primary schoolteachers' initial education and training were to be valuable contributions to a professional debate, in which, however, government politicians previously committed to a radical agenda of their own were in no frame of mind to engage. It will be seen later that further substantial GTC publication followed in 1994 on continuing professional development, setting down markers for the future Council. The work between 1994 and 1997 on professional ethics forms part of a later chapter in its own right.

Meanwhile, however, the prospect of a change of government in the run-up to the 1992 General Election, coupled with yet another change as Secretary of State in April 1992, was accelerating the promotional and political agenda confirmed from the Chair in July 1991, and to these we now return, again with two purposes: the first to record stages of persuasion, steps forward and setbacks; the second to offer a case study for the future reference of all who will help fulfil the potential of the statutory GTC.

COMMUNICATION PROGRAMME

The UCET-hosted initiative had worked towards professional agreement, and whilst it had responded to media enquiries and issued regular Press statements, there had been no wish to promote the GTC in public until agreement had been reached. Indeed, as has been seen, there was no mood in the political climate to launch a public campaign even with agreement. Its technical working party had drawn up a three-year promotion plan in 1987 and updated it in March 1988 in readiness. It would have involved an estimated £327,000, compared with the £56 plus goodwill on which the initiative had worked for four years.

By 1991, with the lead-in to a General Election, the member-associations, now a legal entity as GTC (England and Wales), were much more ready to make public moves, and the Directors revisited the issue of promotion, having before them a revised framework document for publicity (April 1991). There were high hopes of substantial funding, first from the Jerwood Foundation and then from the Paul Hamlyn Foundation. But the first was short-lived, preferring to try a kind of education Oscar award scheme, and the second committed its major funding to the National Commission on Education, and could offer only limited, though very welcome, support to the production of the first GTC flyer for teachers. The framework policy document on publicity could be accepted in principle, but only individual parts of it implemented as outside funding permitted. This was to be revised and developed in November 1991, by which time publicity had been initiated including a two-page *TES* profile of the Chairman and movement (*TES*, 12 September), and a publicity launch on 26 September for the flyer to teachers.

COMMUNICATION WITH TEACHERS

To communicate with half a million teachers in the employment of over 100 LEAs and another half million in the 'pit' (the infelicitous DES term for 'professionally inactive teachers') has always been a problem. They cannot be reached through any one professional association, and their reading of the *Times Educational Supplement* and other journals is not guaranteed. In the wake of the 1998 Education Reform Act, teachers were engulfed in new regulations, syllabi, circulars and pamphlets from government. For the most part, they were reading what they had to read. LEA teachers' centres were already being decimated and time for reflection or open-ended enquiry removed from increasingly government-controlled output-oriented in-service courses. Then as now, if asked whether they would wish to see a GTC, most teachers would answer affirmatively, but without the prospect of it happening it would be low on the agenda of most schools and teachers. Then as now, priorities had to be established with a minimum of expenditure.

GTC Directors wanted at least to make sure all teachers had the opportunity to engage with the GTC, and gave realistic priority to an introductory 'find out more' flyer, to be distributed economically to all schools via member associations and if possible in LEA postbags. John Tomlinson secured the help of the University of Reading's Department of Typology and Graphic Communication in designing the flyer, along with the letterheads which were to be used for the next decade, and in the autumn of 1991, 250,000 flyers were distributed to teachers in all schools as well as being signalled or reproduced in association journals.

COMMUNICATION WITH PARENTS AND THE PUBLIC

During the period of quiet work towards agreement across associations, there had been many enquiries from other associations, individuals and institutions, and the regional seminars in 1989, although not drawing large numbers, had helped to secure a growing list of volunteers. As well as individuals like Gerald Smith with a flair for high profile, there were groups outside the teaching world such as that led by Peggy

Pyke-Lees, whose husband had been a distinguished secretary-general of the GMC, and who was not only encouraging us to adopt a higher profile but was herself corresponding with Ministers and the media, and offering to help with publicity.

At the meeting of Directors on 28 February 1991, it was agreed that Peggy Pyke-Lees and group be invited and recognized as a working party reporting to Directors through the Secretary, with a Director also involved. I was asked to draft a brief for the group, for discussion with Peggy Pyke-Lees, inviting comment and amendment which would be reported back to the next meeting of Directors on 23 April.

From this starting point can be traced three further dimensions to the GTC movement. One was the institution of 'Associates' or 'Correspondents' to whom from time to time a GTC Newsletter would be sent. The second was the appendage to most of the termly Forum meetings of a 'Wider Forum' or 'Extended Forum', often with invited speakers, to which associated individuals and interested associations were invited. The third was a pamphlet for parents and the public. It was not easy to agree the early drafts initiated by Peggy Pyke-Lees, but they were built on particularly by Margaret Tulloch of CASE, who was co-opted as a Director, and the agreed flyer for parents by parents was eventually distributed via CASE, NCPTA and governing body groups in 1993.

COMMUNICATION WITH THE BODIES POLITIC

The imminence of a General Election brought priority to communication with education Ministers and their Shadow counterparts, with individuals and groups on all sides of the political spectrum in both Houses of Parliament, and with the parliamentary select committee. It was not merely a question of persuading them, or encouraging parliamentary questions, but also of establishing what kind of evidence would be most useful to them, and then spoon-feeding. For example, from the updating paper to the Labour Shadow team came confirmation that what was now needed was a detailed draft bill, in addition to the more detailed arguments which were already being prepared to augment the agreed 1989 document. The text reproduced below shows how similar were the questions about a GTC's relationships with CATE or the proposed ESC to those which now have to be worked out between the GTCs and TTA or OFSTED.

EDUCATION ADVISORY GROUP

The proposed General Teaching Council
This paper is offered as an update of the more detailed one used for the front-bench teacher education and training seminar of July 1990. It also examines the boundaries of a GTC and of the proposed Educational Standards Council. In doing so, it addresses the points made in Andrew Smith's first draft paper to the May meeting, and also refers to a personal paper of 25 May from Jack Whitehead.

Update
The Forum of Associations initially hosted by UCET is now a registered company limited by guarantee, with the purpose of promoting a statutory general teaching council

along lines agreed across the profession and its constituency, and meanwhile promoting what would be its main concerns. Membership of the Company is along the lines suggested for a start-up period of the proposed statutory Council itself.

The Forum now has as members of the company, committed to its aims, 30 major associations. These include the six schoolteacher unions and the three from further and higher education, as well as associations representing the private sector, parents, governors, advisers, officers, educational psychologists, teacher-trainers, churches, principals of colleges and polytechnics, and the College of Preceptors.

Other major bodies which have expressed active support without expecting to be part of a Governing Council include the Campaign for the Advancement of State Education, the National Association for Primary Education, and the Association of Principals of Sixth Form Colleges. An advisory support group of individual members of the concerned public has been formed, working to the Board of Directors.

GTC (England and Wales) is now funded for basic administrative purposes by contributions from its member-associations, and has a small base at 27 Britannia Street. The member-associations elect annually a Board of Directors (maximum twelve) and Company Secretary. The Chairperson, elected by Directors, is now Professor John Tomlinson, also currently chairing the RSA.

GTC (England and Wales) is about to take a higher profile and launch an awareness-raising programme of communication, including a flyer to make sure that its actual proposals are known and discussed more widely.

Discussions have been held with CATE which have demonstrated the wrongness of the DES statement that a GTC would involve major upheaval for the existing CATE operation. A GTC would expect to advise (as did ACSET originally) on the criteria to be applied by CATE, and to supervise any development of CATE-type operations in the fields of in-service professional development or re-training. Longer-term organizational *rapprochement* would be evolutionary.

Representations made to Secretaries of State since the failure last year to adopt this major Select Committee recommendation have met with no response. Reluctantly, GTC (England and Wales) may have to make a start soon in discharging some of the responsibilities it proposes, failing a positive response from government. In doing so, it would be intent on preparing the ground for early statutory recognition.

Whilst awaiting any response from the Government here, GTC (England and Wales) has been assisting developments of professional councils, codes or charters in Hong Kong, Canada and Australia.

Principal Points for Legislation

GTC (England and Wales) has NOT suggested a long-term composition or mode of election, but a starting-up mechanism which would ensure the full support of the whole profession and its constituency. What is sought for statutory legislation is:

1. Composition of the Governing Council from the outset to reflect the intended proposed long-term scope of the Council's work.
2. A Governing Council with a majority of representative registered teachers (broadly defined) and with adequate representation of the public interest.
3. No one organized body to have a majority.

Beyond those points, it is for the Council itself to determine, within the parameters established by statute, what should be its composition and procedures, e.g. sub-groupings. Meanwhile, the promoting company articles provide for review of composition every three years.

Personal Comment

Composition and Organisation of the Council

1. In building on the GTC (England and Wales) initiative, Labour legislation does not need to get embroiled in the composition either of the Governing Council or of its sub-groups. In prior discussion, Labour can relate principally to the small board of directors responsible to the whole governing council.
2. The representation available for the start-up period to establish the register of teachers, is through the proffered vehicle of representative associations. The government would decide whether to require the initial Council to come up with a local structure and an ingredient of direct election from it, once it has set up the electoral register.
3. Ironically, representation through associations is the best protection against domination by any of them. In Scotland, by contrast, direct election guarantees domination by the EIS, with pre-meetings of the major union determining outcomes.
4. Representation through associations is also the best means to ensure from the outset the presence of all parts of the educating profession and its constituency. In Scotland, minority groups (heads or inspectors, for example) are not represented, and parents depend on nomination by the government. Reserved places by sector of the education service would be less effective and professionally more divisive.
5. However, a mixed economy of direct election from areas or regions, and national election through representative professional associations, could well become a reality once teachers are registered and able to form local constituencies.

General Teaching Council and Education Standards Council

6. Just as a clear distinction has been drawn between the GTC's professional functions in the public interest, and matters of conditions of service or remuneration which are not its responsibility, the demarcation between GTC (professional standards) and ESC (educational standards) must be made quite clear. The quality promoted through ESC forms the context of the professional expectation, development and ethos promoted by the GTC. Formal links would be appropriate at sub-committee level. The danger of confusion is illustrated in Andrew's draft paper page 15 on induction.

General Teaching Council and CATE

7. It would be unwise to commit the party to extend the functions of CATE in its present form to include induction and in-service development. Nor is CATE to be seen as the body to *set* criteria for its operations. CATE exists to ensure that the criteria are effectively applied. The GTC should be the government's principal source of pro-fessional advice for criteria, whether for initial or in-service education. CATE-type operations across initial training, induction and further professional development would eventually relate to each other in an important sub-group of the GTC.
8. So too, the GTC would be expected to set up appropriate sub-groups for its research dimension. It is in this context that BERA might well be involved (Jack Whitehead's

paper). Action research as a major vehicle of professional development should not however be trapped in a specialised 'research' sub-group. GTC (England and Wales) should bear this in mind in its current preliminary thinking on organization for the initial period.

9. It is wrong to envisage a GTC as yet another *consultative* body. It would bring together such bodies to be the Government's principal source of professional *advice* on professional matters, with the expectation that government would give good reason in Parliament if for reasons beyond the professional domain it were to decide not to adopt it.

John Sayer
July 1991

Chapter 6

Changing Contexts 1991–94

Whilst the positive work of the GTC Trust was being pursued with vigour, the new context of a succession of changes – a new Prime Minister, major legislative proposals between 1991 and 1993, the General Election of April 1992, preceded by yet another Secretary of State – demanded GTC responses and induced new alliances: especially on teacher training.

Increasingly, it was becoming evident that government thrusts were emanating not from Ministers at the DES, or by 1992 DfE, but from 10 Downing Street. The role of policy advisers has yet to be fully charted, but even more marked was the influence on them of pressure groups, vying with each other for claims to the new radical right ground. It was no longer just local authorities and teachers' associations which were to be seen as blockages to reform; if there was little or no immediate effect from national control of examinations and school curriculum, added assisted places at independent schools, inducements to schools to become grant-maintained, CTCs, local management of schools, open enrolment accompanied by league tables, or requirements that governors act as national watchdogs, incorporation of further and public sector higher education to remove them from LEAs, then the root causes must lie elsewhere. The 'educational establishment' included Her Majesty's Inspectorate, which was soon to be truncated in order to introduce OFSTED through the 1992 Education Act; and above all, it was the relative independence of higher education teacher training which became the target of the radical right in the early 1990s.

In 1991, the new Prime Minister's fine sentiments about raising the status of the teaching profession were to be shown to be limited to the mechanisms of salary negotiation and the replacement of the Burnham negotiating committee, a body disliked by the government's advisers not only because of the direct involvement of teacher unions but because of the prominence it gave to local authority employers. The GTC movement was of course not intending to touch salaries and conditions of service, but it did have to emphasize the difference between professional status and pay review. The press release of 16 July 1991 is one example of the disappointment being felt.

Recent government statements still confuse status measured by salary and material conditions for schoolteachers, and proper responsibility by the teaching profession for the development of its service to the public. A Pay Review Body is not the same as a General Teaching Council. Their purposes and functions are quite separate and must be kept distinct.

The finest people will be attracted into teaching not just by recruitment commercials in cinemas, but by seeing a future for well-trained people to take back responsibility for the professional development of teachers, which politicians and bureaucrats should not and cannot properly exercise.

In a statement of 12 May 1991, Directors of GTC (England and Wales) alerted the government and the public to the danger of confusion between the intended recognition of professional status which the Government believes it is reflecting in its new review body for the salary and conditions of service for schoolteachers, and the full recognition of teaching as a profession which is at the heart of the proposed General Teaching Council. This confusion still exists in the most recent statement from the DES to us, dated 17 June, which is being repeated to others even after we have warned of its inaccuracies.

This also illustrates the difficulty which was being experienced in remaining politically impartial. Whilst every effort could be made to extend dialogue with individual politicians across all parties, the government, its ministers and therefore its senior officials were increasingly excluding themselves from dialogue.

THE VOLUNTARY ALTERNATIVES

Because there seemed to be no realistic prospect of persuading the government, GTC Directors considered very carefully whether a first stage as a voluntary GTC should be pursued, in the hope that it might later be accorded statutory responsibility and recognition. The failed precedent of the Royal Society of Teachers, the realization that a GTC 'without teeth' would satisfy nobody but government by its powerlessness in the present climate, the Scottish precedent, the prospect of a General Election and indeed the nature of the agreement which had been reached across the education service to go for a statutory body, combined to persuade us otherwise. Whilst we would try to act as a 'shadow' GTC, we would not and should not be seen as the real thing.

'Nature hath a horror of the vacuum.' It was inevitable that an alternative proposal should emerge, seeking to develop professional consciousness from within. Following a *TES* article in July 1991, Tyrrell Burgess and Betty Adams, both highly respected not least for their championing of records of achievement, one of the significant developments of the 1980s despite not being on the DES agenda, brought together a small group of school respondents to form what they described without seeking to incorporate the title as the Education Council for England and Wales. The proposal was for individuals to agree to act professionally and be accredited as maintaining high standards, to subscribe to a code of conduct devised by the initial group, and so to advance the education profession and its standing.

In early discussion and in subsequent publication, it was clear that the initiators had no faith that a government of any hue would introduce legislation of the kind we were proposing, and that they saw the voluntary route which GTC Directors had set to one side as the only way forward. When asked whether they would not be duplicating the College of Preceptors with its royal charter, they initially saw no prospect of development there. We agreed that a dialogue would be resumed if after a time their initiative had attracted significant numbers.

In June 1992, mindful that a GTC would need to establish sub-committee links with subject associations for teacher-training curriculum, though not expecting them to be in membership for fear of duplicated representation, the GTC Extended Forum was devoted to initiating such links. Subject associations had a very weak co-ordinating body which appeared to be moribund, and one option would have been to offer the GTC as an umbrella. But without a sub-committee structure, the representational overlaps between general and subject associations would have been a problem.

Tyrrell Burgess tried again to promote the Education Council, with a *TES* article using the government's 'decisive rejection' of the GTC. A little later, the government began to respond to continuing GTC overtures by saying there would be no objection to a voluntary GTC, or perhaps a royal college of teachers (again, appearing to ignore the existence of the College of Preceptors). Stuart Sexton, former adviser to Secretaries of State, instigated a Westminster conference to promote a 'College of Teachers', apparently ignoring the existence of the College of Preceptors. Government blessing was not what the 'Education Council' might have expected or sought, but eventually there was to be a *rapprochement*, prompted by Lord Caldecote, with the College of Preceptors and some subject associations, leading to the re-titling of the College of Preceptors as the College of Teachers, and the prospect that it might develop as the co-ordinating body for subject associations. The College maintained through all this process its support for the GTC movement, and did not allow itself to be adopted as an alternative. Officers of GTC, moreover, continued to be involved as the various bodies and personalities converged, to provide the prospect of a revitalized College of Teachers with a distinctive professional role, a broader constituency and the prospect of being able to represent these to the GTC.

It was however a sensitive process, not just because of the possible political and public perceptions of new divisions in a profession which after many years was united for a GTC, but because it touched on questions which are still unanswered, about standards and about the nature of professionality. These will be examined later.

THE 1992 GTC PROPOSALS AND DRAFT BILL

It was Jack Straw's commitment to try to introduce legislation for a GTC in the first session of Parliament should there be a change of administration, together with similar encouragement from Liberal Democrats and from Cross-Benchers in the Lords, which prompted Directors in September 1991 to call for a draft Bill, despite the negative disposition of the Secretary of State. The Chair and Secretary were invited to consult legal experts, but in practice Association solicitors were heavily committed to vast increases of litigation, and parliamentary specialists would have required fees beyond our reach.

It became a matter of wedding years of deliberation and consensus within the teaching communities to parliamentary procedures. Existing legislation was available for the GTC for Scotland, and examples from other professions included the recent strengthening of legislation for GMC, the 1983 legislation for the UKCC, and advice from Lord Walton of Detchant, who was also at that time engaged in draft legislation to regulate osteopathy which served as a contemporary model (King's Fund, 1991), and who as Chairman of the National Commission had shared supportive thoughts with us in the July 1991 Forum meeting.

By February 1992, when GTC Directors and others were invited by Lord Glenamara to a House of Lords Reception drawing in key people from all parties and both Houses, it was possible for the Chairman not only to enunciate what the GTC movement stood for, but to outline the action plan on which we were now engaged. After exchange of drafts, GTC Directors chose a day's retreat in June at Lamport Hall (at that time being proposed to us by Gerald Smith as a grand-style venue for a GTC) to work at the Secretary's draft of the new document including draft legislation, and were able to draw in Bob Morris, now free from his notable AMA education secretary role, to offer comment. Parliamentarians, DES officials and education correspondents were also invited to comment at draft stage, and Mary Warnock was among several who offered helpful amendments. The Proposals document (GTC, 1992) was approved by the Forum and published in August 1992, in readiness, it was believed, for a new government and for general circulation. It was to become the base document quoted regularly in parliamentary debates between 1992 and 1994, when amendment clauses for a GTC were being proposed as an alternative to the annual outpouring of government legislation. Its publication was strongly encouraged by the National Commission Research Committee too, and although the NCE drew back from the intention to publish it themselves, it was seized upon by Stuart Maclure, when used by the GTC (England and Wales) Chair and Secretary at the BEMAS annual conference in September, as the first proposal of substance which was to incline him towards the cautiously positive recommendation he was to make in his commissioned briefing paper (NCE, 1993a) to the National Commission, and which the Commission members were to endorse even more decisively in their composite report (NCE, 1993b).

The 1992 Proposals were to be revised in 1996 to incorporate changes of context, and then to be summarized in Sir Malcolm Thornton's 1996 attempt to secure a private member's Bill. Later chapters will draw out the differences between these proposals and the actual legislation of 1998. Some of these differences are a measure of the future growth still to be striven for if the potential of a GTC is to be realized.

RESPONDING TO PROPOSED CHANGES TO INITIAL TEACHER TRAINING

Just as it has been seen how difficult it had become to remain in at least courteous communication with the current government, up to and even more after the 1992 General Election, it was equally difficult, when government proposals on teacher training were seen to be politically driven, to maintain a distinction between professional activity as a 'shadow Council' and the political thrust which had as its purpose to secure a GTC. The government's political drive would have been entirely acceptable had it been to secure improved training; but it was perceived to be at least in part an assault on institutions, on the 'educational establishment', and it brought together those who felt under attack even when addressing professional issues. Moreover, the succession of Bills to change the structures for the funding, provision and regulation of teacher training were an opportunity to introduce amendments to propose a GTC, sometimes instead of the proposals being made. So the years 1992–95 were, in spite of every effort to the contrary, years in which the GTC movement was perforce opposed to the government's proposals on key matters affecting the professional aspects of teaching. To see why, we must return to the background experienced by teachers themselves.

BACKGROUND OF INITIAL TEACHER EDUCATION AND TRAINING

By the early 1970s, this country had more or less achieved the framework for phasing in a trained graduate teaching force for maintained schools. Existing certificated teachers, those long-service uncertificated teachers absorbed in the late 1960s, and those who had graduated before 1973, remained recognized teachers. For supply reasons, there remained exceptions in the regulations, notably mathematics and physical sciences, but in practice it was by now a recognized career advantage for these too to have undergone prior training. The regulations still did not apply to non-maintained schools. They did not apply to further or higher education teachers, or to pre-school education. Britain still fell short, therefore, of having a trained graduate professional education service. By 1988, the percentage of primary schoolteachers who were graduates had risen to 30 per cent, of secondary teachers 63 per cent (HMI, 1991).

Moreover, the nature of the training received was variable, and it was generally recognized that the one-year Post-graduate Certificate of Education was too short. There were strong recommendations in the 1970s for a two-year PGCE, and the arguments then advanced still apply, although they may by now be considered alongside the argument that the period of probation or induction should be considered as part of initial training, and the further argument that this period should be of two years as in Scotland, and not one as in England and Wales.

The early 1980s brought valuable contributions from HMI (1982), ACSET (1982), HMI (1983), and again ACSET (1984). There was a general professional consensus in favour of agreed guidelines on the content of initial training, and these were largely adopted and reflected in DES Circular 3/84. Partnership was still in the air. There was a particular emphasis on partnership between schools and higher education in covering essential practical professional aspects of preparing to teach, over and above teaching-subject studies, methodology of subject-teaching, or educational disciplines. Beyond the common ground of class management and control, full range of ability, behaviour, social background and culture, the ACSET working group shows an emphasis on group interaction, insight into how a school works, communication, staffroom participation, self-organization, preparation for next stages; HMI on values and continuing professional development; DES on assessment, education system, language, with some rearguard action on specialist help for special needs.

Of the trainers, all three emphasized that higher education tutors must have or be provided with 'recent, relevant and significant experience in schools' (ACSET, 1982).

Of supervisors in schools, the ACSET working group alone expected an understanding of the policy and intentions of the whole course, and it alone insisted on adequate recognition of the professional time and resources required from schools.

The message in Circular 3/84 for the proposed surgery of the 1990s is in a final sentence:

> Opportunities should be provided for students to reflect on and learn from their own classroom experience, and to place their role as a teacher within the broader context of educational purposes.

Through the 1980s, there was considerable progress towards the equal professional partnership of schools and higher education in developing professional competence. Some good collaborative systems were developed, despite the still unrecognized commitment of schools moving into a more disciplined self-costing mode of management. These schemes required a reduction in the number of schools involved if partnership was to be a reality. That raised issues of other kinds, which would grow more acute in the 1990s, when funding to participating schools would be required whatever the partnership pattern. HMI, having gained consent in the early 1980s to inspect university-based as well as public sector courses, was able to publish surveys of both in 1987 and 1988.

The ACSET advice on criteria for approval of initial training courses having been adopted in DES Circular 3/84 (Wales 21/84) and implemented by the new CATE, prescribed minimum periods based in schools. Revised criteria (DES circular 24/89 and Welsh Office 59/89) required school participation in the selection of students, planning and evaluation, supervision and assessment of school-based work. A further report in 1991 of school-based initial teacher training showed up particular weaknesses in the school side of partnerships, which lacked trained mentors or teacher-tutors, and especially in the licensed teacher scheme, introduced against professional advice by the Secretary of State as a new route in 1990, and taken up largely by previously trained and often experienced overseas teachers.

> So far, most licensed teachers have been appointed to schools which are faced with difficulty in attracting and retaining staff. Few such schools are able to provide the time and expertise needed to provide a satisfactory training. Only rarely have mentors received training for their role and few receive enough, if any, extra time in which to carry it out. (HMI, 1991)

HMI, having expressed reservations about this hastily introduced government scheme already rejected in Scotland, would now be included on the radical right agenda as another obstacle of the 'educational establishment' to be removed or reconstructed. However, the immediate effect of their report can be seen to have informed the moves towards more effective school-based initial teacher training.

MORE SCHOOL-BASED INITIAL TEACHER TRAINING PROPOSALS

That is the professional background to the different proposals made, both by the Secretary of State in his January 1992 keynote speech to the North of England Conference, and by the main opposition parties. Both emphasize the continuing role of CATE, which had been and would continue to be under political attack from the political right. Since the GTC proponents envisaged that the proposed General Teaching Council would oversee or incorporate the work of CATE in the future, there was a direct interest in the proposals now being made, and added urgency given to the action proposed for 1992 to follow our substantial statement on Induction with one on Initial Education of Teachers. There was much in the January keynote speech which could have been well received in other circumstances, not least the European context and its emphasis on the teaching profession; indeed, it stands out among such annual declarations as one of the two or three most significant of the 1980s and 1990s. It was, however, also tinged with the pressure-group agenda in seeking to 'break the hold of the dogmas about teaching method and classroom organization which are now being challenged not only by me but by very many other people'. It appeared to use the 1991 HMI report selectively, to drive a wedge between 'schools and institutions' by asserting that it is the former 'that have the direct experience of teaching the pupils', disregarding the conditions laid down in 1984 that teacher-trainers should have recent, relevant and substantial experience of teaching in schools, and slipping towards the already outdated distinctions being chanted by radical groups about 'theory' in training institutions as opposed to 'the thorough, practical experience that can only come from school-based work under the supervision of serving teachers'.

The responses gathered by GTC (England and Wales) to these proposals, formulated as a consultation document later in January 1992, are a rich source of the state of the art and insights from the different branches of the education service and those connected with it. Schoolteacher associations, teacher-training groups, local authorities, providers and parents were speaking with one voice, seeking moderation. Although it was apparent from the January speech that consultation would not change markedly the announced thrust, this was still an opportunity to modify the least acceptable excesses. The GTC advices and comments are appended because they summarized the consensus view and still constitute many of the aspirations of educators. They also include some important issues still to be taken up, such as area training partnerships.

In the event, there were modifications to the original proposals for secondary schoolteachers. The now renamed Department for Education (DfE) Circular 9/92 and Welsh Office 35/92 in June modified the proportion of school-based training, to be two-thirds rather than four-fifths; and this was already the practice in some partnerships, such as the Oxford PGCE scheme. There had, however, been a change of Secretary of State in March, and consultation on professional matters was not to be seen in the next two years.

A DES report on primary schools was sharply commissioned in November 1991 to be delivered within weeks by the 'three wise men', one a respected researcher in primary school education, the second the chief HMI for primary education, and the third the person later to be implanted as senior CHMI. The title given to them reflected the short Christmas season in which they had to make their journey rather than the perceived wisdom of accepting such a commission. Focused on curriculum organization and classroom practice, and seen to support a swing back towards streaming and whole-class teaching, their report had stated implications for initial teacher training. Instead of a consultation paper, the DES issued first a Press announcement on a school-based training project based on City Technology Colleges, with a later letter for information to education bodies, and then not a consultation document but a draft circular in June 1993 on IT for primary schoolteachers. The GTC movement, again drawing on the evidence of all its by now 30 constituents, had to accept that there was not the proper basis for dialogue with government. It did trawl association views, and again the evidence to GTC is a rich source of professional opinion. It did set down at length its comments, and also published them alongside a previously formulated statement of guiding principles and key issues (GTC Trust, 1993) against which any proposals should be judged. But having done all this in the six weeks given, it had in all honesty to preface its remarks as follows:

> This draft circular is not a proper basis for future development. It should be withdrawn. Good quality training of teachers is essential to the quality of education, and its development should be informed by a proper process of consultation. (GTC, 30 July 1993)

It was left to others inside and outside Parliament to draw the conclusions, both positive and negative, which were to be realized seven years later.

> We have never needed a General Teaching Council more. There is no doubt that the profession – both the trainers and the teachers – will be entirely against the more deleterious of the Government's proposals and directions. The question is whether they will develop the unity to select out what is good and to reject what is damaging and will lead to lower standards, not just in training but in the schools themselves. If unity cannot be achieved and the Government, as I am sure it will, fails to convince the profession that it has either their or children's interests genuinely at heart, then we shall end up in the inevitable position of a teaching force progressively less well-trained while remaining as overworked as it is now. The effects on recruitment and retention will be undeniable, but they will not matter within the time-scale of the average short-sighted politician, as their full effect will not be felt in the lifetime of the current Parliament. (Cashdan, 1993)

FINDING ALTERNATIVE ROUTES TO LEGISLATION

The GTC proposals of August 1992 were meanwhile circulating among political as well as professional groups, and were being followed up, wherever possible, across the political board. One helpful new element was the confirmation that Don Foster, the Liberal Democrat who had replaced Chris Patten as MP for Bath, would now act as spokesman for education; predecessors such as Michael Carr had been temporary and insecure. Don Foster was to be an active and strongly challenging supporter of the GTC movement. Not having made any impression on the Secretaries of State, we were seeking advice from other Conservative parliamentarians, not least Sir Malcolm Thornton, whose select committee had been so clearly in support. This extract from our letter to him of October 1992 was written despite the reluctance of some member associations to have anything more to do with the government and its supporters.

> The Secretary of State has understandably enough indicated that he requires new and compelling reasons to depart from the view taken by his predecessors. The Report enclosed offers such reasons, pointing to the Government's own reforms as being the new element which requires such a Council.
>
> We very much hope the Secretary of State will now wish to discuss the document, which he received in advance of publication six weeks ago. Obviously, our preference would be for legislation along these lines to be initiated by the Government. If that is not considered a timely Government priority, we at least would hope to contribute to a climate in which the Government would not by now object to legislation, whether introduced as a Private Member's Bill or just possibly as an amendment to pending legislation. For that reason, we do not want to force negative responses, e.g. to questions in either House or in public gatherings. We do, however, want to make progress, and would greatly value your personal advice.

The advice offered after informal soundings confirmed that it would be extremely unlikely that there would be any sense in pursuing the matter in the Commons, that our approach to the House of Lords offered a much better way forward, and that the sort of rational debate which would take place there would offer a much better chance of success.

Those who had already supported the GTC case in debates in 1989 and 1991 required no prompting; indeed Lord Butterfield and others had been pursuing and encouraging us with enquiries. Supporters included the very significant body of cross-benchers, who invited the GTC Chair and Secretary to address them in March 1993 under the Chairmanship of Lord Dainton. Lord Dainton, a person of great standing within and beyond the education service, whose report on Education for Science and Engineering had had strong impact in the 1960s, and whose services to science, the universities and libraries were to continue over the ensuing three decades, was to remain an extraordinarily effective GTC proponent and friend until his death only days before legislation was introduced to the Lords late in 1998. Among Conservatives, Lord Carlisle reiterated his support but indicated that he was no longer sufficiently involved to take a lead, suggesting other names. The Labour lords were for a time to be led by Frank Judd, who would see and articulate the GTC as the key reform worth pursuing by his party. Helpful discussions were also held with Lord Bishops, who were to add valuable advice to the ensuing debates. The first opportunity came with the second reading and subsequent debates of the Education Bill. This Bill, unlike the one which followed hard on its heels, was not primarily concerned with the teaching profession, but the Lords turned their debate in that direction. Here are some of the extracts from *Hansard* 23–24 March 1993 which serve to show the strength of support and the care taken by the Government Minister Baroness Blatch to acknowledge it.

Extracts from second reading of Education Bill, House of Lords

23–24 March 1993

Baroness Blatch: We see this Bill as another significant milestone in education . . . It will give professional teachers the space and support to practise their art.

Lord Judd: Where is the commitment to create a general teaching council to ensure a sound professional status and reliable professional standards for our teachers?

Lord Ritchie of Dundee: [The Bill] contains nothing to boost teacher morale; nothing such as the Secretary of State being given powers to set up a general teaching council.

The Lord Bishop of Guildford: Parents, teachers and administrators should not be set against each other. They need each other and they look for encouragement to work together. Education without the good will and expertise of the teaching profession is a lost cause. Therefore, I shall be supporting an amendment that will enable the setting up of a general teaching council. That could provide a forum for different groups to work together to improve quality in the teaching profession.

Lord Dainton: One may ask: who are the key players in school in that enterprise? They are the teachers whom we are in danger of forgetting entirely in the legalistic prose of the Bill . . . To be of greatest help to their pupils, teachers must have the training for, and be given the responsibility to adapt their teaching to achieve what they judge to be in the best interests of the individual John or Mary. Teachers have a duty to deliver the best possible service to their pupils in exactly the same way as the doctor has to his patient, the lawyer to his client, the priest to his parishioner, and so forth. In a word, the teachers have to be – and we seem to be forgetting this – true professionals bearing heavy responsibilities from which they must not flinch. To accomplish this, they must be allowed autonomy and discretion to act in the best interests of their pupils . . . rather than being (as the Bill implies to some degree) merely the passive conduits of what is handed down through detailed and prescriptive Acts of Parliament and regulations.

These two alone [the competitive market place, and the National Curriculum and testing] are not enough to make a successful school education system. We also need the active and enthusiastic involvement of good teachers.

I believe that we now have many good teachers . . . teachers today are better educated and trained and anxious to serve. Just like the members of all major professions, today's teachers are ready and willing to take responsibility for their profession's development and for the determination and maintenance of its standards and codes of conduct. If this self-regulation were to be permitted, I believe that there would be a significant and extremely valuable enhancement of teachers' commitment to their jobs. It has been my experience throughout my time in education that giving responsibility invariably liberates new energies and ingenuity on the part of the recipient.

None of what I have said is new. The Scots, mindful as ever of the value of good education, have always accorded a high degree of respect to the dominie. Some years ago they established a Scottish Teaching Council, the performance and value of which have attracted high praise from the Scottish Education Department. We need something in England and Wales which builds on that Scottish experience. There is nothing in the Bill along those lines, and that omission should be remedied. Here I am at one with the Right Reverend Prelate the Bishop of Guildford. I hope that the improvement will come about during the later stages of the progress of the Bill through your Lordships' House.

Lord Renfrew: I was in agreement with everything that the noble Lord, Lord Dainton, said about the active role of teachers. Certainly, it is clear that the quality of education in our schools depends upon the quality of teachers, the quality of their teaching, and the extent to which they are free to teach in an effective manner.

Baroness David: I had hoped to speak of . . . a general teaching council.

Earl Baldwin of Bewdley: Unfortunately there is no mention of a GTC, though we may hear more of that later.

Lord Elton: It will take much to restore the standing of the profession, and acts of statesmanship on both sides to restore the sense of partnership in education.

Lord Dormand of Easington: It can give no pleasure to any of us to witness the low morale of teachers . . . If the Government had any real respect for teachers, they could have demonstrated it in an important way with the Bill. They could have proposed a general teaching council, or whatever they preferred to call it, to compare with parallel professional organizations. Such a body would not only raise the status of the teaching profession in the eyes of the public and parents; it would raise the standards and the morale of teachers themselves.

A number of us in this House and in another place – I know that my noble friend Lord Glenamara has done so – have raised the matter on a number of occasions. The Government's reply has been, 'It should come from the teachers themselves.' That is a demonstration of the lack of interest of the Government. The noble Baroness shakes her head. I was about to say that the feeling has built up in recent months. The proposal now comes from the teachers themselves. We shall see how the Government respond. There is a strong feeling for such a body among teachers. If the Government were to agree to meetings very soon, I predict that a general teaching council would be established within a matter of months. For once, let the Government take the initiative in this matter.

Baroness Carnegy of Lour: The noble Lord, Lord Dainton, identified, as only he can, what it is that young people need from schools and what makes for active and involved teachers. He spoke of the advantages of self-regulation of the teaching profession. As a Scot, and from experience, I agree with him.

Baroness Brigstocke: I was moved by the eloquent support for teachers voiced by the noble Lord, Lord Dainton, and my noble friend Lord Renfrew of Kaimsthorn. Appreciation from two such distinguished academics will do much to raise the morale of the profession.

Viscount Brentford: I wonder whether the Bill goes as far as it can to encourage teachers and to improve their morale generally. I hope that it does. I know from speaking to teachers that it is greatly needed.

Baroness Hamwee: As a noble Lord commented, GTC (General Teachers' Council) is the acronym which is missing from the Bill.

Lord Ponsonby of Shulrede: We also wish to amend the Bill to create a GTC. I believe the noble Lord, Lord Dormand, spoke very eloquently about that topic. Lest there be any doubt, I believe that all the teaching unions support that concept and have approached the Government about the formation of a GTC.

Baroness Blatch: I need no prompting to recognise the worth of professional teachers. No politician in this land can pass legislation without having to depend on the commitment and professionalism of teachers to make it happen and work in the classroom . . . There was considerable talk about a general teaching council. We must return to that subject during the passage of the Bill.

The debate was pursued even more vigorously on 20 April, to an amendment helpfully discussed with us beforehand by Lord Butterfield and withdrawn, having secured assurances of further consideration. On 10 May, a further debate at committee stage was instigated, this time under an amendment (No. 246) by Lord Judd, which would have required the Secretary of State to undertake consultation with a view to establishing a GTC for England and Wales and to report the outcome to Parliament within twelve months. Effectively introduced by Lord Judd and strongly supported across political divisions by Earl Baldwin, Baroness Seear, Lord Walton, Baroness Warnock, Lord Dormand, Baroness Faithfull, Lord Butterfield, Baroness Park and the Lord Bishop of Guildford whilst opposed only by Baroness Cox, Baroness Perry and the Minister, the amendment was pressed to a vote but was lost 114 to 135, the voting pattern showing a division among Conservative peers, some torn between loyalty to government and their personal view. *Hansard* for that day is a valuable record.

A GOVERNMENT TEACHER TRAINING AGENCY

Education Bills were by now becoming an annual event, and 1993 was to be no exception. The Bill introduced by John Patten was seen as a two-pronged assault on higher education, student grants and the higher education funding of teacher training. It had the effect of forging an even stronger alliance between those representing higher education 'providers' and the rest of the education service, and within Parliament the particularly strong higher education lobby was added to those who were already voicing support for a GTC. The Bill brought into being a Teacher Education Alliance, co-ordinated by the official only recently seconded to the National Commission on Education, with an added dimension of co-ordinated briefing and lobbying.

Whereas CATE had no statutory existence, the Teacher Training Agency, which was to replace it, would have powers and duties derived directly from the Secretary of State. It was seen to offend key features of the historical relationship of educators and the State: the aspiration to university education comparable to that of other recognized professions; the aspiration to have a GTC responsible for professional quality issues; and the understanding that teachers should be free from close political or State control. The TTA as a government agency would control teacher supply and training, it would control funding of academic research related to teaching and therefore undermine the independence and impartiality of scholarship and enquiry, and it was perceived as a quango which would remove the prospect of a GTC. Moreover, with a brief to promote forms of school-based training, it would deter universities from the provision already being made.

The Education Bill was very rudely received indeed in the House of Lords, as vigorously opposed by Conservative peers as by cross-benchers and Bishops (*Hansard*, 9 December 1993). It was the subject of an adverse report from the House of Lords Delegated Powers Scrutiny Committee (9 December 1993), demanding added scrutiny from Parliament. It created the *Times Educational Supplement* leader headline: 'Send for a GTC'. It concluded that whilst Downing Street would have its way for the immediate future,

> The ideal solution at the next stage would be a General Teaching Council; if ever there was an idea whose time had come it is the GTC. The more the focus of training is switched to a school base – and that movement is bound to continue – the more we need such a national body to accredit, monitor, co-ordinate and validate. Now more than ever teachers are prepared to assert their right to control entry and standards in their own profession, and are receiving powerful support on all sides. If John Patten craves acclaim for his legislation, he could transform his chances by building in a GTC. (*TES*, 12 November 1993)

GTC (England and Wales) was meanwhile inviting the Houses of Parliament to introduce amendments to that effect, with a detailed series of amendments and explanations, prefaced by a general statement:

> Whilst sharing the general concern that
> a) the partnership of higher education and schools should continue to develop in the initial education and training of teachers, and
> b) there should be a separation of powers as between the distribution of funds and the establishment of criteria for quality control, and
> c) that both should be distanced from the promotion of particular political directions,
> GTC (England and Wales) asks in particular that these objectives be achieved by the creation of a General Teaching Council alongside the funding agencies (13 December 1993).

Letters were written to all who had contributed since 1989 in parliamentary debates on the GTC, and the following extract is typical:

> Part I of the Bill is so directly about the future of the teaching profession and the nature of its service to the public, that the GTC issue will be seen by everyone as crucial to the whole debate.
> Whilst it is most encouraging to witness the unity of independent and opposition groups in opposing the Teacher Training Agency proposals, we would be doubly gratified if the GTC proposal could be seen also by supporters of the Government as part of a better alternative or even merely an expedient last resort. In the long term the proposal for an open and inclusive professional council must depend on political goodwill from all sides, and we would hope that could be engendered by an amendment sponsored by a cross-bench group.

ST GEORGE'S HOUSE, WINDSOR

This legislation was already in the foreground by the time another initiative had come to fruition. The Comino Foundation had offered to support a GTC Consultation, and we had arranged this as a retreat at St George's House, Windsor, involving GTC Directors with parliamentarians from both Houses and other public figures. The Consultation took place on 25–26 January 1994. Its purpose was not just to engage with parliamentarians who might influence the passage of the teacher training part of the Bill introduced before Christmas, but to examine in depth the underlying case for a GTC and the principles involved. The Consultation began with a shared listening session, in which Reg Dyne, the UKCC Assistant Registrar for professional standards and ethics, presented the analogous policy and practice of the nursing profession, whose Council had been strengthened by legislation in the 1980s and again in the 1990s. Discussions followed on the GTC Proposals and how they related to the proposals before Parliament. For those taking part, there were three significant outcomes. First, it became clear to parliamentarians that this was no conspiracy for a mega-union, and that the proposals in fact distanced the GTC from union matters or from any possibility of a GTC being dominated by one interest. Second, for GTC proponents, it was realized that the composition of the Council, whilst safeguarding the public interest, had to be articulated so that this was evident to parliamentarians. Finally, for all participants, the priority of seeking a statement of professional ethics was much stronger.

There were several immediate effects. In the following week, the House of Lords had set aside a day to debate the Report of the National Commission on Education, *Learning to Succeed*, and *Hansard* of 2 February 1994 records not only a further set of supportive references to the GTC, as recommended by the Commission, but specific reference to the St George's House meeting by Lord Butterfield on behalf of those in the Chamber who had taken part. Moreover, Lord Elton, a government supporter, had satisfied himself at Windsor that Ministers should hear the case for themselves, and very promptly arranged a meeting with John Tomlinson and Baroness Blatch, the Minister of State who was introducing the Bill to the Lords. So after four years of Ministers declining to meet GTC, the habit was broken on 17 February, in the company of senior civil servants.

The main concern was to assure the Minister that the principal object of the GTC would be to work in the public interest as a protection for parents and pupils, and as a guarantor of standards; and to emphasize that it would not touch activities related to salaries and conditions of service, and was anything but a 'mega-union'.

Discussion ranged from the idea of starting a GTC as an arm's-length body to move to advisory roles once understood and trusted, to the necessity of including teachers in sharing responsibility for their part in national policy, and having scope for initiatives and professional judgement without which reforms would fail.

There was of course no prospect at this stage that the mind of the Secretary of State, the passage of the Bill or the introduction of the TTA would be affected, although it has to be said that in the ensuing debates, the responses both of Baroness Blatch in the Lords and in the Commons of Robin Squire, that most able and knowledgeable of government spokesmen, were measured and courteous. The impression was left that the GTC case had been pushed an important stage further forward, and that we would need to look a year or two ahead.

A further outcome was the decision by GTC Directors to commission a study of the ethics of the teaching profession; the invitation was accepted by Meryl Thompson, and both the process instigated and the publication of her discussion document are considered in a separate chapter.

Another immediate effect was the issue of a simplified statement of the GTC proposal, for those many parliamentarians who would not take time to study the full proposals document or perhaps even its summary.

THE GENERAL TEACHING COUNCIL FOR ENGLAND AND WALES

There should be formed a statutory General Teaching Council for England and Wales (GTC).

Why is it needed?

- to be a guarantor of the professional quality of service offered by teachers;
- to be a protector of the public interest, as are such Councils in almost all other professions;
- to give recognition of the essential service of teachers to the health and prosperity of society.

The prime object of the GTC shall be the regulation of the teaching profession so as to maintain and improve the quality of education, in the interests of children, their parents, and students of all ages.

To this end the GTC will have a duty:

- to maintain a register of those entitled to teach in schools and colleges;
- to advise on and take account of the standards required for teachers' initial education and training, induction and continuing development;
- to establish and uphold the ethical principles governing the teaching profession and rules of conduct and guidances on good practice derived from them;
- to take measures to ensure that these are observed by all teachers as a condition of being registered, and to have powers to withdraw, review and reinstate names from the register;
- to advise on the supply, recruitment and retention of teachers;
- to consider other matters related to teachers referred to it by the Secretary of State;
- to publish an annual report.

The Council will have powers:

- to raise a periodic registration fee from teachers to fund its work;
- to receive other grants and donations;
- to commission, promote or undertake enquiries and research in pursuance of its objects;
- to publish documents and statements in relation to its work;
- to make recommendations to the Secretary of State, to the public and to teachers on any matter related to that work.

The Council will be so constituted as to enable the teaching profession to take responsibility for acting both in the public interest, informed by insights into all aspects of the profession of teaching, and in the interests of the professional development of teachers throughout the education service.

To this end the Council will have a majority of registered teachers with experience across the education service, complemented by a significant proportion of lay members representing the public interest.

(Statement issued by the Directors of GTC (England and Wales), March 1994)

OPPOSITION EDUCATION POLICIES

John Patten's counterpart as Shadow Secretary of State was by now Ann Taylor. She had made a good impression as someone thoughtfully going about the business of preparing an alternative agenda. It was to be a disappointment when she was moved to another role; she was not prepared to exchange cheap jibes and 'yaboo' with John Patten, and her common sense was accordingly criticized by the media as low profile. She would have been, and perhaps still may be, a worthy Secretary of State. The Labour Party policy statement *Opening Doors to a Learning Society*, which she put before its annual conference, had already committed the party to guarantee that teaching would remain a graduate-entry profession, and that it would put in place a GTC to recognize and promote the professional status of teaching. It was followed in September 1993 by its green paper on education, and both impressed as a genuine attempt to consult across a broad spectrum. The renewed commitment to a statutory General Teaching Council was welcome and encouraging, though much more could have been made of it, and GTC Directors invited the Labour Party to see it as a matter of urgency and an alternative to the non-funding side of the proposed TTA.

Such a commitment had already been given in the Lords by Earl Russell (7 December 1993) on behalf of Liberal Democrats, with the challenge to Labour to do the same. The Liberal Democrat spokesman in the Commons, Don Foster, was, however, to offer an alternative, which would be to make the TTA the executive arm of a GTC.

REVIEW AND FOLLOW-UP

In looking ahead, we were greatly helped by the political wisdom, encouragement and friendship of Lord Dainton. My note of a day's discussion on 3 June 1994 between Lord Dainton with John Tomlinson and myself typifies the strategy and tactics which would now be adopted to introduce legislation for the General Teaching Council, and could indeed be seen in retrospect to have been prophetic.

1. Review of present position(s)
a. political
GTC having drafted a proposal for a private Bill in 1992 had instead been compelled by events to seek amendments to those parts of the 1993 and 1994 government legislation which related to the training of teachers. This had had the effect of including the GTC proposals as a serious part of the debate, and of securing commitments for the future from Opposition parties as well as the supportive cross-bench group. On the Government side, the political imperative of securing at least part of the 1994 legislation

had obscured differences of view about the GTC. There had however been signs and signals of support.

There were those among Government supporters who wished to see a General Teaching Council, but would not be able to support it as the alternative to the Teacher Training Agency (TTA). A private bill would need to be seen by Government supporters to complement the TTA, and by opposition parties to be able to replace it. These differences had to be borne in mind in re-drafting a Bill. They might be reduced once the deficiencies of the TTA became apparent.

b. public

There was support in and beyond the education press, and among those representing parents, governors, public authorities and churches. Public awareness had to be raised.

c. Professional

Teachers were generally supportive, but were overwhelmed by other requirements. There was a need to ensure that teachers generally were prepared for the next GTC move, and could support it actively. Current work on the professional ethic would involve them more strongly. Teachers were no less professionally committed and conscientious as a result of political controls, but their voluntary commitment was too much absorbed in making those controls work.

d. Civil servants

Would seek reassurance that the GTC would not undermine their position, but could add professional insights to the information they must continue to have. Further discussions were needed at all levels.

2. Ways forward

The choice appears to be between waiting for a new administration before seeking new legislation, or building now on progress made. However, the former option would require a new administration (1996/7) to include education in a legislative programme, and it might be the year 2000 before a Government Bill could be put through. There was good cause to keep current cross-bench and Opposition support, and work hard to increase interest or lessen opposition among Conservatives, in order to be able to choose the timing of a private Bill.

A Bill introduced with a General Election in the offing might at the same time find cross-party support and prepare the ground for a government wishing to build without delay on the start made.

Conclusion

The balance of advantage would be to use the next twelve months in multi-pronged political consultation and professional and public awareness-raising, together with visible work on professional good practice. A re-drafting of the proposed Bill should involve updating to take account of recent legislation, and might be presented in terms of a GTC-starting Bill, framed to be capable of extension by stages. A review of progress made on all these fronts might best be made by Easter 1995, with the possibility of introducing a private Bill through the Lords at any time after that.

GTC would take on the task of drafting, if necessary with specialist parliamentary drafting advice. It was appreciated that the task of presenting and carrying through a private Bill of this importance must involve more than one person, but the readiness to be that person was a source of great encouragement to all those involved in the GTC initiative.

Meanwhile, we would be constantly in communication about measures being taken to the above ends, and opportunities would be taken to raise the GTC issue informally with Ministers and civil servants.

It will be understood that Lord Dainton had offered to take responsibility to seek an appropriate opportunity to introduce such a Bill, and during 1995 and 1996 he continued to take soundings and there was constant contact with him for this purpose.

At the June GTC Forum, it was possible to report that all the suggestions made by GTC for amendments to the Bill had been raised in the Lords debate. An amendment proposing the statutory General Teaching Council had been defeated, but the balance of arguments was strongly in favour and the *Hansard* record would be valuable for future reference. The suggestion from a partnership profession that all initial training courses should involve both schools and higher education institutions had been carried, but was being reversed in the Commons standing committee. The Bill had been modified as a result of the Lords debate, but the political imperative to establish a Teacher Training Agency had been asserted. The case for the GTC had been reiterated in the Commons Standing Committee, and was now policy for the two main opposition parties. That, whilst welcome, made it all the more important for GTC to insist on the cross-party nature of its proposals and to build on the support which is also to be found in the government party. The prospect of a further initiative in 1995 would have to be considered carefully, and from the 1994 debates it can be seen what might be the paths worth pursuing:

The debates of both Houses record widespread support for the GTC proposals, although the post-Maastricht political imperative was to salvage at least Part I of the Bill, Part II on student associations having been reduced to a shadow under pressure. Among *Hansard* records, the House of Lords Second Reading, 7 December 1993 (Vol. 550 No. 11) and Committee Reports 10.3.94 (Vol. 552 No. 54), Report (Vol. 547 No. 156), together with the free-standing February debate in the Lords on the National commission report, make important references to the GTC proposal.

The House of Lords Amendment No. 65 was that:

There shall be established a body corporate to be known as the General Teaching Council for England and Wales to advise the Secretary of State on the supply and education of teachers, to advise the Secretary of State on criteria for the accreditation of courses or institutions for the provision of initial teacher education and training, and to maintain a register of those persons qualified to teach in schools.

Although all but a very few speakers were in favour of a statutory GTC, this amendment to create a GTC was eventually defeated under whip in the Lords by a quite narrow margin, and when the GTC issue was reintroduced in the Commons (see *Hansard* 3.5.94, Vol. 242 No. 95), it was resisted by the government at Committee stage, and the April–May reports of Standing Committee E record these debates. However, even among those who voted against, there was strong support in principle, and on this we could continue to build. The general disposition can be gauged by these cross-party quotations from debates in Lords and Commons:

From the Lords:

Baroness David: A general teaching council would give the teaching profession a standing body to safeguard standards.

Baroness Lockwood: I can only lament the fact that the Government did not take the opportunity to establish a general teaching council rather than establishing another controversial agency. It would have given a new confidence both to the teaching profession and to higher education. One must ask: why is it that the Government always seems to believe it knows better than the profession for which they seek to legislate?

Lord Dormand: The case for a GTC, like the case for nursery education, is unassailable and not in dispute by anyone who knows anything about education.

Lord Walton: We need and indeed must have a general teaching council for England and Wales . . .Why are the Government so implacably opposed to the proposal in the light of the cogent and responsible documents prepared by those in the teaching profession promoting the establishment of such a body? What has happened to the hallowed and cherished principle of professional self-regulation, fully accepted by government in relation to other professions?

The Lord Bishop of Ripon: I am no supporter of professional isolation . . . teachers need to look to all sorts of other people who are involved in education: to parents and to others in the community. But all of this involves a strong profession at the core.

Lord Plant: While we are undertaking one strategy to professionalise the nurses, we are going down a different path which may de-professionalise the teachers.

The Earl of Limerick: Teaching is a graduate-level profession and one would assume that standards in teaching are best set and delivered by teachers.

Lord Judd. The establishment of a GTC, possibly at a stroke, would repair the morale of the teaching profession and reverse the decline in the public perception of teachers.

Lord Beloff. It is an extraordinary anomaly for those who believe in the importance of teaching . . . that in every other profession one can look to a central body . . .Teachers should feel that they are valid.

Lord Dainton: Professional people who have to give a service to others, whether they be doctors dealing with patients, lawyers dealing with clients or teachers with children, will give of their best if they are invited . . . to accept a responsibility and are entrusted with a measure of discretion in its discharge; if they feel they have some influence on who may be allowed to join their ranks and share their responsibilities; if they are permitted to establish a professional code of conduct; and if, out of their experience, they can formulate advice and proposals for the improvement of the delivery of their service to which the Government would at least listen. The best means for doing that in the case of school education is the general teaching council proposed by the amendment.

Baroness Warnock. There is an absolute reason for it to be a statutory body . . . There already is a non-statutory general teaching council under Professor Tomlinson, which is flourishing and which is supported by a large number of teachers.

Lord Elton. I am a friend to the general proposition that there should be a general teaching council because I believe that it is a means by which teachers could earn that change in self-regard and public regard.

Lord Glenamara: Now all the teachers' unions and the bodies interested in this council have come together and reached agreement. It can be done. I have never known morale in the education system to be as low as it is at present. If the Government want to improve it they could begin by creating a general teaching council. I can assure the noble Baroness [Blatch] that it will do an enormous amount to raise morale in the teaching profession. Even if she cannot accept the amendment, I implore her to say that she will at some point produce some kind of plan for establishing a general teaching council.

Lord Annan: Although I am in favour of a general teaching council, I think that we need to have a draft constitution . . . the way forward is for those who are in favour of such a proposal – I would willingly support them if I could see such a constitution – to introduce a Private Member's Bill either in another place or in your Lordships' House.

Lord Murray: We really cannot spend half our time denouncing the teaching unions and their members for irresponsibility and the other half of our time denying them any responsibility . . . I am sure that offering members of the profession the opportunity to be involved in shaping their own future, establishing their own conditions and enforcing their own standards of conduct would be enormously helpful.

And in the Commons:

Mr Wyn Griffiths: On all sides, we can agree that there should be means by which teachers become well qualified and enter a stable environment in which a conscious effort can be made to ensure that learning in the profession is a continuous process. The evidence is that a General Teaching Council would provide an excellent framework to carry out the Bill's objectives in a superb manner.

Ms Estelle Morris: For any issue under discussion today that impinges on education, we can argue that a general teaching council would be important as a forum through which to contribute . . . to improve the quality of our teachers we must consider reprofessionalising the teaching profession . . . A GTC can improve the profession of teachers and there is no disagreement that that needs to be done.

GTC OFFICERS

GTC (England and Wales) was started on a shoe-string, and continued that way, depending on voluntary service for all but the clerical functions of convening meetings and dealing with enquiries. However, by 1992, the Chair and Secretary were committed well beyond what might originally have been envisaged. John Tomlinson, as Director of the Institute of Education at the University of Warwick, was at the centre of the pressures affecting all teacher-training establishments, not least because of the government proposals; and I had already moved from running the Education Management Unit at London, to European Union development work for Central and Eastern Europe, working from Oxford. Having intimated in 1992 that the position of Secretary should be reviewed, and having given eighteen months' notice, I was succeeded as Honorary Secretary in September 1994 by Roger Haslam, who had previously become involved as a UCET working party member and then as a GTC Director, also editing the GTC CPD document, and who was now retiring as Head of Settle High School; and Malcolm Lee from our host association NATFHE took part of the role as honorary treasurer. I was invited to become Vice-Chair to share some of the pressure. That foursome was to continue by annual election for the next six years.

They were years in which the context had changed drastically and would continue to do so. The argument for a GTC had been won; the profession across all sectors, the major providers of schools, further and higher education, the public, the media, and most parliamentarians of all hues would have wanted it; but it was not on the government agenda. The TTA had been installed instead, and would have in some of its functions to be either replaced, advised, supervised or subsumed by a GTC. The GTC Secretary had meanwhile written to the Chair-Elect of the Teacher Training Agency, previously known as a supporter of the GTC movement, and cordial working relations were established, as they had been with the now superseded CATE, without touching the controlling politically appointed councils of either body. In another transformation of the context, the radically changed national inspectorate had been given a role for teacher-training institutions which was akin to the visitations by the GTC in Scotland. However, the Secretary of State, having inherited and pursued a programme with apparent relish in antagonizing anyone in the way, even to the point of being successfully sued for libel, had to go in July 1994; but the agencies once created were there to establish their roles.

Chapter 7

Towards Legislation 1995–97

The review with Lord Dainton and in the June Forum of GTC associations provided the agenda for the next three years, across political, public and professional activities. A Bill introduced with a General Election in the offing might at the same time find cross-party support and prepare the ground for a government wishing to build without delay on the start made. The balance of advantage would be to use the next twelve months in multi-pronged political consultation and professional and public awareness-raising, together with visible work on professional good practice. A re-drafting of the proposed Bill should involve updating to take account of recent legislation, and might be presented in terms of a GTC-starting Bill, framed to be capable of extension by stages. It was realized that the programme we wanted to pursue would be beyond our resources, but the quest for funding for a Development Officer was not successful. It was to be a period requiring all the skills of chairmanship and the background of finding mutually acceptable positions to overcome both the frustration of political thrusts and the tensions inevitably caused by exploring unresolved issues such as professional ethics.

COMMUNICATION WITH TEACHERS

The third GTC Newsletter was circulated to associates, subject associations and other correspondents in the autumn of 1994. The pamphlet for teachers was updated and reissued to schools and through professional associations in the autumn of 1994, with the assistance of sponsorship from Commercial Union, a major insurer for teachers. A policy for relations with subject associations was agreed which, on a model akin to the medical profession's, kept the GTC distant from an umbrella function for subject associations, but acknowledged the need for channels of communication. This also left the way open, as has been seen, for a parallel College of Teachers initiative.

ETHICS

Through the 1980s and 1990s, it had been recognized that a mark of a profession with a measure of responsibility for its public service was a statement of the ethics of teaching. John Tomlinson had made a point of this in accepting the GTC chairmanship. There had been many such statements, from individual associations, from CATEC, from JCH, from the College of Preceptors, from the Education Council. An adaptation of the UKCC code had been offered by Malcolm Lee after the St George's House Consultation, and he was later to influence the declarations of FENTO. Most of these statements or codes could have formed the basis for a GTC declaration, but there were three immediate and related obstacles. The first was timing, the second ownership, and the third definition.

There were misgivings among some members about a code of conduct being promulgated before the statutory GTC could control its use. The argument was related to the concern about double jeopardy, if a code of conduct were used by employers to justify dismissal. Moreover, although GTC (England and Wales) and its Trust were the nearest available body to being representative of all teachers in all sectors, it was not the body it sought to have established, and had no wish to be identified as more than a shadow of that. The third problem was definition. Was conduct to be construed as minimum acceptable, or as the ideal to which imperfect mortals aspired? Was this to be a code or rules, with the implication that to violate the code was to jeopardize membership of the profession? Or was this to be a general statement of what teaching stands for, and recommendations of good practice? Nigel Harris, in his diligent directory of professional codes of conduct in the United Kingdom (Harris, 1996) had attempted to disentangle codes of ethics, codes of conduct and codes of practice, but had acknowledged that 'each of these expressions is used in a variety of different senses and in ways that overlap'.

For a year or two, GTC Directors could make no progress, for one or other or a combination of these three reasons. By 1994, however, it could be seen that in order for the future GTC to have some preparatory basis for its responsibility for professional ethics, the timing was appropriate for a considered discussion document. It was also recognized that if GTC Directors did not instigate such a study, others could attempt to impose a code. A brief was drawn up by the Chairman, and a grant from the Comino Foundation enabled the Directors to invite two of its alternates to research and write the discussion document on professional ethics. By this time, Michael Barber had been lured into new academic posts and could offer only limited initial support, but Meryl Thompson was part-seconded to undertake the study. This was not to be a definitive statement, but a study in depth to be used as a basis for nationwide professional discussion.

The process was difficult in the extreme. If the discussion document were to be written on behalf of the GTC Directors and Forum and to be recommended by them to the profession and public at large for debate, it would be pursued with their full participation. Every effort was made by Meryl Thompson to secure that, and the more the participation, the greater was the frustration as different educational philosophies were seen to emerge. The document, as will be seen in a later chapter, drew on major works and was itself a significant contribution to thinking about the profession; but that also released objections to the academic tone and could, ironically, have resulted in a consensus to use a very much more simplified summary statement of the kind previously drafted from St George's House and considered premature. The commissioned document was completed and published (Thompson, 1997) with a supportive foreword from John Tomlinson, but had to be seen as a document *for* GTC Directors rather than, as had been hoped, on behalf of and endorsed by the GTC movement for nationwide discussion. Perhaps we had all become so sadly used to 'consultation' documents which were not open to change that the ethos of professional discourse was still not seen by some to be realistic. The document awaits nationwide discussion. A future GTC will be alert to the problems experienced, and all the better able to pursue this task. Certainly, any attempt to impose a professional code of conduct without consensus would be a contradiction in terms.

LINKS WITH OTHER NATIONAL TEACHING COUNCILS

GTC aspirations in the 1970s and 1980s south of the border had long been fuelled by the existence since 1966 of the General Teaching Council for Scotland, which was also providing an example for initiatives in Australia and New Zealand, Eire, Ontario, British Columbia and elsewhere. It was to Scotland above all that we turned for precedent, example and advice. The GTC for Scotland was not a model. We were shown, for example, how difficult it had proved for primary legislation to be amended to extend the GTC's work into continuing professional development or regulation in further education; this informed our proposals, which were perhaps closer to what Scots colleagues would have wished to see as legislation for the 1990s rather than the 1960s. It could also not be a model because of the differences in context: the predominance of one professional association (EIS), the absence of universities from higher education teacher-training institutions, and the dependence of public interests (including parents) on appointment by the Secretary of State are three obvious examples. It had a turbulent start, from which it moved through consolidation in the 1970s to development and adaptation in the late 1980s and 1990s. During the period of confrontational government, it also did not seem prudent to point too frequently to the Scottish precedent: a government which did not wish to accept the case for a GTC in England or Wales could have used the anomaly to question the existence of a GTC for Scotland. We had been advised in 1994 that the GTC for Scotland was not popular with Conservative politicians; no doubt its rejection of the licensed teacher scheme, even though coupled with an acceptable equivalent to promote wider access to teaching, had not endeared it to a government intent on central control.

However, the support of colleagues in the GTC for Scotland was constant and invaluable. Ivor Sutherland, the Registrar, was also drawing BEMAS into the GTC debate and encouraging its renewed and further study of the idea of a profession. Moreover, it was to Scotland that DfEE civil servants and politicians turned for a living example of what was being debated to the south. In Scotland, the Council has 49 members, of whom 30 are elected from primary, secondary, further education and teacher training by national election, together with fifteen representing bodies including churches, universities, regional directors, employers, and the non-university sector of higher education. Four are nominees of the Secretary of State for Scotland,

and there are two assessors from the Scottish Education Department. Teacher associations have no direct role, but it is not difficult for the EIS, for example, to influence elected individuals, most of whom are also its members. The roles and functions are similar to those proposed for England and Wales, though with less scope for advice on continuing professional development, and with a much more direct role in the accrediting of training institution courses by visitation, and in the control of the probationary period which, as we have seen, was extended to two years at the time that it was being abolished in England and Wales. The Council is again trying to agree a code of professional conduct, not having been able to do so in the 1970s. It advises on teacher supply, and although not involved statutorily in teacher recruitment, has a separately funded recruitment unit under its wing. As well as the statutory committees for investigation and discipline, it has standing committees for ITT accreditation and review, probation, education, further education, and communication, together with a committee of convenors (i.e. committee chairs); it also has *ad hoc* committees on such matters as partnership in teacher education, code of conduct, and premises. The 30 years' experience of the GTC for Scotland has been readily put at the disposal of colleagues south of the Border and from other countries.

DISCUSSION WITH CIVIL SERVANTS AND GOVERNMENT AGENCIES

CATE

Since 1992, there had been GTC discussions with CATE, whose Director, Sir William Taylor, was well disposed to the idea of a GTC, and indeed was to contribute to its thinking in 1995. GTC had brought together the views of its member associations to show that the competence approach to teacher qualification was considered too limited. One of the most promising CATE developments was the initiation of area training consortia for monitoring and scrutiny, and it was disappointing that the government put an end to these, no doubt wishing to exercise more direct central control over accreditation rather than peer review. GTC's evidence on initial teacher education had made a strong plea for area professional bodies. So I had written to the CATE area professional committees which had indicated that they would wish to continue to meet voluntarily, inviting them to consider whether this might sensibly be in association with the GTC initiative. Their interest was to be overtaken by events, CATE being replaced by the legislation for a teacher-training agency; however, the question remains: what could and should be the local or regional presence of a GTC?

The Teacher Training Agency, meanwhile, was expected to respond to government demands with a minimum of delay and therefore, in its early years, with unreasonably short time for consultation. The new Secretary of State, moreover, was to accept that it should extend its work into the area of teachers' continuing professional development, beyond its initial legal brief. In 1994, it was already launching the Headlamp voucher scheme for newly appointed headteachers, and picking up where CATE had left the profiles of competences expected for newly qualified teachers. GTC Officers met the TTA Chairman and administrative officer in December 1994, and were able to show just how much further the GTC movement had progressed since 1989, when Geoffrey Parker had been involved. The GTC documents on induction and CPD were made available to TTA, and it was made clear that GTC was already working on professional ethics, which we thought might otherwise have become a TTA project, despite the unsuitability of a government agency for such an exercise. TTA was invited to send a representative to the GTC Extended Forum meetings, and did so. Anthea Millett, a highly respected senior HMI, when appointed as TTA chief executive, was invited as the GTC guest speaker in June 1995. John Tomlinson agreed to contribute in a personal capacity to a TTA committee. The relationship remained cordial, despite the 1993 political background, when TTA was seen to have been established instead of a GTC, and despite the awareness that it was operating in what eventually must become GTC areas of responsibility. An informal understanding of respective roles was to emerge by 1997, when it became evident that the new government would not be removing or radically changing the agency.

In turn, the Directors of SCAA and FEDA, and the OFSTED Head of Teacher Training were invited to contribute to the GTC Forum in 1995 and 1996. It was possible to explore what would be the right relationship between SCAA (now QCA), charged with advising on curriculum and assessment for pupils, and the training requirements for teachers, on which a GTC would advise. With OFSTED moving more systematically into the inspection of teacher-training institutions, similar questions of relationship would have to be explored.

The exploration with FEDA was and will remain crucial. From the outset, the GTC movement had to consider whether its eventual remit should be for teachers in all sectors, even if it might begin with schoolteachers and those who trained them. Further education and higher education were already involved, and were debating through the 1980s and 1990s whether this was in their teacher-training capacity alone, or also as teachers. One-third of teachers in further education were found also to be qualified schoolteachers. The GTC would also expect to be involved as the competent professional Council in any Education Lead Body which eventually emerged from current discussions, and would have an important role in matching competences required, and training, both in a National Vocational Qualification context and in trans-European recognition.

We had already held discussions in 1992 with DfE civil servants on the Lead Body proposals, which the Department was then resisting despite the pressure of the Department of Employment. By 1994, Michael Harrison, former CEO for Sheffield, was assisting in the creation of a Lead Body for education, the last major public field without such a framework, and it was clear that further education was seen as the point of access, with NVQ Level 5 qualifications and with implications for competency teacher qualifications in higher education and in schools. Gillian Shephard had been a champion of NVQ qualifications during her stay as Secretary of State for Employment. The link with the TTA consultation on schoolteacher competences was obvious. Ruth Gee, for the Association of Colleges, was calling for a strategy to 're-professionalize' FE lecturers. Stephen Crowne, the FEDA chief executive, reported that Ministers had clearly decided the FE sector was ready for a new teacher-training framework. GTC Directors had shared discussion with Michael Harrison, and the GTC Forum was aware of the whole-profession context when meeting Stephen Crowne in 1996. Whilst the Lead Body development may not have been as rapid as envisaged, training bodies for FE and HE lecturers were soon to develop very rapidly indeed. In the universities, CVCP had initiated an inquiry leading to the Booth

Report, from which emerged the initiative to create an Institute for Learning and Teaching in Higher Education and the intention to ensure teaching quality by requiring preparatory training for new lecturers. For further education, a new national training agency, FENTO, was to be negotiated, and the GTC was represented in its planning and articulation of national standards, through our Treasurer. The future would demand either the involvement of these new bodies in a GTC or some form of strong linkage across them, or both.

The Lead Body developments were also seen to have European currency. Since the 1992 European Union Maastricht Treaty, and the implementation since January 1993 of professional mobility rights, increasingly recruitment and retention would be seen in the European market, not just in a national one. There would have to be a European dimension to forecasting, and the open professional market would also have an effect on disparate salary and promotion arrangements. This would no doubt be marginal in terms of overall teacher numbers, but would be likely to have more importance in subject-shortage areas, including those from which graduates were being drawn into other careers. It would also have a considerable effect in geographical areas to which it is more difficult to attract native teachers, especially whilst some virtually bilingual European countries are producing more trained teachers than they will need. This was already seen at the tail-end of the late-1980s supply crisis in London boroughs.

Machinery in England and Wales to gauge the appropriateness of qualifications and experience gained in other countries had been extremely weak; indeed, it had consisted largely of approaches from the DfE for an opinion from the British Council. In Scotland, the General Teaching Council was already available as the appropriate body, and accrediting qualifications and experience from the wider European dimension is just an extension of the procedures already in place to regulate supply from England and Wales.

Quality control of supply from other countries, the European Community in particular, would have to be matched by promoting worthwhile experiences in other countries for teachers trained in England and Wales. A General Teaching Council should be promoting international professional enrichment as well as regulating it. One appropriate function of a General Teaching Council would be to give a whole-professional view of such opportunities. Another would be to provide the badly needed reliable framework through which good practice could develop in the employment and if need be retraining of teachers returning from teaching abroad.

LOCAL AUTHORITIES

Although the GTC proposals had from the outset envisaged the involvement of local authorities as employers in a statutory body, the local authority associations had been slow to become involved. The first was WJEC, which continued to be active in its contributions. ACC sat on the fence until 1994, its chief executive having taken a pragmatic view, as an ex-DES civil servant, that there was no scope for negotiation. AMA had been less favourably disposed, at the time when Stephen Byers was in its chair, and it was only through its education secretary Bob Morris that it had become persuaded that the GTC proposal was not just for the sake of 'providers', by which was understood teachers. Early in 1996, AMA became much more strongly interested in becoming involved, held a careful consultation with its members, and after a meeting with GTC officers was welcomed into the Forum. The local authorities would shortly re-group as the Local Government Association (LGA) and play a full and concerted part in the GTC negotiations.

PUBLIC AWARENESS

Agreement on a pamphlet for parents had caused difficulty since the initial proposals, not least because of rapid changes in NCPTA, but Margaret Tulloch, co-opted in 1993 as a GTC Director, had now produced a draft modified from the pamphlet for teachers, which was to be distributed through parent groups and governing bodies in 1995.

REVISED PROPOSALS

In 1994, Directors called for a revision to the GTC proposals and draft bill, both in anticipation of the General Election and in readiness for any opportunity for a private Bill in the Lords or Commons. In revising the 1992 GTC Proposals, we were now able to consult several of the parliamentarians committed to a GTC, having already taken account of their observations during the 1993–94 deliberations. After examination of sections through the spring and summer of 1995, by the autumn a new draft document was ready for Directors to amend and then offer to the member associations for deliberation and debate. It was found possible to make allowances for changes in context since 1992 without having to re-negotiate the agreements on which the proposals were based.

POLITICAL AND PARLIAMENTARY DISCUSSION

By the autumn of 1994, although we had written a courtesy letter to the new Secretary of State, and the Chairman had had useful discussions with the Downing Street policy unit, there was no immediate prospect of a government change of mind. At the same time, a letter was sent to the new Shadow Secretary of State, David Blunkett. Meanwhile, Sir Malcolm Thornton had requested an update on the GTC initiative, for a speech at his party conference, and was continuing to seek a change of heart there. He was keen to put a Private Member's Bill for the establishment of a GTC should the opportunity arise. In the House of Commons, there is scope each year for only a dozen Private Member Bills, drawn at random, and in the autumn of 1995, Sir Malcolm was not among the twelve to be successful.

GTC Directors met David Blunkett and the new Shadow education team on 17 May 1995, and were able to use the revised draft proposals as a basis for discussion. The Shadow team all had a teaching background, and the commitment to try to introduce GTC legislation early in a new administration was confirmed, although in follow-up correspondence David Blunkett clarified that this could not be assured and that a cross-party private Bill was an interim option which would have his support. In 1995, they were joined by Peter Kilfoyle, who would be the main spokesman for school education in the run-up to the General Election. By the autumn of 1996 he had been including questions about the GTC in school visits, and when I met him in October he had been impressed by the strength of teacher opinion. He may also have had a wider vision for the GTC than some other colleagues, and he had informed himself so well in the run-up to the General Election that it was a disappointment that he was to be moved to another responsibility.

Contact and meetings had continued with Liberal Democrats, and the GTC Vice-Chairman and Secretary were invited by Don Foster to the well-disposed Liberal Democrat Education Group in November 1996. Don Foster had a firm grasp of the main issues, and had pursued discussions with the GTC secretary and with me, challenging in particular our views on professionality. For all we knew, we might in a hung parliament be talking to a Minister for Education, and that was no sorry prospect. In the same month, we responded to an invitation to the House of Commons by the Conservative Backbenchers' Education Group. The House of Commons Select Committee had returned to the topic of the status of teaching, was receiving evidence in 1996 from many GTC associations, and was confidently expected to reiterate its recommendations for a GTC.

Everything was happening. Whilst this increase of political activity on all sides was in the period before a General Election, GTC was maintaining its hope that there would be an opportunity to introduce a private Bill in the House of Lords. The new Proposals document, printed and distributed early in 1996, was referred by Lord Dainton to the Clerk for Private Bills in readiness for re-modelling in parliamentary form. There was constant debate among members about the wisdom of a private Bill just before a General Election which might produce an administration committed to GTC legislation anyway. A private Bill would be a paving or enabling Bill, and it was uncertain who would be the Secretary of State 'enabled'. Instead of a short enabling clause, of the kind already tried in amendments to legislation, it would have to contain all the principles of the fuller legislation to ensure that it was not misused. On balance, however, it was seen as a further opportunity for bringing the proposals to the fore, for being seen to seek a political consensus and perhaps enable the much less confrontational Secretary of State to modify the government stance: and if the proposals reached the House of Commons, for testing the position of MPs before they faced the electorate.

One November morning I was taken by surprise by a telephone call from Sir Malcolm Thornton. This year, he had been successful in the draw for the dozen Private Member Bills, and was already fending off lobbyists wanting to use him for a whole range of pressing concerns. He was determined to demonstrate his commitment to the GTC, but would need an immediate drafting for a Bill. It was fortunate that our revised document for full legislation was ready, and that some thought had been given with Lord Dainton to a shorter enabling version. Lord Dainton readily advised that it would now be more profitable to pursue a Bill in the Commons, though he remained prepared to introduce it in the Lords instead. It was possible to draft the Bill and to discuss it with Sir Malcolm on 17 November. He gave notice of this with sponsorship secured from across the three main parties. He took soundings on two options: the first, to make a full proposal, with our document, to secure a full debate and raise the profile, even if there would be no chance of such a detailed proposal running the full course of legislation before May; the second, if it appeared that the present government would remain neutral or even show some positive encouragement in principle to a consensual approach, to make a framework Bill, including the main principles, functions and eventual scope. It would have the disadvantage of raising less debate, but if it raised no objections it could just possibly be put on the fast track, and benefit from the special end-of-term arrangements in May whereby legislation still in train is either nodded through or not.

GTC Directors' concern was to try to ensure that the principles on which we were agreed were incorporated in such an enabling Bill. In the event, this was the option taken by Sir Malcolm, and from the end of November through to early January there was detailed consultation on the wording of the Bill, before entering into a series of very helpful exchanges with Paul Silk, the Clerk for Private Members' Bills in the Commons. This Bill is a convenient summary of the legislation we were looking for in 1992 and 1996, to compare and contrast with the eventual government bill.

The 'Thornton Bill' was supported across parties by Don Foster, Alan Beale, David Jamieson and Gerry Weinberg as well as three fellow Conservative MPs, Sir Peter Fry, Sir Alan Haselhurst and David Porter. That in itself was remarkable. The 'Thornton Bill' was printed and issued on 15 January. Sir Malcolm and some of his supporters met GTC Directors on 16 January, to discuss final details and possible outcomes. Sir Malcolm had hopes that the Secretary of State would seek and gain Cabinet assent at the weekend Chequers meeting when final Election policy was to be decided. If so, the government party would not oppose the Bill, and it could be nodded through. Three Bills were to be introduced on one day, this being the third, and after negotiation there was a good prospect that it would be given just enough time for a first reading. The private Bill was due to be tabled on 24 January, and it was a question of negotiating adequate time for the Bill to be tabled and go through preliminary stages, i.e. ensuring that the preceding Bills did not extend to 2.30 p.m.

In the event, that government assent was not secured, the negotiated time to introduce the Bill was talked away, it could not be tabled before 2.30, and was therefore not presented, and a brave attempt had been thwarted – brave in particular, because this was a time when Sir Malcolm's neighbouring constituency, Wirral, was beginning a landslide by-election change, and much of his time would now be devoted to campaigning to arrest it. (In the General Election, Sir Malcolm was to be defeated at Crosby with a similar swing, the largest in the country.) However, the Bill had been published in Parliament, and was being used extensively by its proponents and others, when yet another opportunity arose for a GTC amendment. The Labour and Liberal Democrat education spokesmen, with the prospect of a cross-party Private Member's Bill, had been invited to give priority to that if it had a chance of making progress; but they had earlier in the autumn indicated that they would look for the opportunity to put a GTC amendment to the government's Education Bill.

This was the Government's 1996 Education Bill being hurried through Parliament. Both in Standing Committee D, 16 January, and in the second reading on 28 January, Peter Kilfoyle introduced a new Clause (23 and 10 respectively) for a GTC, drawn from the GTC proposal wordings, and for the first time, debates in the House of Commons matched those of previous years in the Lords. In Standing Committee on 16 January, after a debate notable for the more conciliatory response of the Minister, was withdrawn at that stage, and could have given way to the Private Member's Bill had that been tabled on 24 January. The events of the weekend Cabinet deliberations at

Chequers, or rather rumours and press statements about them, together with the vote of Monday 27th on another clause of the Education Bill, changed the climate. On that Tuesday, the Opposition reintroduced its GTC amendment, and after again constructive debate, pressed it to a vote, despite requests not to do so by those GTC supporters who would be forced to divide on party lines.

We could all see, whatever our political persuasion, the imperatives on all sides which caused this to happen. The vote, in which the Government survived, had nothing to do with the content of the amendment. The chances were now that if the cross-party private Bill were reintroduced, or if the next government included a GTC in its early legislation, which by now had been made much more likely, it would be in a climate of goodwill to the principle of a GTC itself, less affected by the win-lose transactions which are the stuff of pre-election strategies. As will be seen in the next chapter, that on the whole was what next happened.

Part III: Issues for the New GTC

Chapter 8

Creating and Carrying Out the Teaching and Higher Education Act 1998

The commitment to introduce legislation for a GTC had been a consistent one for both Labour and Liberal Democrat parties over the decade before the 1997 General Election. Labour's landslide victory on 1 May brought in a new ministerial team to cover the very broad area of education and employment. The shadow team had included Peter Kilfoyle and Bryan Davies, both of whom had become familiar with the GTC issues and had made their mark in parliamentary debate on the GTC earlier in the same year. In the event, Peter Kilfoyle was moved across to a more general public service brief, and the Minister for School Standards, with a far-reaching brief which included the General Teaching Council, was Stephen Byers, who had not been involved in pre-election debate or deliberation. As Chairman of the Association of Metropolitan Authorities some years earlier, he had presided over an employer body which at that time had been opposed to a GTC, although it had since changed its view and had become very active in the GTC movement from 1996. Stephen Byers had in the run-up to the election of course echoed his party's policy to legislate for a GTC, but could be expected to be cautious, especially with teacher associations.

At first, under pressure from all sides, he did not wish to meet and discuss, but David Blunkett wanted him to meet the GTC Directors, and this happened on 16 September, whilst consultation was still under way. This was a friendly, open and courteous review, in which it became apparent that the kind of GTC we were proposing would extend beyond his schools brief, crossing into the territory of Estelle Morris, the Under-Secretary to oversee teacher training, qualifications and supply, teacher misconduct and appraisal, and into the territory also of Baroness Blackstone, responsible for further and higher education and qualifications. Both of these colleagues, moreover, had been involved in previous GTC discussions and debates. It became evident from our meeting that Stephen Byers had not envisaged a GTC extending beyond the schools sector which was his remit. He also expressed the view that we should disregard anything that had happened before 1 May. We could only hope that our meeting might have modified that approach, for the consultation documents had included questions about the scope of a GTC to include pre-school, further and higher education. In retrospect, this initial stance and limited view of the new Minister can be seen to have caused problems; some of them were resolved in

Parliament, others in the detail of implementation; but the Bill as originally prepared would have been unacceptable not only to Parliament but to the teaching profession, and the government was able to retrieve credit only by being seen to be influenced by consultation and debate.

The White Paper *Excellence in Schools* was issued in July 1997, confirming the government's commitment to setting up a GTC, and inviting views on its role and composition. It was followed in the same month by a consultation document on the GTC: *Teaching: High Status, High Standards,* issued to 'organizations concerned with teaching standards in England', already showing that the Welsh Office would be consulting in the principality. The document confirmed the commitment to introduce legislation that autumn, and asked the obvious questions on GTC roles, scope, relation with other bodies, composition, modes of election, and funding.

The analysis of responses was issued on 3 December, after the first reading of the Teaching and Higher Education Bill, which was introduced in the House of Lords to run parallel to the School Standards Bill introduced in the Commons. How far the wording of the Bill was affected by responses is not clear, but amendments made during the progress of the Bill certainly reflect some of the messages received.

THE DEBATES IN PARLIAMENT

The debates on this section of the Bill were remarkable for their spirit of cross-party consensus to strengthen the GTC remit. Whereas until January 1997 Conservatives had been required to resist calls for a Council, they were now able to point back to Sir Malcolm Thornton's all-party Bill and to ensure that the Council was given real powers. On 11 December, in the second reading in the House of Lords (where the Bill had been introduced) there was all-party support in principle for the establishment of a GTC. It was a poignant moment, for it was overshadowed by the death of Lord Dainton, who would have been speaking on behalf of the GTC movement, and to whom tribute was paid by Lord Butterfield, assuming that mantle, and by others. Both in the second reading and in the committee stage (20 January 1998) there was all-party support for its strengthening and for reducing the powers of the Secretary of State. It should not be a 'toothless poodle of the Secretary of State' (Lord Tope), whilst Lord Glenamara who as Ted Short had thirty years before tried in vain to introduce a GTC, considered the government Bill 'an ungenerous way to make the provision'. As he put it: 'This body should govern the teaching profession. Therefore it must control ingress to the profession and egress from it and not simply be able to give advice on those matters.' Baroness Blackstone, the Minister charged with steering the Bill through the Lords, confirmed that 'it is important that we should give responsibility for standards to the profession and involve teachers in ensuring that we have the highest possible standards', but Glenamara continued to insist on powers for teachers to decide on fitness to teach, not just advice which leaves power in the hands of the Department for Education or the Secretary of State as 'a great super-national nanny'. Others made sure that the Bill, which started by empowering the Secretary of State to enable or control the Council by regulation, should be amended so that Parliament should scrutinize the regulations by affirmative procedure, or that the Secretary of State should be required to give powers to the Council. Another important theme was touched by Lord Peston, trying to shield the government from accusations of introducing a Council without sufficient powers:

> I regard this as the first stage in setting up the teaching council . . . I hope that my noble friend will confirm that this is an evolutionary matter. We are not setting it up once and for all but in order to get the matter started and to gain experience. I believe that we are setting it up partly in order that teachers themselves can gain experience in becoming self-regulating as a profession. Again, I had not read the Bill . . . as saying that in due course the general teaching council will not evolve to do many more things on an obviously self-regulatory, professional basis . . . this provision gets us started with something that is dear to our hearts. There is more that I would like, and once this provision has been achieved, it may well be that I and my noble friends will ask to have other matters added as the basis of experience. (*Hansard*, 20 January 1998, p. 1393)

But how was this to happen, asked Earl Baldwin? Will there be another Bill? He was reiterating what had been stressed by the GTC movement, not least on the negative experience of Scotland: that primary legislation must give scope for such extension, not make it dependent on further primary legislation. Others wishing to remove powers from the Secretary of State invoked the Privy Council. Glenamara came back to the GTC initiative:

> For some years now, a body organized by the teachers themselves has been planning a general teaching council. I cannot imagine why the Government have not followed its model in the main, but there it is. I believe that we should have tried to follow that model which is very different from this proposal. (*Hansard*, p. 1396)

The over-cautious stance of Stephen Byers was becoming exposed. Glenamara and others on the Labour side continued to insist, as did cross-bench, Liberal Democrat and Conservative peers, on a teacher majority and self-regulatory powers for the Council.

The Minister conceded, presenting herself as a 'Fabian gradualist', and offering the parallel consultation as justification for not yet giving firm assurances. It is important to record the assurances given by Baroness Blackstone in Parliament about future scope for the Council, for these will have to be the basis for future additional legislation.

> We must approach this matter with care. We must build. It may well be that in 10 years' time the final shape of the general teaching council will be rather different from what it is when established . . . it is sensible to approach this from an evolutionary basis. I have no doubt that as the council establishes itself and beds down, it will build on its own work. It may start with a slightly more limited remit compared to its eventual remit, but it is extremely important that at this stage we do not limit the power . . . In the long term it may be that new legislation will be required. (*Hansard*, pp. 1397–8)

Other Ministerial statements in that debate will also be noted for the future.

There will be scope to review the relationship between the GTC and the TTA once the GTC is established. If experience shows that we need to consider the balance of statutory duties performed by the GTC and the TTA then we may return to that in the next Parliament. (*Hansard*, p. 1437)

By not recognizing the long-term aim of self-regulation for the whole teaching profession in whatever sector of the education service, the Minister was in some difficulty. At one point, she claimed that 'no part of the Bill . . . which relates to teaching falls within my policy remit', and because teaching was being presented as school teaching in maintained schools, she was able to resist amendments to transfer from the Secretary of State to the GTC powers to bar or restrict employment under Section 218 (6) of the 1988 Act, because:

The existing powers cover anyone working in a school who has regular contact with children, not just teachers. And they cover further education colleges and independent schools as well as the maintained sector. So the Secretary of State has powers to bar a range of people who do not fall within the GTC's remit. (*Hansard*, p. 1448)

That was precisely the point which the government had missed by a mixture of accident and design in the GTC proposals, and which was not allowed for in the wording of the legislation: that in the long term these matters should be covered by the GTC.

Baroness Blatch made good the largely negative response to a GTC which she had dutifully made when Minister for Education, now sharing with cross-benchers the insistence that the Secretary of State's powers should be curbed: she pressed for key regulations to be subject to affirmative resolution in Parliament, i.e. to be under parliamentary scrutiny; insisted that the GTC should have self-regulatory powers, and secured an assurance that the Secretary of State would usually respond publicly to advice given by the Council. Each wave of amendments proposed and withdrawn brought from the Minister more positive assertions of the powers of the GTC as proposed, including 'maintenance of qualified teacher status', which Lord Whitty asserted 'may well include career development and continuing in-service training at a later stage' (*Hansard*, p. 1474) and that it should be for the Council, not just the Minister, to decide what information it required. It was left to another former Minister, Baroness Young, to propose a detailed amendment giving regulatory powers, and in doing so to attempt even to invoke Sir Keith Joseph as someone who 'when he was Secretary of State, tried hard to set up a general teaching council' (*Hansard*, pp. 1449–50). So even the legendary Sir Keith had now been posthumously converted to the cause, having refused to countenance it when able to do so.

The January 1998 House of Lords debate also drew from the Minister what had previously been curiously missing, a statement of the aims of the Council:

(a) to contribute to improving the standards of teaching and the quality of learning; and
(b) to maintain and improve standards of professional conduct amongst teachers, in the interests of the public. (*Hansard*, 23 February 1998, p. 438)

Further pressures drew from her the repeated statement that 'the Government wish to see a strong and independent GTC giving independent advice to the Secretary of State. It would defeat the object if that were not the case' (*Hansard*, p. 451). By 26 February, she for the first time expressed herself 'happy to accept in principle that serving, qualified teachers should form a majority on the council' (*Hansard*, p. 802) without waiting for the result of the further DfEE consultation document on Council composition. Crucially, this was coupled with the view that the teachers on the Council should be qualified teachers with recent experience of teaching.

From all sides of the political spectrum had come the insistence that the Council should have regulatory powers, not at some time in the future requiring further primary legislation. Although this pressure had drawn much more positive assurances from the Minister, it was no surprise that the amendment reintroduced by Baroness Young to put the Council's authority into the text of the current Bill, was carried on 12 March by a significant majority, 137 votes to 112.

At first, government voices asserted that it would cast out this amendment when the Bill reached the House of Commons. It was an anxious time for the GTC movement; without such powers, as Baroness Warnock had with unusual vehemence stated in the Lords, a GTC would be a fraud, and the GTC Forum of Associations not only could not have accepted it, but would most probably have been compelled to speak out against the legislation it had worked for over so many years. In the event, the messages from inside and outside Parliament had been strong, and pragmatism won the day. Stephen Byers on 16 March was able to announce that, after further consideration, the government would bring in its own amendments to give the GTC 'powers over, rather than an advisory role in, professional misconduct matters' (*Hansard*, p. 1042). Although he retained for the government decisions related to child protection (justifying this by the wider-ranging child protection legislation just introduced), and restricted GTC to the advisory role for such cases, even here he was able to suggest that 'over time, as the [GTC] is tried and tested, the House will want to consider giving it further powers'. He was also able to announce a second consultative paper on the composition of the Council.

The debate showed members on all sides seeking to ensure that this improvement to the Bill should not be diluted in committee, and there were constructive contributions from all sides: Jacqui Smith signalling the need for the GTC to look at the key tasks for teachers and those which could be undertaken by support staff; Andrew Lansley for the majority of teacher members to be elected, the Chair to be independent of government, and Council nominees of the Secretary of State to be independent and represent legitimate interests in education provision and improvement; David Chaytor to point to the anomalies if sixth-form and further education colleges are excluded.

In committee, on 31 March, Phil Willis for Liberal Democrats pursued without receiving complete satisfaction the point made to him by the GTC movement that there should be a clearer definition of what is meant by a 'teacher'. Amendments relating to the composition of the Council were thwarted by the promise by about that date to produce a consultation paper on the topic. He also introduced what was to become the main thrust of the committee stage, the attempt to reduce the powers of the Secretary of State and confer them where appropriate on the GTC. Stephen Byers was resistant to further powers being conferred at the expense of existing agencies:

'there is no doubt in the Government's mind that one organization – namely, the Teacher Training Agency – should have responsibility for qualified teacher status' (*Hansard*, 2 April 1998, Standing Committee F, p. 38). It remains to be seen what is to be understood by responsibility, and whether such a statement will survive further reviews. In distinguishing between teaching methods and competence, he was also drawn into stating that the Council should deal with teacher competence, a controversial matter still to be clarified, and that it should produce a code of conduct, whereas many would consider the Council should decide whether and in what form statements on conduct should be made.

By now, following the initial consultation, it had become clearer that whilst the legislation covered England and Wales, the working assumption was no longer one council later to become two, but two from the outset. Somewhat different scope was being suggested, and parliamentarians were able to query discrepancies and secure confirmation that the two councils would establish their own reciprocal arrangements. They were also able to pursue definitions: what is to be understood by the councils' responsibility to give 'general' advice? This was clarified by the Minister as 'to prevent any danger of the GTC commenting on individual teachers' (*Hansard*, 2 April, p. 47); and 'not intended to deny the GTC the opportunity of drawing attention to specific cases to illustrate a particular point' (p. 48). There was also a useful attempt to clarify procedures: in cases of gross incompetence, 'an individual would have to be dismissed by his or her employer before the GTC could consider the case. With misconduct, that would not necessarily be so' (p. 55).

There were still moments when the Minister showed the lack of confidence in the GTC which had bedevilled the earlier stages of the Bill. So in response to a Liberal Democrat amendment on regulations relating to registration, Stephen Byers was drawn into insisting that:

> It is appropriate for the Secretary of State to determine whether someone has qualified teacher status and is therefore able to enter the teaching profession. It is for the Secretary of State to determine whether individual teachers should be registered as qualified or not. To hand over that power to the general teaching council . . . would not assist our efforts to raise school standards. It would allow the general teaching council, by regulation, to take over responsibility for what is an important power. That would not be appropriate. (Hansard, 2 April, p. 58)

And yet again, he later hedged this with the timing argument: 'Over time, we may feel that it is appropriate for additional responsibilities to go to the general teaching council, but we do not need to do it all from day one', and suggested flexibility was needed.

A year later, it remained to be seen whether or not the initial regulations, which would be subject to a third consultative paper, would be restrictive or reasonable.

The GTC provisions were only one part of the Bill, which also contained important provisions for induction and headteacher qualifications, both of which will be part of a GTC concern; all three of these provisions were accepted in principle, and the amendments in debate had reached a stage when the proposed starting role of the GTC could be accepted, subject to the regulations being approved by affirmative resolution. The major and most controversial part of the Bill, however, was that which related to tuition fees in higher education, and it was this which caused the Bill to be blocked on its return to the House of Lords, and which for a time towards the summer recess threatened to topple the whole Bill; it was only by a last-minute patching up and undertaking of further consideration on aspects of student fees that the Bill squeezed through and the Act was given the royal assent on 16 July 1998.

IMPLEMENTING THE ACT: CONSULTATIONS ON COMPOSITION OF THE COUNCILS

The Act required regulations to be made for the composition of the Council which ensure a majority of registered teachers and which also have regard to the interests of employers of teachers, providers of teacher training, those with special educational needs, religious bodies, parents, commerce and industry, and the general public. Further consultation documents on composition for both England and Wales were published during the later stages of the Bill. Parliament decided that it wished to scrutinize these regulations before they were applied, and approved the Minister's proposals, by now amended after detailed consultation, in debates on 15 April and 10 May 1999.

An additional consultation was to follow from April to June 1999 on the detail of powers and functions of the GTCs. Regulations are also to cover the process of election and appointments, including Chair and Chief Officer. The first Chief Officer and temporary Chair would be appointed by the autumn of 1999, the first elections to the Councils would be early in 2000, and the first full meeting by autumn 2000.

The consultation paper for England, entitled *Teaching: High Status, High Standards – The Composition of the General Teaching Council* was published in April 1998, and a Welsh Office paper with the same title appeared in July. Both were welcomed as a fair reflection of the stage reached in the progress of the Teachers and Higher Education Bill through the Houses of Parliament, and for their clarity of presentation. GTC (England and Wales) which had since the 1980s borne the burden of arguing the case for a GTC on behalf of the teaching profession and its constituencies, was able to welcome the strengthening of the Bill during its passage through Parliament, in particular the government acceptance only after debate that there should be a teacher majority, without which the legislation would have been plainly unacceptable. The parliamentary debates had shown how much the Thornton Bill had influenced Conservatives, now able to demand greater powers for a body they had dutifully voted against when in power. Almost everyone now supported the statutory GTC as initiated in law. There remained the need to give scope to allow the GTC to develop further in the ways already indicated by Ministers in debate.

There were differences between the two sets of council composition proposals in the consultation documents for England and for Wales. The insignificant TTA presence in Wales added weight to a Welsh GTC influence on recruitment and more clearly worded continuing professional development. Another important difference was that whereas in England, where a regional framework for the GTC might bring it closer to its electorate, there was no such proposal; in the much smaller area of Wales, regional and no doubt language differences prompted an initial proposal for regional structure for elections. Different voting systems were proposed: a single transferable vote for England, an alternative vote system for Wales. Despite the government acceptance in parliamentary debate, the proposals for Wales did not show a clear teacher majority, although one would be assured after nominations by representative bodies and the Secretary of State. The proposals were made under the working assumption that the two Councils would start in the year 2000.

AIMS, SCOPE AND COMPOSITION

Consultation on details of composition was however being conducted somewhat awkwardly before the conclusion of debates or further consultation on powers and duties which would give fuller meaning to composition. The consultation documents on powers and duties were not published until April 1999, and would lead to draft instruments that autumn, by which time the dust had settled over composition. However, the introduction to the consultation paper was welcomed as a general statement of GTC role, future extension, funding, and further consultation seeking consensus. What follows is the gist of responses by GTC (England and Wales) on composition.

A general warning was and is that although the government is committed to inclusive education and to a continuum of lifelong learning, it has not yet given the Bill scope to include teachers of all phases of education. It is vital to the public interest that all teachers in whatever sector of the education service should be involved in some way. So far, only teachers in maintained schools and independent special schools are to be required to register: teachers in independent schools, in advisory, education officer or support service roles, in the youth service, further and higher education and teacher training are not yet to be required to be registered. GTC (England and Wales) had to warn that there was a danger of creating permanent divisions in the education service if the initial composition of the GTC were unduly limited or if unnecessary constituencies were created within that initially limited range.

It could be accepted that the first stages of registration would be for those who teach in primary and secondary education (not only in schools), but we wished also to see required registration at that early stage for those with substantial input to the professional aspects of initial teacher training. We looked in vain for a declared long-term aim for registration across the whole education service, whether by extending the scope of the GTC as we had previously proposed, or by developing professional bodies for other sectors of the education service, or by a combination of the two. Whichever route is adopted, a close association across the teaching profession as a whole will be needed, so the initial composition of the GTC should in some measure and in one way or another reflect the whole profession.

This is also why we had recommended that the definition in the Bill of what constitutes a teacher should allow scope for extension from the government's very limited starting point, and we still urged that provision for this wider scope to be envisaged should be included from the outset rather than be subject to later primary legislation. The scope of the Thornton Bill had not been replicated.

Composition of the Council

Because required registration had been sought, so far in vain, also for those in higher education institutions (HEIs) who train teachers for primary and secondary education, we wanted them to be able to elect representatives. It also could be argued that since DfEE regulations for initial teacher education require a close partnership between schools and HEIs, those engaged in pre-service professional training of teachers for primary and secondary schools maintain a familiarity with the schools, assume a major responsibility for the quality of teaching, and help to create the climate of professional service and development which would be reflected in the work of the Council.

Transition

GTC (England and Wales) had recommended a three-year transition period, and reiterated the need, because neither we nor the government, according to parliamentary statements, would wish the GTC to be confined to the scope of its initial responsibilities or to the detail of its starting composition. We wanted the first Council to be able to review its needs and make recommendations for changes, for example to appointments to ensure balanced representation of major interests. Whilst it might be considered appropriate for a first tranche of thirteen members to be appointed by the Secretary of State, some of the subsequent appointments would preferably be made on the recommendation of the Council, leaving the Secretary of State with the specific role to ensure that the DfEE and its agencies are appropriately represented.

We acknowledged the 'working intention' to establish two separate Councils by the year 2000, but this would make it all the more important to ensure a close working relationship, and to have this reflected in the composition and cross-representation of both Councils.

The role created by the Government for the GTC to act as an appeal board on decisions related to completion of the teachers' induction period (see Chapter 10) would require a statutory committee which we had not envisaged. There would also have to be close definition and shared understanding of 'serious professional incompetence' if this were to be a ground for GTC de-registration. We also noted that later decisions would be needed on the GTC role related to medical fitness, in order to clarify the nature of sub-committees regulated for statutory responsibilities. It was problematic to be considering consultation before finalizing functions or stating long-term aims. However, the document did start by seeking views on underpinning principles, with which it was possible to agree.

Principles

A full profession is one which provides a major and essential public service, which is founded on a body of knowledge and skills for which a long training of high standard is essential, and which exercises a significant measure of responsibility for the service it provides. The GTC, as reflected in the composition of its Council, must be authoritative, balanced, effective and independently responsible. For the public and the teaching profession, it is important to see that the GTC operates independently of any one organization, and of government; this will be reflected in the balance of composition, which will reflect responsible partnership. Whatever the eventual composition of the Council, these were principles which would have to be upheld.

Whilst teaching in schools constitutes the major element of initial public education, it does not constitute the whole of the teaching profession. A GTC must be able to draw on direct and up-to-date experience of teaching at all stages, and its balance must reflect the full range of teachers, not just schoolteachers. This was reflected in the consultation document Section 2 §10 better perhaps than in its wording of principles. It is difficult to offer analogies: but the GMC is not just for general practitioners, although they constitute the first, largest and most obvious public face of the medical profession; hospital nurses do not constitute the UKCC. To accept this is not to diminish the importance of general practice, hospital nursing or schoolteaching; on the contrary, it is important that these are seen to relate to specialized professional sub-groups in the same professional body, which speaks on behalf of the whole service. Whilst wishing to endorse the underlying principle that recent, relevant and substantial experience of teaching should be a criterion for elected Council membership, we were looking for representation of those smaller groups also, and in the long run this should not depend on the Secretary of State.

Size of the Council

Until further regulations clarified how far membership of committees (e.g. investigating committee, professional conduct committee, possibly medical fitness committee) would be limited to members of the Council and what would be the powers and limits of co-option, we did not believe it would be wise to regulate a maximum of 60 members as was suggested. We agreed that many interests might be involved through co-option, sub-committee, joint working party etc., but a general principle would be that no teacher should be without a channel for representation on the Council, whilst specific interests (teaching subject constituencies would be an example) could be additionally served by consultative or committee arrangements. Because we recommended that there should be representation on the Council from all parts of the teaching profession, we believed that an effective and fully representative Council for England might need to have scope to be a little larger than suggested. We also recommended that the Council should have the capacity to review its size as part of its regular review. Again, it was difficult to respond in advance of the statutory instruments on powers and duties which would specify scope for co-option.

Routes to membership

We could endorse the principle of securing a balanced Council embracing all the interests to make it the [rather than 'an'] authoritative voice of the profession for the responsibilities it is to undertake, and all the skills to make it effective. Independence from any single person, institution or interest group can best be ensured by that all-embracing composition, and this is yet another reason for ensuring that teachers whose work is not in schools should have representation.

Our own proposals had been for an initial transitional period, in which a wide range of professional associations (whether or not also unions) would offer themselves as constituencies for elections and appointments to enable a Council to function even before the register is established. Whilst we still believed there are difficulties in the alternative proposed, we had to recognize the likelihood that initial election through existing bodies would not now be the major route adopted.

On routes to membership, our first comment followed from the concern already expressed that all teachers, not only those in schools, should be represented from the outset. Second, a clearer distinction should be made between appointments or elections of teachers (again in the broad definition) by representative bodies, and appointments or elections of providers and other public-interest groups. Third, for reasons already given, we believed that elections and/or appointments and/or co-options should seek from the outset to reflect the eventual scope of the whole teaching profession, to include further and higher education, support services and early-learning teachers.

Teacher elections

We welcomed the government's response to consultation and parliamentary debate which had both confirmed that there must be a teacher majority on the Council. Whilst the consultation proposal was for a smaller majority than established for most other professional councils, we accepted that this might in practice be increased by further appointments. We recommended that the Council membership should be broadly representative of not just schoolteachers but teachers as a whole. This could allow for the government's initial suggestion of twenty elected schoolteachers and nine teachers elected or appointed from the main schoolteaching associations, to which could be added representatives from further and higher education, associations of teacher trainers, support services, and other bodies such as ISC, the College of Teachers, and Early Learning Associations.

Electoral constituencies were envisaged in the consultative document as one way to ensure a broadly representative Council. We emphasized however the case for the constituency covering teachers in further education; it is no solution for them to be eligible to vote in the secondary constituency, and there could be misgivings about that suggestion both among secondary and among further education teachers. Over one-third of teachers in further education are estimated to hold schoolteaching qualifications. This is a very large body, which deserves its own franchise, even if this is not practicable for the first Council's elections.

We noted the parallel developments in further education of FENTO, with which we would expect there to be cross-representation, and similarly for the Higher Education Institute for Learning and Teaching, and considered these should be borne in mind in determining appointments, co-options and cross-representation.

Separate electoral constituencies were proposed in the document for headteachers. It was necessary to point out that there are problems in creating a separate constituency for headteachers, which would require careful consultation with all teachers. Given that headteachers' representation would be assured anyway by NAHT and SHA appointments, we had to question why a further constituency would be necessary. The GTC is about professional practice at all levels, including management, which is a responsibility shared differently in various organizations. Many headteachers could be expected to wish to represent their colleagues as teachers, and should not be debarred from teacher elections by a misguided division in the regulations. Teachers should be able to vote for headteachers as their Council members if they so wish. It could well be in practice that more headteachers would be elected to the Council if there were not a separate constituency; that should be for teachers to determine. Moreover, if there were to be a separate electoral constituency, should it include deputy heads? If the issue is a distinctive body of professional leadership and management, then the comparison with Directors of Education had to be made. We therefore warned of serious issues to be addressed before adopting this proposal.

There were strong reservations about the proposal to establish a separate constituency for teachers of children with special educational needs. This might not be consonant with the government's policy of inclusion (by which is not meant necessarily integration or mainstreaming) and the professional partnership across a spectrum of schools services providing for individual needs. At least 90 per cent of children with special educational needs are on the role of mainstream schools and further education colleges. All teachers qualified since the mid-1980s, whether in ordinary schools, special schools or colleges, are trained to help meet their needs. To distinguish between teachers in special schools, 'special needs teachers' in ordinary schools, and other teachers meeting needs would be invidious and run counter to professional practice and government policy. Teachers in special schools may well wish to be eligible for election by all teachers, and not to be debarred from such responsibility. We recognized that there had been political debate on ensuring representation, but considered this could best be ensured by such appointment or co-option as might be considered necessary after reviewing the elected membership and other appointments.

We had to accept that it would not be practicable at this stage to arrange for regional constituencies. Initially, a balance across regions could be a factor in appointments by representative bodies or the Secretary of State, or in co-options, but was not likely to be a major factor. The option of regional constituencies could be left to depend on the views which emerged from the first Council, on the experiences of the GTCs for Scotland and Wales, and on future government intentions relating to a regional dimension of government. Regional boundaries could correspond to the European economic regions, which already have significant impact on education and training. The numerically smaller sub-groups could be represented in other ways than through the regions.

We therefore recommended at this stage that the elected teachers for the first Council should be from equal primary and secondary constituencies; that careful consideration of all views should be given before creating a separate constituency for heads and deputies; that there should not be a separate category for teachers of children with special educational needs; and that there is a case for a further education constituency even if not for the first Council.

Asked for an opinion about the single transferable vote, we believed it would be an acceptable option to most professional groups. More importantly, however, whatever may be the voting system, procedures would be needed for being accepted for nomination. Without either regional or association constituencies, the option of preliminary elections is not available. A requirement of a certain number of nominations may be no problem for teachers in secondary schools, but could be to the disadvantage of teachers in small schools.

There remained further questions relating to the 'constituency' in which qualified teachers vote, if they are not currently on the staff of primary or secondary schools. This affects not only qualified teachers in further education, but teacher trainers in higher education, advisers and officers, together with the very large number of teachers temporarily not in post. We recommended that in such cases the voter should decide on one constituency.

We recommended that those standing for election should be able to demonstrate recent, relevant and substantial experience in their teaching field. 'Very recent experience in the classroom' was not a recommended formula: recent experience may or may not be substantial. Our view of what constitutes teaching extended to home tuition, and to subjects and activities outside the classroom, and we considered that teachers casting their vote would be better able to decide on appropriate teaching experience than any regulation.

Appointments by teacher associations

We had already put the case for additional appointments and/or elections through associations representing teachers in further and higher education, but otherwise endorsed the proposals for nine members drawn from the schoolteacher associations. We agreed that qualifying criteria for teachers from associations should be as for elected teachers.

Appointments by other representative bodies

We agreed with the general approach to be adopted here, but suggested that the case for religious interests in the GTC is to be seen in terms of provision of teacher-training institutions, not only in terms of provision of schools. We recommended, therefore, that the Churches Joint Education Policy Committee would be the appropriate body rather than two of the separate denominations.

There should be further clarification of what is meant by employers of teachers. Some of the bodies mentioned seemed inappropriate. We believed that an involvement of the proposed FENTO would be essential not only in the longer term. This might also apply to the HE Institute for Teaching and Learning.

A distinction had to be made between teachers' professional representation and representation by providing bodies or other public interests. We considered that some appointments should be made under the heading of 'other representative professional bodies', e.g. of education advisers/inspectors, officers and psychologists, and possibly independent schoolteachers if they can be represented through ISC.

Similarly, whilst we wished to see CVCP, UCET and SCOP represented, there is a distinction to be made between CVCP as a body representing principals of institutions and UCET as a body representing teacher trainers as part of the teaching profession. Asked about SCITT, we saw it as a mode of organization, involving schools and training institutions in partnership much as other modes of initial training do, and therefore not requiring separate representation. Indeed, there would be serious questions of equity if this were provided for distinctively rather than through the more general representation available.

The employment interest would best be served by representation from both CBI and TUC. No doubt there would be negotiations with the several associations representing governors before deciding how governing body interests should be included. There are similarly several bodies from which parent members would nominate a parent or parents.

Whilst acknowledging that it might be appropriate to nominate a person or persons to represent those working with children with special educational needs, if in the view of the Council this field is not already adequately represented among elected teachers, we considered such nomination could be instead of and not in addition to an electoral teacher constituency.

Secretary of State appointments

Whilst it might be considered appropriate for a first tranche of these appointments to be made by the Secretary of State, we considered that some of the subsequent appointments might preferably be made on the recommendation of the Council, leaving the Secretary of State with the specific role to ensure that the DfEE and its agencies are appropriately represented.

Once the Council is in place, it should be seen as part of its responsibility to identify gaps and needs for balance, and it would diminish the Council for this still to depend on the Secretary of State or to be subject to any sudden political change. After the first Council, therefore, we recommended that the Secretary of State should ensure that the DfEE and appropriate government agencies are properly represented, but that most other appointments or co-options should be by the Council, or at the very least on its recommendation. We suggested therefore that after the first Council the Council could recommend a further seven voting members and the Secretary of State could nominate six members to represent the DfEE and related agencies.

We further recommended that the Council should have powers to co-opt a limited number of non-voting members to the Council. In addition, regulations should provide for powers of co-option to those committees required for statutory functions.

Terms of appointment

We were in broad agreement with the suggested terms of appointment. However, we recommended that there should be provision for members of the Council to report regularly to their constituencies and receive communication from those who have elected or appointed them.

Given the emphasis on serving teachers and/or recent, relevant and substantial experience, we believed it to be essential that Council members' expenses should include payment for cover in their schools, and that this should be made known well in advance of elections. Without this, there would be reluctance and resistance for the best available teachers to stand for election, and undue pressure on school staffing.

Chair and Chief Officer

We were in broad agreement with the proposals for a Chief Officer to be appointed initially by the Secretary of State and subsequently by the Council once in being, and for the Council to elect its own Chair from among its members. We suggested that the first appointment as Chief Officer should be for five years and renewable by the Council; subsequent appointments should be for whatever term the Council may decide.

Additional Comments

We had considered questions of gender balance and minority representation on the Council, and believe these legitimate concerns should best be entrusted to the wisdom of teachers in casting their votes and to the Council in recommending additional appointments and making co-options.

The Council should have the public duty of annual report and regular review, and must have the power to modify its composition, within the principles established under regulation, and to make recommendations for any modification which may require a change of regulations.

OUTCOMES OF THE CONSULTATION

The summary of over 300 responses received in response to the consultation document on composition for the English GTC was published with the decision, ten months later. It showed a majority in favour of the four proposed routes to membership, though with a frequent request for a larger teacher majority and fewer nominations by the Secretary of State. There were a variety of views on having separate constituencies for headteachers or for teachers of those with special educational needs. The DfEE was able to show that the decision taken was reasonable in view of either the weight of opinion or the differences to be reconciled.

THE COMPOSITION OF THE COUNCIL AS APPROVED BY PARLIAMENT

The Council composition decided by the Secretary of State is:

- 25 elected teachers (the original proposal had been for 20): 11 teachers of 'senior pupils' (over 12), 11 teachers of junior pupils, 1 headteacher of a secondary school, 1 headteacher of a primary school, 1 teacher of a special school.
- 9 teachers appointed by the main teaching associations (as originally proposed): 2 from ATL, 2 NAS/UWT, 2 NUT, 1 NAHT, 1 PAT, 1 SHA.
- 17 people appointed by major representative bodies (originally 13): 3 from LGA, 1 ACEO, 1 AoC, 1 CES, 1 CoE Board of Education, 1 CRE, 1 CVCP, 1 DRC, 1 EOC, 1 ISC, 1 NCB, 1 NGC, 1 SCOP, 1 UCET.
- 13 members appointed by the Secretary of State, including 2 or more representing the interests of parents; and having regard to the Council's membership including persons with experience related to teaching persons with special educational needs, and reflecting the interests of the general public.

Elections are to be for four years, and the members of the Council elect a chair from amongst their number. Subsequently, the English regulations were amended to provide for the prior appointment of a temporary Chair. The initial appointment as Chief Executive was for three years in the first instance.

The result of consultation on the Welsh GTC was not published by the same time, but on 22 March 1999 draft regulations were laid before Parliament. There were to be twelve elected members: four secondary, four primary and four head or deputy headteachers. Thirteen would be appointed by the Secretary of State from two lists: four from a list of eight unions including NATFHE, five from a list of 26 other organizations, four more of his choosing, and the Secretary of State was to assure a registered teacher majority. The initial Chair as well as the Chief Executive would be appointed pre-Council.

A COMMENTARY ON THE COMPOSITION OF THE GTC FOR ENGLAND

In general, these decisions show that account has been taken of the consultation responses. Given the restricted framework adopted in legislation, this is a reasonable starting arrangement. Positive features are:

1. The size of the Council is sensibly extended somewhat to provide for four more representative bodies and five more elected teachers.
2. There is fortunately no separate sector created for special education needs, but provision instead for the election of a special schoolteacher, and scope for membership appointed by the Secretary of State with experience in relation to teaching persons with special educational needs. This formula may well satisfy the parliamentary imperatives without undermining inclusive policies.
3. Rather than specifying school sectors as constituencies for teacher election, the formula is sensibly adopted of teachers of senior and of junior pupils, thus allowing for the inclusion of teachers working pre-school, outside schools or across 'special' and 'ordinary' sectors, and also intended to include teachers in sixth-form and further education colleges, despite the term 'pupils', which might have to be reconsidered.
4. There are some valuable additions to the representative bodies proposed by GTC (England and Wales) to the government: Commission for Racial Equality, Disability Rights Commission, Equal Opportunities Commission and National Children's Bureau.

Less fortunate, but understandable within an initial formula:

1. Separate appointments from Roman Catholic and Anglican bodies have been preferred to a Joint Council which could have encompassed Free Churches (also as providers of institutions) and conceivably other faith schools.
2. Teachers in further and higher education (other than teacher-educators) are unfortunately not represented, unless nominated by the Secretary of State.
3. Instead of NATFHE or SEO, there are provider or management bodies, such as the

Association of Colleges and the Association of Chief Education Officers. Similarly, the CBI is there but not TUC. The tendency, then, for non-school representation is towards the managerial rather than the practitioner representation.

4. Continuity after the first term is provided for only by the possible five-year term for appointments by the Secretary of State, and not yet by elected teachers.

5. It is possible but unlikely that from the thirteen members appointed by the Secretary of State there may be teachers from further and higher education, and from LEA services outside schools. This may also be a means of access for such bodies as SCETT, or the College of Teachers, in recognition both of its long-standing advocacy of a GTC and of its recent attempt to extend its role to subject associations.

6. Parent bodies as such are not represented; instead, it is for the Secretary of State to appoint two or more members to represent parent interests. In the long term, it would be preferable for parent bodies themselves to be represented, as are governors through NGC.

7. The number to be appointed by the Secretary of State is high, and still leaves government to determine the balance of public interest rather than the Council itself.

FOR THE FUTURE

Co-option or observer arrangements for the full Council are not yet specified; there is scope for the GTC itself to draw on other bodies in its non-statutory committeee and sub-committee arrangements. It is not yet clear how membership arrangements will be reviewed, either in the course of a Council (e.g. if bodies cease to exist or are merged) or from one Council to the next. Reciprocal arrangements with the other GTCs, with FENTO and ILT have to be negotiated. The composition of the Council is now clarified, but the means of election (nomination, presentation) and of communicating with electorates have to be worked out. The Council will have to address the question of continuity in election years and whether later to have phased elections. It is to be hoped that after the initial term of office the Secretary of State will have sufficient confidence in the Council to confer before making at least those appointments which are not directly representing government or its agencies, and that at a later stage some of these can be nominated by the Council itself. For England, a regional dimension has yet to be considered. The ability and willingness of teachers to stand for election will be affected by arrangements to support them or their schools for absence. Primary legislation will be needed to extend the scope and elected composition of the GTC to other sectors of education.

ORGANIZING THE GTC ADVISORY ROLE

The GTC unit set up in the DfEE to conduct consultations and prepare for the new Council could more readily attach importance to and plan for the registration functions (some of which would grow out of existing DfEE operations) than for the advisory responsibilities set out in the Act. At a late stage, when drawing up a business plan for the preliminaries and the start of the Council, the GTC Team invited views on the scope and costings of the GTC's advisory work, and the comment they received is below.

The Teaching and Higher Education Act 1998 sets out the advisory functions of the GTCs for England (Section 2) and for Wales (Section 9). To exercise these functions, and to have credibility with teachers and the public, it will be essential for the GTCs to have organized themselves internally and externally for such purposes. Much which is suggested here for the GTC for England will apply to Wales and then Northern Ireland. Whilst understandably the DfEE team and GTC Unit has been initially preoccupied with those GTC functions which will be transferred from the Department, to establish the register and to enable elections to proceed, the preparations for advisory functions will be no less demanding in the transition years.

External factors

The majority of teachers on the Council will be elected by national ballot from sectors of teaching: primary, secondary, etc. Whereas in Wales they may be accessible to other teachers, in England once elected they are on their own unless and until the GTC organizes communication among them and with their constituencies. A minority of teachers drawn from associations will be able to seek and if they wish to represent association views, with access to teachers through existing channels. Most Council members representing other interests will be able to do so too. For the majority of elected teachers to play their full part, they will need to work through systems established by the GTC. A regional dimension in England is not an option for the first Council: nor are field officers. The GTC members must have immediate access to and for all teachers, whether through a much more frequent equivalent of *Links,* the GTC for Scotland newsletter, or through Internet or both. So the external communications must be set up beforehand. Teachers and the public should expect within the first two years substantial position, discussion, consultation or guidance documents on each of the advisory areas.

There are ambiguities which probably have to be lived with until the Council is fully active, but which have to be signalled for its attention and that of other organizations. For example, the Council will be expected to advise the Secretary of State on the initial education and training of teachers; but so will OFSTED, having this duty under the 1996 Act. A *modus vivendi* will be needed, and perhaps a distinction made between advice which describes the standards found on inspection, and general advice on what those standards should be and how to maintain and improve standards of practice. Moreover, the Teacher Training Agency will have views arising from its funding, accreditation and monitoring procedures, and even if it will not continue to be the prime source of advice to the Secretary of State, it will be important for these views to be channelled. It will not be easy for a new body to communicate with established agencies, or for these to modify their practices to make way for it. In the DfEE itself, such issues are most clearly seen in the arrangements for registration and discipline, at present located in Darlington. But there will be no less need for close liaison and exchange of information on teacher supply and other DfEE statistics located in London. To undertake the responsibility of advising the Secretary of State, the GTC must have access not only to the information which the

DfEE considers it needs (this was the case with the Advisory Committee on the Supply and Education of Teachers) but the information the GTC itself considers it needs in the form it needs. The administrative liaison related to advisory functions may be as significant as the liaison with DfEE for registration, discipline and appeal.

A third element of external organization is related to the legal requirement that the Councils for England and Wales should exchange information. There will obviously have to be systematic arrangements for the two Councils to confer, to act in concert, or where there are compelling reasons, to make decisions or provide advice which is distinctive or at variance. Access to teacher training and to most teaching roles is open across England and Wales, as is access to higher education and professional careers in general. The political imperative to create the Welsh National Assembly moved the legislation from the proposal initially to create a joint GTC and only later to create a separate one for Wales. This original proposal would have allowed time to develop shared policy and practice internally, but the enthusiasm in Wales for an immediate start to its GTC brings with it the need for immediate liaison systems. It may well be found, moreover, that a separate Welsh GTC will be more expensive for its smaller numbers; the proposals for the Republic of Ireland with 40,000 teachers to be members, are for an annual registration fee of £50. Some joint services across England and Wales may be financially desirable as well as professionally appropriate.

This aspect, which may well require some form of overarching co-ordinating committee as well as mutual Council observer access, joint working groups on specific topics, a joint registration machinery, and possibly joint committees for investigation, discipline or induction appeal, may also become part of a wider though not necessarily so detailed co-ordination with Northern Ireland, and with the GTC for Scotland. Moreover, there will have to be at least mutual observer and administrative links with the training body now set up for further education, FENTO, and with the Institute for Learning and Teaching in higher education, with which there will be such overlap that the GTC movement had envisaged the GTC as eventually encompassing them all.

Internal factors

To have credibility both with the profession and with the public, the GTC will be expected within two years of its establishment to have conducted a thorough review of existing criteria and expectations across the range of its advisory remit, and to have either confirmed and assimilated these to be part of the GTC's advice or conducted appropriate enquiries and consultations in order to advise that standards should be modified or updated. It will reasonably be expected within those two years to have established a fuller business plan for developing its advisory functions.

The major headings for the GTC's advisory responsibilities are not discrete. Supply and access, qualifications for entry to training, standards to be reached during initial training, recognition of EU and overseas qualifications, criteria for induction, expectations for continuing professional development, re-entry updating, qualifications in the course of a teaching career, preparation and development for headship are part of a continuum of professional expectation and education. Whilst only the Council itself once elected will be able to determine how it should best proceed, preparations, facilities and budgets must be there to enable the Chief Executive to go ahead, making ready a working arrangement which can be adopted or modified once the Council is established.

Council members coming individually from their schools will need facilities to form working arrangements and interest-groups, and should have an information bank and resource centre available to them. The administrative costs of servicing their capacity to advise will be high.

It is at least likely that the GTC will have panels or sub-committees for each of its advisory areas, perhaps as sub-committees of a major committee for the education and training of teachers. These panels or sub-committees would have powers to co-opt *in rem*. They should be envisaged for initial education and training curriculum programmes and qualifications, EU and overseas qualifications, induction, continuing professional development and further professional qualifications, teacher supply and demand, professional ethics and code of conduct, and possibly for age-phase, special educational needs, and school leadership. A research committee will be needed to promote, commission and support research in or across any of these areas. So perhaps ten panels or sub-committees beyond the organizational, executive, investigative, disciplinary and appeals arrangements will be needed. Such arrangements are indicated by what has been found appropriate in Scotland, but the advisory function in England will be wider, whilst the corresponding GTC accreditation functions in Scotland will no doubt remain with the TTA. Initially, the panel or sub-committee activities will be frequent and demanding, and it should be envisaged that each advisory panel will need to meet four or five times in each of the first two years.

In a Council of 64, even if those representing interests beyond the education service were to take a full share in sub-committee work, it would be difficult to envisage Council members involved in more than two advisory panels each, bearing in mind that many will also be involved in the statutory committees and that most will be in full-time employment without secondment for Council service. The size of panels will vary, as will the number co-opted. They might average ten to twelve. Each will require professional and administrative servicing. So perhaps 50 days of meetings per year, 600 council member-days, 150 days administrative servicing, over and above statutory committee, executive and administrative functions. The professional servicing might in the first year or two take the form of short-term secondments to produce or draw together state-of-the-art papers for the consideration of the Council, on each of the advisory functions indicated. These might take the form of published discussion or consultation documents of the kind commissioned in 1992–93 by GTC (England and Wales) Trust, which would have immediate impact in the teaching community and engender shared responsibility for the subsequent advices issued by the General Teaching Council.

All these advisory responsibilities require budgets within an overall financial control which itself must be sustained, initially by government and later largely by registration fees. The otherwise excellent report of the steering committee for the Irish GTC (1998), based on study of comparable Councils including Scotland, contains a full survey of estimated administrative and financial requirements, but does not provide adequately for advisory functions. It is hoped that a fuller anticipation will have informed the DfEE's estimates and the government's provision for start-up costs and arrangements.

INITIAL OUTCOMES

The draft business plan for the Council in February 1999 incorporated in summary form most of these recommendations, and it was possible to build in estimates for the initial funding of the GTC advisory role, although the Minister for Schools sought to restrict the initial staff size.

Chapter 9

Teacher Supply, Retention, Morale, Social Standing and Public Image

A feature article in the Education Supplement of *The Independent*, 28 January 1999, illustrates all too well the mood among teachers. The headline: 'No daughter of mine is going to be a teacher'. It is written by a deputy headteacher. 'Everyone has said to Joanna – and I mean everyone – "Don't become a teacher. It would be such a waste."' Sadly, her father agrees.

> There should be no finer or more important duty than that of helping to shape and inform the minds of the future. It should be seen as a great responsibility which requires imagination and wit and intelligence, all the things our best young people have. Except that today, we don't think teaching is a suitable career for them. The profession always needs good new recruits. It needs the vibrant enthusiasm of youth. I have seen the way in which talented young teachers can transform a department and a school. They are the transfusion that the lifeblood of a school needs. But where are they going to come from, when it seems to me that so few teachers would ever advise their own children to join this profession? . . . If teachers are discouraging their own children and also the children they teach from entering the profession, isn't there something fundamentally wrong? (Ian Roe)

Yes, there is. So what can be done? Until the 1970s, little was done to advertise teaching as a career. Some professional associations and some local authorities began to respond to the 'milk round', in which large commercial and industrial complexes were attracting graduates into lucrative openings. The Department of Education and Science followed suit, leading to the establishment of TASC, soon to be superseded in England by the TTA, one function of which is teacher recruitment, as cinema-goers are aware. It should not be the purpose of a GTC to be the instrument of government recruitment to training, although such an information unit is attached to the GTC for Scotland and provision is made for such activity in Wales. The GTC for England will, however, expect to be in communication with the government recruitment agency, and would project a whole-professional view of the vocation of teaching, and the qualities and competences required, and be able to advise potential teachers of suitable channels of information.

It has been noted in earlier chapters that the GTC proposals include a function to advise the Secretary of State on the recruitment of teachers. The Teaching and Higher Education Act 1998 includes this responsibility: for the GTCs for England and for Wales there is a responsibility to advise on recruitment; for Wales, moreover, powers are conferred on the Secretary of State to require the Council to undertake activities designed to promote recruitment. No doubt the difference is derived from the existence of TTA promotion activities in England. In Scotland, a unit for promoting teaching is attached to the Council and funded by the Scottish Office.

This chapter, whilst drawing on earlier work (Sayer, 1993) seeks to update the need for the General Teaching Councils to work on all aspects of teacher supply, recruitment, retention and retrieval. Adequacy of supply must be determined by good-quality professional practice in the public interest, and therefore the GTCs must establish how they are to advise at the same time on developing teaching quality and on the general issues of supply. The political and economic issues of government or government agency control of initial supply numbers have to be informed by advice on professional morale and its influence on motivation, retention and retrieval of teachers. Advice must also be related to the general professional and public expectation on school organizations to staff schools according to the activities which they are intended to perform, and to regulate their budgets accordingly. It must have regard to professional mobility within teaching, between teaching and other occupations, and across the European Community in particular and the international market in general. There is a particularly strong relationship to be fostered with the General Teaching Council for Scotland. To be able to advise, the GTC must be able to promote or commission research related to teacher supply.

The General Teaching Councils as now established should be expected to exercise their responsibilities by advising the Secretaries of State on the numbers needed for entry to initial education and training in order to implement public policy for the education service, such advice covering national totals, age-phase and curricular areas, and the most appropriate balance of modes of training or re-training. Their recommendations will be coupled with advice on necessary standards of proficiency for entry to training and for the competent and safe practice of teaching. The Councils for England and Wales will have to co-ordinate their work so that overall supply issues are addressed together, leaving such distinctive questions as Welsh language teaching to the Council for Wales. There may well be a case for further co-ordination with the Councils for Scotland and Northern Ireland, and for a consultative procedure with the new Council for the Republic of Ireland.

The GTCs will have the duty to respond to the government's questions on teacher supply implications of reforms and other developments, and indeed to advise on such matters as they consider appropriate, without waiting to be asked. Arrangements will be essential for the GTCs to have the continuing resource of government statistics and forecasting of teacher supply, potential and needs. The GTCs should be in a position to offer advice on recruitment and on advertising to that end. They will in effect be the regulatory body to advise on adequacy of supply, and on appropriate interpretations of such notions as shortage or surplus.

As such, they will through their general advice to the Secretary of State inform government agencies such as the TTA which are there to execute policy. The evidence of those carrying out policy must also be made available to the GTCs, along with the evidence from members and the constituencies they represent. No doubt the working groups or sub-committees for questions of teacher supply will co-opt to complete their whole-service perspective.

GOVERNMENT POWERS AND GTC RECOMMENDATIONS

It has been pointed out (National Commission on Education, 1993) that a GTC will be usefully involved in teacher-supply questions only if a government is prepared to listen to its advice. That is patently true: indeed, any government not prepared to listen to advice about teaching from the whole teaching profession is not fit to govern in such matters. That does not mean that in all circumstances a government should follow professional advice; there may be other political priorities. It would seem to be common sense that those having to take ultimately political decisions would be involved anyway in GTC deliberations, and it should be clear to the GTC what are the parameters of the politically possible before it makes its recommendations. That kind of collaborative problem-solving has not been evident in recent years, has been badly needed, and is now even more badly needed when supply problems have again become acute.

The Councils (which include the voices of government, employers and others directly affected) will have the responsibility to advise on supply and related issues, not to determine how many teachers should be recruited. It remains to be seen how the Councils and government interpret the cautious legislation which states that 'any advice given by the Council on matters falling within subsection (2) shall be advice of a general nature'. The advantage to the government must be that no stone be left unturned in reaching the right solutions; and that, if things still go wrong, no stone will be seen to have been left unturned. Teacher supply is a poisoned chalice; a GTC will have to be prepared to accept a share of the blame for mistakes made: that is professionally acceptable. Teachers are more demoralized and much less willing to rally round if mistakes are made in decisions in which they have not been involved but could and should have been.

It is one of the major achievements of the education service in post-war Britain that teaching in schools is becoming a graduate or graduate-equivalent activity, and entry to the profession is at trained graduate level. The normal requirement of length of higher education study in Britain is still not as high as in other major economies in Europe, but for the moment is recognized as just adequate for recognition and professional mobility.

Demographic change and economic fluctuations cause severe problems of teacher supply, and these in turn affect the nature of the teaching 'force'. The average age of teachers in secondary schools, for example, has risen above acceptable levels, whilst age related to subject balance is even more distorted.

THE EXPERIENCE OF ACSET

The GTCs will also have benefited from the experience of the Advisory Council on the Supply and Education of Teachers, which resumed the work of the earlier similar body

(Advisory Committee for the Supply and Training of Teachers) set up following the recommendations of the Weaver and James Committees. Despite the initial difficulties surrounding them (including the understandable unwillingness of the NUT to take part until the latter stages) ACSET did good work, developed its own professional dynamic, and indeed made such clear recommendations for the future that the Secretary of State used this as a reason for not reconvening, pointing out that ACSET had given the Department an agenda for action for some years ahead.

ACSET was the last representative professional national advisory council or committee for the education service before the establishment of the GTCs. It was unwieldy, over-dependent on the DES and its inadequate information, and limited to responding to the questions which the government chose to ask. It did manage, however, to engage the whole maintained education service in deliberating together with central and local government on important questions of supply and training, and its recommendations still stand, some of them awaiting satisfactory response.

ACSET functioned with sub-committees, cross-representation, and exchange of papers prior to main committee decision-making. With all its limitations, it involved teachers and their representatives with employers and government in making joint recommendations in a responsible and consensual advisory mode, and demonstrated the potential benefits of the fuller involvement which a GTC would bring.

The GTCs will include an even wider range of interests, including for example parents, governors and the independent sector, which absorbs about 10 per cent of teachers to serve about 7 per cent of children.

MORALE, RECRUITMENT, RETENTION AND RETRIEVAL OF TEACHERS

It was seen in an earlier chapter that the House of Commons Select Committee addressed the issue of teacher supply in the wake of the problems and apprehensions of the late 1980s and that one of its major recommendations was that a General Teaching Council should be established.

A crucial point made by the Select Committee was that supply questions cannot be solved by government alone, but only by concerted work together, including the encouragement of schools to potential teachers to undertake training, and to existing teachers to continue to develop in the profession.

Although the GTC should not become the government's recruitment agency, its activity should be expected to improve the morale of serving teachers, which has been so low in the perception of pupils that it has been a deterrent to contemplating a teaching career. It is reasonable to expect, moreover, that once teachers feel they have a significant responsibility in determining the quality of their profession, the average length of a career in teaching, which was declining again by the late 1980s, may cease to decline, and that an adequate framework may be found for promoting the return to teaching of those who are qualified to teach but are not at present doing so.

There will have to be consortia and alliances across all those agencies which offer a resource for training and development (among which schools are deeply involved individually and collectively), and these can best be developed under the aegis of the GTCs. The equivalent council for the nursing profession, UKCC, offers a parallel, both in its close linkage with the health service special training agency, and in its powers to require updating and re-training. It is in the interests of the general public that there should be comparable opportunities in all parts of the country and in all kinds of schools and services for professional training, re-training, re-entry and development for teachers, wherever and however they are at present employed, and indeed prior to re-employment.

CONFIDENCE, TRUST AND MORALE

Professional needs are closely related to questions of motivation and morale. In 1990, the House of Commons Committee for Education, Science and the Arts (ESAC, 1990) noted with concern the contrast between the Houghton Report (1974) assertion that 'after the family, the teacher is the most important influence on the next generation' and the statement from Her Majesty's Inspectorate that many teachers 'feel their profession and its work are misjudged and seriously undervalued'.

It therefore sought ways to improve the morale of the profession, and one of its principal recommendations (as seen in an earlier chapter, the one not to be adopted by the government of the day) was the creation of a General Teaching Council for England and Wales (Scotland's GTC was established in the 1960s).'We believe that the positive effect on morale from a properly constituted and effective council warrant such effort'.

Generalizations about morale across well over half a million teachers are difficult and dangerous, but the HMI and select committee statements were well founded, and there is little doubt that morale plummeted from the low point of the 1980s. In the 1993 Oxford Employment Life survey (Gallie and White, 1993), teaching was found to be the most stressful of the professional occupations, along with social work. Part of the problem was beyond education: from the early 1970s, a weakening British economy requiring scapegoats, together with falling school rolls, combined to lower the public priority given to education and to add to the difficulty of maintaining confidence. The industrial disputes of the mid-1980s were a symptom rather than a cause, but certainly did not improve either public confidence or teachers' confidence in themselves or each other. There may have been 'a deep professional and public commitment to an underlying unity of purpose' (GTC, 1992), but there were times when coming to the surface and being visible might have been more to be desired than the depth of burial.

It has also to be said that high professional morale is not an end in itself: rather it is to be seen as a prerequisite to the kind of public service which teaching aspires to offer and which at its best it provides. Moreover, the raising of morale is not usefully to be seen as strengthening the 'feel good' factor without attending to the underlying causes of disenchantment. So, for example, a General Teaching Council will not by itself raise morale and motivation. It will contribute to the conditions required to do so; with the GTC will come a sense of ownership which will have to be reflected also in management styles in schools, in which teachers will have a real influence on content and policy, be it in schools or in the nurture of their profession as a whole.

RECOGNITION OF THE TEACHING ROLE

In wanting public appreciation for their work, teachers are faced with a dilemma. They are exasperated and demoralized by the perception of teachers as having short hours and long holidays, whether it is expressed in the jovial bantering of neighbours or for their own purposes by the populist media or politicians. But there is also a professional satisfaction in concealing the necessary background preparation, administration, follow-up, and sharing only the direct transactions of teaching and learning. The reward of teaching is the achievement and fulfilment of learners, enabled by teachers but not owned by them. So the efforts they have made behind the scenes are not their first concern for praise. What teachers want appreciated and celebrated is first and foremost learning. In this they differ from some other professions. It would be difficult for a defending lawyer to celebrate the innocence of the client rather than the skill with which that verdict has been gained. The lawyer's prime concern is not a change or improvement in or by the client. In the medical profession, there are different emphases of professional satisfaction as between consultants, surgeons, family practitioners and nurses. The former will derive high professional satisfaction from the exercise of special skills; the latter will have a higher level of satisfaction in enabling patients to share and take over the business of recovering health.

EUROPEAN PROFESSIONAL MOBILITY

Increasingly, recruitment and retention will be seen in the European market, not just in a national one. There will have to be a European dimension to forecasting, and the open professional market will also have an effect on disparate salary and promotion arrangements. This is still marginal in terms of overall teacher numbers, but is likely to have more importance in subject-shortage areas, including those from which graduates are being drawn into other careers. It will also have a considerable effect in geographical areas to which it is more difficult to attract native teachers, especially whilst some virtually bilingual European countries are producing more trained teachers than they will need. This was already seen at the tail-end of the late-1980s supply crisis in London boroughs, and in the overseas uptake for the licensed teacher scheme.

Machinery in England and Wales to gauge the appropriateness of qualifications and experience gained in other countries has been extremely weak. In Scotland, the GTC is already available as the appropriate body, and accrediting qualifications and experience from the wider European dimension is just an extension of the procedure already in place to regulate supply from England and Wales.

Quality control of supply from other countries, the European Community in particular, has to be matched by promoting worthwhile experience in other countries for teachers trained in England or Wales. The GTCs should be promoting international professional enrichment as well as regulating it. They could give a whole-professional view of such opportunities, especially in the context of the government's recently declared intention to increase substantially the number of teachers exchanged with other EU countries. The GTCs could provide the badly needed reliable framework in which good practice could be encouraged in the employment and, if need be, re-training of teachers returning from teaching abroad. The GTCs will also, of course, be involved as the competent professional councils in any Education Lead Body which eventually emerges from current discussions, and will have an important role in matching competences required and training, both in a National Vocational Qualification context and in trans-European recognition.

THE GTC, INDUCTION AND RETENTION

One of the key recommendations made to the government by GTC (England and Wales) was that its initial measures and funding announced to encourage good practice and partnership in induction must be shown to be part of a long-term policy of support for professional improvement and reduction of wastage of recently appointed teachers. The 1992 GTC document quoted evidence from the former DES and from other surveys of increased wastage rates in the late 1980s, especially for teachers under 25. Once normal mobility affecting any form of employment is taken into account, including considered decisions that a person's future is not after all in teaching, the problems of initial overload, general conditions, and attitudes within schools and among the general public are seen to have a serious impact on retention.

> A good induction programme cannot solve the education service's greatest problems but it can ameliorate them, stress the positive, build strengths and commitment, and thus retain and motivate quality people. A bad or virtually absent programme could mean needless sacrifice of people the service can ill afford to lose. It is in everyone's interest, not least of national government and the governors of schools, to support this vital contribution to a healthy profession and education service. (p. 25)

This is just one further example of the intimate connection between qualitative professional improvement and questions of supply.

In another chapter, it is proposed that the GTCs could and should provide a suitable cross-professional regional or local framework for professional development and re-training schemes beyond the proper scope of individual institutions. In Wales, a regional framework was proposed for the GTC legislation; in England, where it is even more badly needed, it must be created. This is particularly necessary for those teachers who for whatever reason are not at present teaching. They may number 350,000, nearly as many as those teaching in schools. It is true that the 'PIT', the DfE acronym for professionally inactive teachers, includes some who may teach beyond the statistical reach of the government, and that many are not potential returners. Nevertheless, it is the largest potential source of qualified teachers, and should be cared for at least as carefully as the market for potential new teachers.

Routes back into teaching are recognized as important, and both the TTA and some enlightened employers have developed policies and strategies to make a return easier. LMS in its present flawed form has worked to their disadvantage: for a full-time post, a school might in any case be looking for a newly trained and practised entrant rather than someone returning to a very different world from the one experienced some years before; but if budgetary pressures determine that preference anyway, equal opportunities are not in play for either employee or employer.

The most common route back into teaching is through part-time work for those becoming free of family commitments. Part-time teachers are badly treated, professionally and socially as well as contractually. Part-time teachers rarely figure in professional development priorities. They rarely return to the level of responsibility they had before, let alone to a level to which they might have aspired if family commitments had not come first. Professional meetings and professional training days may not be at times when they are available. Those on minority time and temporary employment contracts are the most likely to be left to the end of timetable planning because of permanent contract resignations and appointment deadlines. They are the most at risk from budget pressures at the end of each school year. The GTCs, in developing professional expectations for the nurture of potential returners and their re-introduction to schools, must increase the likelihood that teachers in the PIT would choose to return and resume their teaching careers.

There are related professional concerns about the position of supply teachers. They may account for between 2 per cent and 3 per cent of the teaching in our schools, a very significant percentage in itself and one which includes a much higher potential of retrieval through transfer to more permanent employment. Nothing could be less conducive to attracting teachers back to more substantial teaching than the present supply arrangements. The variety of demands to which supply teachers may respond with or without notice has gone largely uncharted. Arrangements are haphazard. Some supply teachers have been recruited to local authority lists and the local authority may have provided an agency service to 'its' schools. That already uneven and diminished practice is increasingly unlikely to survive. Large schools have built up their own supply lists, and may be able to build them to some extent into regular commitments and timetable plans. Small schools are unlikely to be able to do that.

Newly qualified teachers will not be required to register for up to one year of supply teaching. Thereafter, the GTCs will include teachers not in regular employment in its registration, its codes of conduct and its recommendations for induction, re-training and professional development. The development of good practice in the use of supply teachers will be an increasing priority as employment practices become more flexible.

PROFESSIONAL MOBILITY AND DEVELOPMENT ACROSS SECTORS

There are new needs for a GTC arising from the shifts of public funding and employment responsibilities in recent changes to the education system, notably the removal from LEAs of the public sector higher education institutions and then the incorporation of further education colleges. The need has always been there: to recognize that the teaching profession exists across maintained and independent schools, across schools and further education, across schools and the truncated local authority administrative and advisory services, across schools and teacher training institutions – and that teachers may well move between them. That has supply implications for all parties. Whatever the other factors, undoubtedly, one of the attractions presented by private education is the generally smaller size of classes. That may attract parents and it may attract teachers. Certainly it requires more teachers, as does boarding provision, now mostly in the private sector. Likewise, in further education, into which sixth-form colleges have now been drawn, there are different staffing practices and different notions of supply.

More often than not, teachers in independent schools have been professionally isolated from re-training and professional opportunities from the public purse, and to some extent independent school groupings have developed training programmes for their own staffs. Similarly, further education colleges and schools have been artificially separated by different regulations and habits. For some purposes, this may be appropriate, but the separation should not be artificially imposed, and there are resources for mutual support and learning which are being blocked.

The GTC movement's proposals are for all teachers in all sectors. However, the legislation is limited in the first instance to maintained schools and independent special schools, whilst FENTO is being launched (January 1999) for further education, and higher education is creating its own Institute for Learning and Teaching. A professional council must have the support of all sectors, and must contribute to good practice across them. It is vital that in developing policies and practices to ensure that recruitment and retention correspond to educational needs, representatives of all these sectors should pool their proposals and their resources in a general concern which transcends their particular interests, and which depends on their collaborative insights and concerted action. The systems must be in place to ensure that this happens.

GTC CAPACITY TO ADVISE ON TEACHER SUPPLY

As explained earlier, Section 7 of the Teaching and Higher Education Act enables the Council to advise the Secretary of State whether a person is a qualified teacher, and to maintain records on categories of persons other than qualified teachers. Section 13 requires the Secretary of State to consult the GTC before making or varying regulations about the standards required for qualified teacher status, whilst Section 14 requires both the Secretary of State and the GTC to supply each other with 'such information as he considers it to be necessary or desirable for them to have' or 'such information as he may request' for their functions relating to teachers. It also usefully requires the GTCs for England and Wales to share information necessary or desirable for their work.

It has been pointed out (GTC Trust, 1999) that this does not give the GTC power to require information from DfEE that it considers necessary or desirable. However, in practice the database of teachers currently maintained by the DfEE will now be maintained by the GTC, and will be updated in the annual registration process. It will be possible to have different categories of registration from which more accurate estimates of potential supply can be gauged: those teaching and in which field; those not at present teaching but registered with the intention to return; those registered but unlikely to return to schoolteaching; those with overseas qualifications and temporarily registered; those on ITT courses; and NQTs in the induction period. The database could provide details by subject specialization, age, sex, ethnicity, region, additional qualifications. Above all, it could give accurate updated addresses for communication. Much of this will be new to England and Wales.

This places the GTC in a well-informed and potentially very powerful position to advise on most aspects of teacher supply which have eluded the DfEE and its predecessors or for which they have had to depend on sampling methods. Not only will it have better information than has existed in the past; it is also a 'forum of all stakeholders' bringing together perspectives and insights and capable of motivating action. It becomes more than wishful thinking that the teaching profession will move on from 'no daughter of mine is going to be a teacher'.

Chapter 10

Professional Induction

INTRODUCTION

It has been seen in an earlier chapter that the previous required probationary period of one year for newly qualified teachers had been unadvisedly swept aside in England and Wales, whereas in Scotland the same government had allocated a grant to enable the GTC for Scotland to extend probationary service there to two years. Only in Scotland was probation systematized across institutions and regions under the aegis of the General Teaching Council. The longer, two-year period of probation in Scotland, was and is also permissible in non-maintained schools. During a professional vacuum in England and Wales, Scotland has continued to provide the experience and evidence of good practice in probation and induction, and of partnership between the GTC and the government (Scottish Office). So in 1993 the Scottish Office was distributing at the same time its leaflet on teacher competences and the GTC's booklet *Assessing Probationers*, an addition to the GTC guidance for headteachers on the assessment of Probationer teachers (GTC, 1990) and the research reports, training units and videos distributed through teachers' resource centres by Moray House. More recently (1997/98), it is the GTC for Scotland which has commissioned and published studies showing the unacceptably high proportion of newly qualified teachers engaged in short-term supply posts of 'creeping permanence' because of local authority cut-backs.

In 1992, GTC (England and Wales) Trust concluded its publication on the induction of newly appointed teachers with recommendations which still stand and against which the new induction arrangements in England, which have started in September 1999, can be measured.

A. To the Teaching Profession

1. The induction of newly appointed teachers should be an explicit part of the general responsibility of all teachers, and the key tasks of induction should in each case be the designated specific responsibility of appointed teachers in each school.
2. Individual teachers must have the prime responsibility for taking opportunities to further all stages of their own professional development, including induction into new posts.

3. Profiles enabling teachers to compile their own professional records should be developed across the education service. Profiles from initial training should be capable of being adapted for the period of induction and form a basis for initial stages of professional appraisal.
4. The continuum of training and development across institutions and career phases should be developed by local consortia bringing together all the agencies for initial training, induction and continuing development.
5. Arrangements for induction and induction training in each consortium area should be under constant review, and there should be formal evaluation in each area at least every three years.
6. Whilst a link between induction and appraisal may make for progression and continuity once teachers are appointed, much has still to be done to develop the continuum from the initial education and training of teachers. This must involve cross-service collaboration to develop good practice in progression and continuity across the initial and continuing education of teachers.
7. The role of a General Teaching Council should be considered as an essential complement to regulatory action, in providing the framework for developing good practice in profiling and for support in the acquisition and improvement of professional competences; in promoting local arrangements for continuing development of good practice; and in the review and development of professional policy and practice.

B. To Schools

8. Policy and practice for the induction of newly appointed teachers should be explicit and built into the school's development planning and organization.
9. An induction programme should be negotiated well in advance for each new teacher, and built into timetabling arrangements.
10. Newly appointed teachers must have specific time set aside for the necessary shared activities of the induction period, and for individual planning, observation and reflection.
11. There should be a clearly understood designation of roles and responsibilities in the school (or across schools) for professional tutoring and mentoring activity related to induction of new teachers.
12. Adequate training provision and time allocation must be made for these responsibilities to be carried out to the highest professional standards.

C. To Training Institutions

13. The responsibility as partners in initial training should be seen to extend to the period of induction.
14. Profiles and records of teachers in training should by negotiation with newly appointed teachers be adapted as a basis for teachers' own records in the induction period.
15. Where new teachers are appointed beyond the area which can be covered by the training institution, arrangements should be made through the local consortium to ensure and facilitate the involvement of another training institution in the induction programme.

16. The connection and the distinctions between the designation and training of mentors for partnership in initial training and the training of mentors for induction should be made explicit in arrangements made with schools and in the support offered for the training and development of mentors and professional tutors.

D. To Employers and Governors

17. All employers of teachers, whether local authorities, trusts or governing bodies should have an explicit and published policy for the induction of new teachers into the profession as a whole, and a statement of good practice which will be expected and supported.
18. The induction of new teachers must be seen as a key part of induction arrangements as a whole, including the induction of supply teachers, returning teachers, and those appointed to new responsibilities.
19. Employers must ensure that adequate training is available for teachers appointed to take responsibility for induction, and that the funding and arrangements made for their work are appropriate.
20. Employers should ensure that their schools are well represented in local consortia for the development of good professional practice in induction as part of the continuum of professional training and development.

E. To Government

21. The expressed wish of the Government to have continuity developed across initial training, induction and career-long professional development, and the initial measures and funding announced to encourage good practice and partnership in induction must be shown to be a part of a long-term policy of support for professional improvement and reduction of unnecessary wastage of recently trained teachers.
22. The additional costs for the new arrangements for induction, beyond the initial development period being funded in some areas through Grants for Educational Support and Training, should be clearly identified, and specific provision should be made to ensure that policy can be transmuted into practice in all schools and in all areas.
23. The quality of induction in England and Wales under previous regulations has depended much on the priorities of individual schools and local authorities, and on the time and training given to new teachers and those who supervise them. This is perceived to have been variable. Recognition of experience in further education, overseas, and outside the maintained sector of schools is still an area of uncertainty. A consistent policy of induction across the whole education service is now required.
24. The longer, two-year period of probationary service in Scotland, also available in non-maintained schools, should be noted in the development of the new induction proposals for England and Wales.
25. The new schemes being introduced for funded improvement of induction within the framework of professional appraisal should be reviewed after three years, and development work should be initiated in those areas in which further

improvement is needed. The special responsibility for induction would remain whatever future changes were made to appraisal regulations in the light of experience. That special responsibility could be discharged effectively and systematically within an appraisal framework only if appropriately modified appraisal involved all new teachers in their first years of teaching.

26. The government's desire for more systematic and effective induction of new teachers and identification of their needs is welcome. An extension of appraisal to new teachers requires guidance, preparation and modification of the aims of appraisal as formulated in Statutory Instrument 1991 No. 1511, to make Education (School Teacher Appraisal) Regulations 1991 consistent with effective induction.

27. The special nature of the induction period must be fully recognized as a significant *extension* of the appraisal scheme now being introduced, in which the distinctive purposes of induction must be incorporated. It should be noted that under current regulations formal appraisal will be mandatory only in maintained schools (para 5). The GTC will be concerned with good practice in induction across all sectors and phases of the education service.

28. At this stage, parallel DES guidances, e.g. on the authorization of overseas-trained teachers (Statutory Instrument 1991, No. 1134) should be borne in mind. In particular, attention is drawn to references there to designated mentors. Mentoring for induction has to be systematically planned, with structure, adequate time and prior training.

Conclusion

29. Such considerations add to the need for non-statutory guidance. GTC (England and Wales) is happy to contribute to such guidance, and a future General Teaching Council should be expected to develop it.

30. Were these recommendations to be in place, with every new teacher assured of high quality provision for induction into a school or college and into the profession, through the concerted action of all agencies in local consortia, appropriately funded and professionally driven, then the government, employers and teachers together would have contributed to a significant improvement in the education of the coming generation.

A NEW START FOR INDUCTION IN ENGLAND AND WALES

The Teaching and Higher Education Bill, introduced in December 1997, and the consequent Act given royal assent in July 1998, made provision in Section 13 for the Secretary of State to make regulations requiring newly-qualified teachers to have served a satisfactory induction period as a condition of being employed in a maintained school or a non-maintained special school in England and Wales. This could be seen to restore the probationary period there, which had been peremptorily removed in 1992, and to be more consistent with practice in Scotland, where in 1992 probationary service had been extended to two years. It was more than restoration, however, giving new strength to the guidance. support and development aspects of induction as a professional activity of schools.

The DfEE consultation document *Induction for New Teachers* (April 1998), signalled that this would apply to all beginning teachers in maintained schools and independent special schools from September 1999, and envisaged they would have provisional registration with the GTC, to become full registration on successful completion. It made clear that this was not merely an assessment of probationary service, but one which would require schools to offer a full programme of structured support and guidance. The induction period would be one year or its part-time equivalent. It was proposed that newly qualified teachers should have a teaching load reduced to 90 per cent of the school's average, with 'Standards Fund' support from the government. Draft standards to be met by new teachers were proposed, together with assessment arrangements. A new element was the proposal that the GTC once in being would be the body to deal with appeals against decisions on induction. Independent schools offering the statutory National Curriculum and providing the necessary support could opt into the induction arrangements. The future GTC key role was set out in advising on appropriate standards and quality assurance for induction. The TTA was given the task of developing the detailed arrangements once responses were received. A similar consultation was initiated by the Secretary of State for Wales.

GTC (ENGLAND AND WALES) RESPONSE, JUNE 1998

Drawing on the views and evidence of its membership, GTC (England and Wales) welcomed the restoration of a statutory induction period and the general approach taken in the consultation document. Its publication: *The Induction of Newly Appointed Teachers: Recommendations for Good Practice*, which was produced in 1992 to fill the vacuum caused by the previous government's withdrawal of the probationary period in England, had included detailed recommendations largely compatible with those in the consultation document, but went further in setting out responsibilities of all concerned to ensure that the induction period is one of professional learning and development, and not only of probation and assessment.

The government's commitment to provide for the statutory General Teaching Council to be the body to advise on all aspects of induction was of course welcomed, and it was accepted that this would include issues of registration, de-registration, conditions for re-registration and forms of appeal. Since by this time it was already apparent that the GTCs for England and Wales would start as separate bodies, it was emphasized that for induction, as for other purposes, it will be vital that the General Teaching Councils for England and for Wales work together to ensure consistency of advice and criteria.

Particular issues addressed in the response were:

1. Proposed implementation of induction period

The new standards for completion of initial teacher training were noted as confirming good practice and relating to new curricular priorities. It would be for the GTCs regularly to review such standards, and to ensure that advice on induction represents a continuum of quality provision and expectation. Confidence was expressed that all schools would wish to be party to the development of good practice for the induction of new teachers, and this reflected the GTC hope that all independent schools would become committed to induction practices. It was accepted that the minimum statutory induction period would initially be the equivalent of one academic year in full-time teaching, but in view of the longer period for teachers in Scotland, that the GTCs for England and Wales should review and recommend any future extension.

2. Appropriate first appointments

The DfEE statement of normal expectations was accepted, but it was anticipated that schools under pressure may have to offer appointment to difficult situations, and therefore the view was strongly endorsed that in such circumstances the support and guidance should be correspondingly greater. Beginning teachers undertaking supply work before finding a suitable full-time appointment would require particular care and support. It would be for the GTC to recommend good practice. In no circumstances should employers offer fixed-term or temporary contracts to NQTs for a post advertised as permanent.

3. Completion of induction in a set time after initial training

The proposal for a set time was questioned: some beginning teachers will enrich their future potential by taking teaching posts abroad and should not be discouraged from doing so; others may wish to have an immediate break for personal reasons or to develop experience in other occupations. However, the demands on teachers' skills and knowledge will be subject to constant change, and it is unreasonable to believe that successful completion of initial training can be guaranteed as adequate for a first appointment after an interval of a number of years to be prescribed after further consultation. It was therefore suggested that after such an interval there should be a requirement of concurrent updating in addition to the normal provision for induction. It would be for the General Teaching Council to advise on the situations and circumstances in which this requirement should be applied or waived. This recommendation is consonant with the expectation that at any career point a person returning to teaching after such an interval should have access to additional support and re-training.

4. Career entry profile

Having previously recommended (1992) the adoption of profiles, their introduction was welcomed, despite the haste with which this had happened, and the GTCs should review and advise on their further development. The uses envisaged for profiles as a starting point for the induction period were agreed, and also their use in the continuum of induction and further professional development. However, the targets set during initial training should not be used as a measure of successful completion and care must be taken to ensure that the profile is primarily a tool for development and not envisaged as a criterion for assessment.

5. Elements of induction programme

Previously recommended (1992) details for an induction programme were signalled, and the government's inherited fascination with the use of 'best' 'magnet' schools was discouraged. We had yet to be convinced that experiments of using the 'best schools in the area' should be generally applied to induction programmes. The priorities should be an element which could draw on practice in other schools without these having been prescribed. Access to mentoring would also require a recognizable training of mentors for the purposes of induction; small schools in particular are likely to benefit from the involvement of experienced teachers in other schools. Regulations should not attempt to prescribe induction experience with special educational needs. There should be interaction with other teachers engaged in meeting special educational needs; whether this involves visits to and from special schools, specialized units attached to mainstream schools, or schools with other modes of organization will depend on local situations. In some larger schools, management responsibility for induction and professional development might have been distributed, and it is not necessarily the headteacher in person, as suggested in the DfEE document, who would best observe and comment.

Networks with other new teachers can be the most valuable part of an induction programme, and one which LEAs and groups of schools should facilitate. Other essential elements were highlighted such as information about the school organization, policy and practice, the opportunity to manage one's own workspace, support in form tutoring (whether or not the new teacher has a designated tutor group) and work with parents.

6. Change of induction school

The DfEE suggested that on successful appeal a new teacher should be eligible to have an extended induction period and/or serve a further induction period in another school. It had to be pointed out that there are several difficulties here. NQTs have and should have a substantive contract with one school. The LEA has no power to intervene. Whilst local agreements across schools in an LEA area might facilitate such transfer, this would be an unreliable arrangement. Agreed transfer of school for induction purposes would require new contracts and designated contingency funding, and should be used only in cases where proper supervision has become impossible. In some circumstances, it may be appropriate to defer or extend the induction period to allow agreed contractual transfer to a suitable school in the second year of teaching.

7. Teaching 'load'

The language of loading is symptomatic of the teaching situation in this country. It was agreed that it is good practice for a beginning teacher where possible to have a substantially reduced teaching timetable, but it is difficult to prescribe percentages of an unknown quantity in contexts with other variables. It is for example desirable that as far as possible the beginning teacher should not be used to cover the lessons of colleagues absent or otherwise engaged. Some regular times designated for induction support should be included in the timetable.

8. Contribution of training institutions

A major contribution of training institutions will be in the training of mentors. Training institutions within reach of the school can provide access to library and subject teaching materials, inputs to training programmes, and facilities for peer group meetings. Without prejudice to the autonomy of trained teachers and without the expectation of being 'alma mater', the training institution of origin can play a positive role in the review of development, not least with reference to the career entry profile and action plan. It is suggested that this could be a formalized consultation in cases where the successful completion of induction is in doubt. It was also recommended that the training institution of origin should be kept in communication, and have feedback on the outcome of the induction period, for its own records and in order to review its own outcomes.

9. Funding of induction support

The announcement of formula-based funded support for induction was welcomed. This would enable schools and employers to restore and build on good practice where it previously existed. There is a strong case for funding schools which appoint new teachers in much the same way that schools are funded for their part in initial training. In addition to a formula to cover the reduction in teaching time for the NQT, schools would have to be funded for the professional time required for the training and release from other teaching duties of mentors and others involved to provide an induction programme of quality, and to purchase courses and other induction activities beyond the school.

10. Draft professional standards

Interestingly, comment was not invited on the drafting of professional standards, and should therefore be seen as provisional pending careful consultation across all parts of the teaching profession involved. In due course the GTCs should be expected to review and recommend such standards. It must be remembered that career entry profiles had been introduced and completed this year in undue haste: the process had not been trialled; the targets might not always represent the fully shared reflection which should be expected in future; and they would certainly not have been drawn up as criteria for the assessment of induction. The TTA draft standards, as amended after this general consultation, might be used, therefore, as guidances in the first instance, pending review.

It was seen as unreasonable to expect beginning teachers to have 'consistently met all the standards of QTS throughout the induction period'. Adjustment to new school situations must be allowed for. It would be more reasonable to expect beginning teachers to have met such standards for a substantial part of the year. What would be the position of a teacher who had shown excellence in meeting most of these standards but not had the opportunity to meet one or two others (e.g. in a school which included no pupils with special educational needs?). Standards and assessment should demonstrate rigour, not dogmatism. The induction period is one of professional development, to be assessed in terms of having become a successful teacher, not having been successful from day one.

Many of the standards suggested had already been included in QTS standards for initial training and should not be emphasized out of proportion to other aspects of the quality, skills and knowledge of teaching. It was also pointed out that there was as yet no mention of capacity to work collegially and collaboratively with other teachers. In setting standards it must be clear how they will be assessed: how will new teachers be assessed, for example, in keeping up to date with research and development in pedagogy? How should such assessment relate to this element in the appraisal of experienced teachers? In general, the advice was that the draft standards required further careful consideration, and that in the first instance a resulting set of provisional standards should be used as guidances pending further review by the GTC.

11. Assessment arrangements

The provision for regulations in Section 19 of the Teaching and Higher Education Bill were seen as appropriate, and it was suggested that these regulations should specify the employing authority as the appropriate body to which recommendations should be made whether or not a new teacher has met the expected induction standards for inclusion on the GTC register of qualified teachers, and that the GTC would be the body to which an appeal might be addressed.

There was general agreement with the proposal that it should be the immediate 'line manager' or a person designated by the line manager who should have formal responsibility to monitor the new teacher's development through the induction period. This person and/or a designated mentor should also have training and designated time to support and monitor the new teacher's development through the induction period. However, if in a small school the line manager is the head, another person would usefully be involved after consultation between the head and the employing authority to consider with the head what further support or action is needed, and to share in the final interview with the head to review progress. It is important that decisions about induction should be the result of shared professional assessment.

In a larger school with a senior management team having designated responsibilities, whilst the ultimate formal responsibility is with the head, it may well be that another member of the management team will be the person to observe the new teacher at first hand, and at least to share in final interview. The deployment of management responsibilities is a matter for the school. This option in no way detracts from the importance of induction; on the contrary, it embeds it in the management of the institution.

The rhetorical tone in parts of the DfEE document, such as the 'clean and clear' judgement of suitability, was criticized. It is by no means always clean and clear whether shortcomings in performance are caused by failings in the school, in the new teacher, or in the relation of the two. Life is messy for new teachers in new teaching and living environments, and judgements have to be made with full understanding and evidence of situations as well as performance, in order to be rigorous, fair, transparent and objective. This is not a matter of 'giving them the benefit of the doubt' or 'making assumptions about further experience'. There should be a full analysis of all factors, and if this leads to the professional view that a period of induction should be extended or that this extension should be in another school or with another line manager, this should be one available option. It must also be remembered that the proposed induction period is very short, and where appropriate a period not exceeding the two years in Scotland should be available.

It was agreed that appeals against induction decisions should be referred to the GTC once it is established, and that the appeals panel established in the interim should also be independent and reflect relevant interests and insights.

12. Quality assurance

Whilst the new statutory appraisal arrangements would not apply to new teachers in their induction period, it is important to ensure consonance across induction and appraisal criteria, and the GTCs would no doubt wish to address this question of consistency and continuity and advise the Secretary of State as necessary. It was agreed that the employing authority would have an important role in ensuring that schools have effective induction arrangements, and training institutions should be involved in the development of mentoring and monitoring, especially where schools are also in partnership with them for initial teacher training. It would be the duty of the GTC to advise on all aspects of induction arrangements, and therefore to have access to relevant data and evidence from employing authorities, and where necessary to initiate research.

13. Independent schools and induction

Although initially there will be no statutory requirement for teachers employed in independent schools (other than special schools) to have completed the statutory induction period, policy and practice should be guided by the principle that the public interest is best served by consistent professional standards in schools of all kinds. The arrangements made by the GTC for Scotland for induction in non-maintained schools were to be noted, and may be equally applicable south of the Border. Although adoption by a non-maintained school of the National Curriculum may be a current criterion for statutory induction arrangements, there could also be a case for recognizing non-transferable induction in schools such as Steiner schools which have a radically different curricular approach. The same general standards of induction programme and support should be expected in participating non-maintained schools, and there should be the same right of appeal to the GTC.

14. Special schools and induction

The trend for special schools to employ new teachers should not be encouraged. Where they do, induction should be made possible through linkage with partner schools and access to the full range of induction opportunities. Induction should operate in the same way for all schools including special schools, and appeal procedures should be the same.

15. The GTC and induction

The proposals related to the GTC were endorsed in summary:

(a) The statutory General Teaching Council is to be the body to advise the Secretary of State and others on all aspects of induction, and we accept that this will include issues of registration, de-registration, conditions for re-registration and forms of appeal.
(b) It will be vital that the General Teaching Councils for England and Wales work together to ensure consistency of advice and criteria, and liaise with the GTC for Scotland, the body proposed for Northern Ireland and other equivalent bodies and authorities in the European Union.
(c) It will be for the GTC for England regularly to review standards for the completion of initial training, and to ensure that its advice on induction represents a continuum of quality provision and expectation.
(d) In view of the longer period for teachers in Scotland, the GTC for England should review and recommend any future extension.
(e) In some circumstances, including supply teaching, support and guidance should be greater. It will be for the GTC to recommend good practice.
(f) For those entering a first appointment some years after initial teacher training, it will be for the General Teaching Council to advise on the situations and circumstances in which a requirement of concurrent updating should be applied or waived.
(g) The GTC is to review and advise on the further development of career entry profiles and their continuation in and beyond the induction period.
(h) The GTC is to review and recommend required professional standards.
(i) The GTC will maintain the register of qualified teachers, and will be the body to which appeals for registration, against de-registration or for re-registration will be addressed.
(j) It is important to ensure consonance across induction and appraisal criteria, and the GTC will no doubt wish to address this question of consistency and continuity and advise the Secretary of State as necessary.
(k) It will be the duty of the GTC to advise on all aspects of induction arrangements, and therefore to have access to relevant data and evidence from employing authorities, and where necessary to initiate research.
(l) The same general standards of induction programme and support should be expected in participating non-maintained schools, and there should be the same right of appeal to the GTC.

As implied in previous sections, it was considered that there will be cases where it may be appropriate to extend the period during which teachers are entered on the provisional register, whether by recommendation or as a result of appeal.

THE TTA CONSULTATION DOCUMENT: INDUCTION OF NEWLY QUALIFIED TEACHERS

The Teacher Training Agency, having had delegated to it the task of making recommendations on monitoring, support and assessment arrangements for induction, was able to take acount of responses to the DfEE document, and of its own feasibility studies. It adopted the more open consultative approach advocated by the new government, and this was reflected both in drawing up its document and in the consultation process which followed it.

Its recommendations were very much in line with the responses made to the DfEE, and a considerable improvement on the earlier document. GTC (England and Wales) was this time able to confine itself to recommendations which would affect the operation of the GTCs once established. In particular, the appeals procedure was discussed in a meeting between GTC, TTA and DfEE officers on 9 January 1999. It was evident that the likely scope of this had not been sufficiently evaluated, that its relationship with the new DTI 'Fairness at Work' industrial tribunal legislation would have to considered, together with the European Union Social Contract measures, that neither the likely costs of appeals hearings nor who should pay for them had yet been assessed, and that much still had to be considered around the interplay and sequencing of employment and professional appeal procedures plus judicial review. It became clear that regulations for the committee structure of the GTCs would have to include not only investigative and disciplinary committees for cases of professional misconduct, but in addition a structure for the GTC induction appeals role. This was expected to emerge in the regulations on GTC scope and powers, but strangely was not included in the April 1999 consultations.

FUTURE ISSUES

Induction of newly qualified teachers is a major element, but by no means the whole of a school induction policy or programme. A school culture of welcome and induction for colleagues will encompass the new teacher, experienced newcomers to the school, supply teachers, returning teachers, teaching assistants, and those newly appointed to different responsibilities whether from within or outside the school. It has been recognized that provision should be made for the induction of newly appointed heads and newly qualified teachers, but the whole range of intermediary and ancillary positions needs to be encompassed by the school and by linkage with training institutions, local authority support, and other schools and services.

Because of the different contexts, the new arrangements for England and Wales leave the GTCs with a general advisory role and also with an appeal hearing role for the induction of teachers, whilst arrangements are made through the Teacher Training Agency and carried out by schools. In Scotland, and in the proposals for the Republic of Ireland, it is the GTC which sets out the procedures, ensures they are followed by schools, and makes decisions on satisfactory completion of probationary service. In the course of time, it will make sense for these alternatives to be reviewed together, and no doubt to contribute to the development of best practice across different contexts elsewhere in the European Union.

The GTCs for England and Wales must be in a position to review the new arrangements being made in their absence, and to confirm or recommend changes to criteria for assessment and standards of good practice. This will not be easy with the TTA and OFSTED already commissioning longer-term review studies, and there may well have to be a firm understanding of roles once the GTCs are established. The TTA Quinquennnial Review published in May 1999 was a welcome first move.

FURTHER QUESTIONS ON INDUCTION

Whilst its main thrust is for the renewal of induction into first teaching posts in schools, the new induction requirement must be related to a culture of induction in other sectors and levels of the education service. Governmental shakings of the kaleidoscope, in local government, inspection services, financial delegation, appraisal and powers of governing bodies, have affected not just the specific targets of initial education of teachers, induction into first posts, and continuing professional development, but the balance of management across these.

There have been examples of good practice in individual LEAs and schools, but they have depended on forms of governance now dismantled. It is essential that good practice should continue to be developed according to firm principles under new regimes. According to what good practice is to be encouraged, there has to be a new shape to the governance of induction, manageable in relation to trends in training and supervision generally.

Whatever formal systems of management are set up in and around schools and colleges, the informal support and positive atmosphere of staffrooms will exercise a strong influence on incoming colleagues. Indeed, many applicants for jobs will have this as their main criterion, and will simply not wish to join an uncongenial environment. Much is now changing in the school staffroom, and the 1998 Green Paper initiative on this is welcome.

The increasing numbers of dissatisfied teachers leaving the profession and the belated realization in government that a shift of national curriculum had to be matched with teacher supply has also prompted additional schemes of training teachers on the job and recruiting abroad in shortage areas. This brings an added responsibility for introduction to systems of schooling and professional relationships here. Professional mobility across the European communities from 1992 will also have effects as yet uncalculated. So there is no clear distinction in a staffroom between teachers in training, teachers newly qualified, teachers moving from other schools, those re-introduced to teaching, and teachers introduced to new roles. Mobility across schools and further education sectors is likely to increase. What is it like and what should it be like in future dispensations to join the staff of a school?

STAFF APPOINTMENTS

The way a school is presented to those looking for the right job is and will continue to be as important for those who present as for those who are at the receiving end. This is equally true of written descriptions and of presentations on the spot. The actual process of teaching and non-teaching appointments is as good an indicator as any, of the real staff relationships in the school. Formal procedures may have become more standardized, and more consistently school-centred, but there are very obvious differences between schools where the needs of applicants are properly considered and those which expect them to accommodate to whatever they find.

Heads and deputies continue to have a central role in the appointment of colleagues to the school, and this is shared with governors, including staff and parent governors. School management of resources gives greater flexibility in the choices to be made, and may reveal the values and priorities of the place. There may well be local policies of positive action to balance the teaching community; with or without these, each school has its own adjustments to make to achieve a balance of age, gender and ethnic background, in appointments and in promotion.

Interviews are too often described and indeed treated only as personnel selection: that indeed was the distorted brief given to researchers by the Department of Education and Science. Yet an interview is just what it says, two parties to a potential contract and therefore two equal parties viewing each other, needing each other, wanting each other. An appointment is at least as much a matter of school and career selection by individuals, and should be arranged with that in mind.

A new appointment is also an opportunity to adjust and adapt to a changed set of relationships, as a part of the professional development of those there already and not just of an incoming colleague. Mutuality of professional assessment and appraisal starts here. For the selected person and the selected school, therefore, interviews are the first stage of induction, to be built on by a continuing programme.

THE GOALS OF INDUCTION PROGRAMMES

Induction programmes may have a variety of goals. As far as possible, these should be negotiated and shared if those involved are to be committed to making the programme work. Too often, they are seen to be 'provided'. Self-induction is more vital than having a programme laid on, which in itself could be patronizing and de-skilling. There is the story from Tagore of the beggar picking up grains of rice from passers-by, until one day the carriage of a prince is seen, the beggar's hopes are raised, the carriage draws up, the princely potentate even descends, and then, wonder of wonder, extends his hand – and asks: what can you give me? The beggar, hopes dashed, can think of nothing to give but a grain of rice from his pouch. That evening, he discovers among the grains of rice a grain of gold. If only he had given the whole pouch-ful!

The goals most likely to be held in common are to improve competence and confidence, and to promote well-being and positive attitude. Those welcoming a newcomer will also wish to transmit a professional culture. On another level, there may be the wish to reduce drop-out rates, both from the school itself and from the teaching profession. This will be realized both in recognizing new strengths and achievements, and in a team adjusting to those strengths. There is at the same time the need to identify gaps in knowledge, skills and expectations, face them and do something about reducing them. So there are both monitoring and supporting aspects to induction, which are not necessarily part of the same remit.

INDUCTION INTO NEW ROLES

Any supervisory responsibility for other teachers, such as mentorship, team-leadership, departmental, or administrative responsibility itself requires induction, along the lines suggested for new teachers, but with the focus on the new job specification. There is much to be said for the proposition that all teachers become mentors to each other. Beyond the school, this is established practice in parts of the education service: Her Majesty's Inspectorate used to have a clearly defined and rigorous mentorship; local inspectors and advisers have established codes of practice. There are other sectors of the service, however, which show weak supervision and support: advisory teachers, co-ordinators, short-term development officers are in a more precarious position. There may be a mentorship element in teams; but just as often, the team is a paper grouping of people working in isolation or even competition. The value of peer mentorship for newly appointed heads of schools has been recognized, and translated into structured plans, now being strengthened.

PARTICULAR NEEDS OF SUPPLY TEACHERS

Two categories in particular require attention: the supply teacher, and those contemplating a return to teaching. Both consist mostly of women, and largely of women who have moved from teaching to bring up an infant family. There is considerable overlap between the two categories.

The supply teacher's role is as vital to schools as the fire service is to the community: it is an on-call role. People drop what they were intending to do in order to respond to an emergency. At best, they may be in a permanent supply position in a school which, with delegated funding, has realized how much more valuable it is to incorporate an element of supply in termly or annual contracts, and to build up a group familiar with the situation, known to the children, and in essence engaged in long-term cover for colleagues. These teachers can feel and be felt as part of the school community and have the same professional commitment to colleagues and to the ethos of the place as those in broadly permanent positions. Induction can be arranged for them as for any new teacher in the school, with an additional recognition of the versatility required in their job.

Some local authorities still manage to appoint a number of peripatetic supply teachers, including headteachers. Their position is more difficult, but is capable of being structured and supported. They are likely to be experienced and to have highly developed coping skills. They are more likely than others to be employed for specific purposes in which they have competence and regular practice. They are more likely to be called upon for long-term supply, such as covering for secondment. It is becoming increasingly difficult for local authorities to support such appointments.

The 'typical' supply role, however, beggars description. It will be in response to last-minute emergency. Teachers may have done their professional best to leave work, or if they are taken ill, a colleague will have tried to do so for them; but without knowing who will cover or with what subject-competence, this is never easy and sometimes impracticable. The supply teacher may be one who has recently retired; one who has returned from abroad or wishes to return whilst still bringing up an infant family; one who has not yet secured a permanent position, and may be insecure in a variety of ways. Most schools, if they have the chance, will not place people in precarious positions; but the exercise of cover is one of constant crisis and can often include snatching at the option of having someone in front of a class rather than nobody at all. Responsibility for cover is continuous, unrewarding, and stressful. In the larger school, computerized programs for cover may help with the basic administration of equity across regular teachers' non-contact time, which will be subject to thousands of invasions per year. But the computer does not have much to offer the casual supply teacher, other than the knowledge that this is a last-ditch call.

Even if the supply teacher copes, as many do, against the odds, the experience is one of coping and not much more. The supply teacher may remain unfamiliar with the school, most colleagues, most pupils, most of the teaching programme, and often has no framework within which to become familiar with them and be more than a crisis cover next time. Successful intermittent coping is no basis on which to build, is inadequately recognized, and is an insufficient recommendation for a permanent position.

There is, then, a strong case for a GTC to work on rigorous codes of practice in supporting the supply teacher. Even if it is not always possible, we have to work towards a better situation, and reduce the incidence of people being placed in an impossible situation, which can do no good to anyone, and can do irreparable damage. Teachers in schools are well aware of this, are as sensitive as their situation allows, but are under undue pressure.

The need may be for a strong induction programme, introducing all potential supply teachers to situations before they occur, creating networks of people who can help release each other in emergency, giving training according to identified needs. The shadowing, the team teaching, the observed practice lesson and reflections on it, the curricular updating, the social involvement, can all be undertaken before cover is needed. But it is unlikely that one school, unless it is large, can develop such a programme as a priority. Nor should the supply teacher be confined to one school in a neighbourhood. It is much more probable across a cluster of schools, and this is an attractive professional exercise, also enabling schools to assist each other with their practices.

RE-INDUCTION OF RETURNING TEACHERS

It will be noticed that supply teaching is at present one of the main routes back into teaching. The majority of those involved are women teachers able to contemplate and prepared to try some resumption of teaching in combination with the care of young children, perhaps those who are beginning at nursery or more usually primary school. There is certainly a connection, then, between the induction of supply teachers and the re-introduction through supply of those who may be looking for a return to a more permanent career. There is a responsibility on schools and local authorities to encourage and help with that return. Even the economics of teacher supply point in that direction, given that there are nearly as many trained and qualified teachers in the 'PIT', as there are in schools, and the major problem of our age is not recruitment to initial training through wider access schemes or TTA advertisements, but retention and recoupment of existing teachers.

There may well be benefit for teachers contemplating a return to teaching to be involved in local induction programmes for supply work. But they are entitled to much more than this, and I argue elsewhere for a break from teaching to be seen as a stage of professional development and to be accompanied by opportunities for career enhancement rather than treat returning teachers as though they had to start again from scratch. An induction process for supply teachers should include, therefore, the identification of potential for career development and access to courses and other means of returning not to the starting point, nor even to what may have been the point of departure, but to the point of a career which would have been reached without the added experience of bringing up a young family.

The management of local programmes is one which demands policy commitment and financial support either from a local authority or from a pooling of funds devolved to schools. It benefits from a link with initial teacher-training institutions as well as any accessible surviving teachers' centres. We should be looking, then, at school clusters resourced not only from their combined budgets and expertise but by a larger grouping of the profession, an area professional development consortium, and which is the bridge between schools, authorities and higher education. Back down to earth in each locality, a crèche is among the first essentials. Even more essential is an attitude change across the profession, not so much to recognize the need, which most are all too acutely aware of, but to have confidence in meeting it.

INDUCTION INTO NEW SPECIALIZED ROLES

In the future, we should be anticipating and planning for much more mobility across the education service, between primary, secondary and further education sectors, between teaching, training, research and development, advisory and administrative services. All the more important that in each of these areas there should be clear principles and procedures for the induction of colleagues. Because each organization or service has its own culture, there can be no blueprint for good practice other than the very firm expectation that induction should have been planned, that the needs of newcomers and the organization's wishes for them should have been identified, and that an adequate response should have been made in every case.

In most cases, this is simply not happening. Some steps have, however, been taken in some areas. The National Association of Educational Inspectors and Advisers produced a document on the Induction of New Advisers (NAEIA, 1991), ironically but even more necessarily at a time when their future role was again being subjected to governmental shakes of the kaleidoscope. The NAEIA document illustrated a continuum of existing LEA models, from the minimalist job visiting and meetings, through those which added assured information transmission to a mentor-attached apprenticeship mode, to a structured developmental approach. It identified nearly forty activities which may be included, and turned identified skills and task-needs into a management audit. That may well be something for a GTC to develop and extend across the whole profession.

Individual services and local authorities provide examples of a similar continuum of good intentions, unevenly applied or honoured in the breach. The unevenness can be attributed largely to a failure to insist on resources of time despite the pressures to get on with the job before knowing what it is, and also to a failure to negotiate the responsibilities of induction in job descriptions, performance review, and organizational structure. There appears to be a universal acceptance that it would be a good investment to convert ideas into disciplined applications, which will occur only within a framework of professional expectation and controlled management practice.

That is the kind of discipline needed in every branch of the education service. It should be promoted as good practice within the framework of the General Teaching Council and adopted as part of organizational expectation and management audit, whatever may be the future framework for quality control. It should be seen not as a separate activity, but as part of the continuum from initial preparation to professional and organizational development.

Chapter 11

The GTC, the 1998 Green Paper and the European Dimension

The coincidence of the GTC consultations and the Green Paper *Teachers Meeting the Challenge of Change* in December 1998 caused delay in the announcement of the composition of the Council, at least in part because the DfEE did not want what seemed to be an uncontroversial outcome of consultation and consensus to be associated with a much more controversial document. The situation illustrates a more general distinction, between proposals affecting the career structure, salary and conditions of service of teachers, which are largely a matter for negotiation among employers, unions and the government, and those matters which are the responsibility of the teaching profession and are now being vested in the GTC. It is a general distinction which has to be made but which also has to be recognized as impossible to maintain in detail. The Green Paper is predominantly about the future structure of school staffing, about salary incentives, salary thresholds and ways to cross them. So the parallel GTC innovation is given no more than a passing reference; yet the drive behind both is to raise 'standards', and this Green Paper is offered as a new vision of the teaching profession, with incentives for excellence, a culture of professional development, strong leadership, non-teaching support, and a way forward to improve image, morale and status, recruitment and motivation – the same slogans also offered for the barely mentioned GTC. Moreover, the headings used are sometimes the same: what, for example, is meant by career and performance management in the Green Paper and at the same time in the GTC legislation?

This chapter does not seek to debate the proposals in the Green Paper: its focus is on the connections of this paper with functions of the General Teaching Council, which is alluded to only in §124 and the accompanying caption. It is essential to envisage before the GTCs are elected and begin their work in the year 2000 what will be their role in relation to the new proposals, and to make provision for them to be able to carry out their functions.

This was not a Green Paper in the sense of being a preliminary consultation to be followed by a White Paper heralding legislation. It was a document presented to Parliament. There will be no White Paper before introducing the proposed changes. Unlike one or two recent consultation documents, on which far-reaching questions have been asked and responses have been taken into account in subsequent action, this Green Paper (coloured green anyway) spelt out firmly that the structural changes will be made, and simply asked whether people agree or disagree, or have other comments. There was more scope for detailed response at an operational level on the technical document on pay and performance management, but on the whole the response documents are more likely to have elicited market survey information than informed comment for further consideration.

The major headings for the GTC's advisory responsibilities are not discrete. Supply and access, qualifications for entry to training, standards to be reached during initial training, recognition of EU and overseas qualifications, criteria for induction, expectations for continuing professional development, re-entry updating, qualifications in the course of a teaching career, preparation and development for headship are part of a continuum of professional expectation and education.

All of these areas of responsibility are affected by the Green Paper, and the GTC will be expected to advise on the modifications proposed for each of them. There are in particular four aspects of the new proposals for which the GTC will have to be in a position to advise with sound judgement; one of these is considered in a separate chapter on induction. The other three are new routes into teaching, performance development, and training for school leadership, including the proposed national college.

1. NEW ROUTES INTO TEACHING

The proposals for new routes of access to teaching (§§ 113–19, 138–45), include transitions from qualified teaching assistant to qualified teacher status, access from other graduate employment, and fast-track training. The GTC will have to advise generally on what constitutes and distinguishes the responsibilities of teachers and teaching assistants in schools, and should have the extended role of commenting on training and qualification for teaching assistants. But it is the accompanying proposal in the Green Paper to 'make it easier for teaching assistants who want to do so, to train as teachers' (§138) on which the TTA has already been instructed to report and for which funding is offered, which merits particular GTC attention.

The proposals for teaching assistants to become qualified teachers are linked in the Green Paper to the 'more flexible employment-based routes' into teaching proposed in §115, and with recognition of relevant experience. 'We are determined that employment-based routes into teaching should be recognized as providing high quality preparation for entry into the profession, open to those who may not be able to pursue a more traditional teacher training programme.' There are already, since October 1998, new incentives to schools to accept trainees on these routes, and further expansion of this option will now be encouraged, possibly by 'funding students directly, rather than the course providers, to put together the elements of training in the way that best suits them'.

The exploration of routes giving wider access to teaching is to be commended and will doubtless continue. So far, however, the evidence has been that training on the job (for example in the variations on licensed teacher schemes) and school-centred initial teacher training have not generally resulted in high quality. What are described as 'more traditional' courses have been transformed since the mid-1980s and again since the mid-1990s, and there is a surprising lack of incentive to existing course providers to widen access. Another thrust of the Green Paper is to assure that all teachers are well prepared in information and communications technology (ICT). Here again, this would seem more likely to be achieved through larger-scale providers of initial training courses than by fragmented provision; but it will be for the GTC to advise on what should and could be achieved.

The various suggestions that funding could be re-routed, whilst they may secure the position of the TTA, are in danger of so undermining the higher education providers that they would be compelled to withdraw their service. This would be a self-defeating exercise. The majority of intending teachers who are looking to postgraduate conditions, status and university qualification for their initial teacher training could be put off coming into teaching at all if this route became less accessible, at a time when the government is desperate to improve teacher recruitment. In Scotland, when the previous government attempted to introduce licensed teacher schemes, the existence of the GTC made it possible for something much more professionally acceptable to be negotiated so that the aim of wider access was achieved without reduction of standards. That is the kind of scrutiny which would be expected of the GTCs south of the Border. There need not be a problem, but to continue the undermining language of the previous government would again create problems. A reasoned estimate of the numbers who might be expected to secure provision through alternative routes would probably help to show that there is no major problem; but this is an area in which a market economy would undermine confidence all round. Instead of recycling the language of 'traditional' and 'radical' alternatives, much more will need to be done to ensure that the whole resource of initial training is promoted, encouraged to meet the challenge of social change, and related to induction and continuing professional development strategies.

2. CONTINUING PROFESSIONAL DEVELOPMENT

The Green Paper is introduced with the aim to 'engender a strong culture of professional development'. This new focus on CPD is at various points elaborated under headings of performance development, including the new training framework, professional development aspects of appraisal, skills updating, individual learning accounts, the role and training of external advisers and assessors, criteria for transition through professional teaching levels, a national code of practice for training providers, and inspection of training. Performance management through a new start to appraisal is further expounded in the Green Paper's technical consultation document.

The Green Paper proposes to support commitment to professional development through a contractual duty for all teachers to keep their skills up to date; a new focus on professional development bringing together national, school and individual priorities; a national code of practice for training providers and a new inspection programme; more training out of school hours to minimize disruption to children's education; a review of training arrangements for supply teachers; and continuing emphasis on equipping teachers with good ICT skills. Individual Learning Accounts for all school staff are to be piloted. In §128 it is clarified that there is no intention to extend the formal contractual obligation beyond the five days already provided for, but that teachers should be paid if they are expected to take further training courses outside directed time; however, in §129, teachers making a significant investment in their personal development through higher degrees should be expected to contribute more to the training cost. This does not yet sound like a cultural transformation.

The GTC is to be expected to consider

> how the proposals in this paper might be reflected in the Code of Practice it will issue to lay down standards of professional conduct and practice expected of registered teachers. The Council may wish to consider whether there should be a professional duty for teachers to keep their skills up to date, which would underpin the new contractual duty. It may also want to consider how teachers' achievements against the new career framework might be recorded on the new register of teachers. (Green Paper, §124)

That is the kind of postulating which could damage the purpose and credibility of a GTC. To be expected to underpin contractual duty with a professional code could jeopardize the independent professional judgement of the GTC, which should be expected to examine critically and advise with considered judgement in order to improve thinking and practice.

GTC (England and Wales) had already made general recommendations for good practice in the introduction to its 1993 document on the continuing professional development of teachers. These, it will be noted, were framed at a time when the government had blurred induction and CPD.

1. individual teachers should take active control over their personal continuing professional development;
2. senior managers in employing schools, colleges and services should establish structures and systems for the formative review and further development of each individual member of their staffs, and should garner and target funds to enable teachers at all stages of their career;
3. such funds should be allocated and directed to meet the needs of individuals as well as the needs of schools and colleges themselves, as advised by a committee of staff under the direction of a member of the senior management team;
4. appraisal and inspection reports should be used by senior management teams to assist professional development committees and individuals to identify and plan to meet their needs;
5. the government should allocate sufficient funds for initial teacher training institutions and their partner schools and employers to allow the new ITT schemes to establish new teachers in an ethos of continuing professional development;
6. this funded induction should include supported self-study, experiential professional learning, observation, course attendance and studentships to properly trained, experienced and inspiring mentors;
7. new teachers should be encouraged to build up development profiles, which will also be of use as a curriculum vitae throughout their career development.

The Trust's recommendations to specific bodies were:

1. To members of the profession

Our continuing professional development is our own responsibility. We must ensure that it happens. To neglect this is to fail ourselves, our profession, and ultimately young people. We must develop and foster our professional links, seeking and expecting assistance from local schools, colleges and providing agencies.

2. To schools and colleges

You have a duty to each member of your staff to assist them to develop themselves professionally. This can often be achieved alongside your own school or college development needs. Ensure that you have the structures and systems to guarantee that this occurs and is seen to occur fairly and at least adequately.

3. To training institutions

You have the opportunity to guide and direct new teachers into paths of expecting and attaining continual professional development, and have a role to play in ensuring that active (and also apparently 'dormant') teachers and schools and colleges in your locality have access to apt and appropriate training.

4. To employers and governors

You have the responsibility to ensure that each school, college or other part of the service has appropriate structures and systems for it to develop successfully and also develop fully the staff who work for you. It is also your responsibility to ensure that those who manage those systems have adequate funds to provide for continuing professional development.

5. To government

Quality assurance and control demands that your inspection and audit systems should check that employers, governors and managers have established and do maintain structures and systems to enable schools, colleges and individual members of the profession properly to pursue their own continuing professional development. You have a responsibility to the future of the nation to ensure that there are sufficient funds available to guarantee success.

6. To all concerned

We must all work together to ensure that resources and energies and research endeavour are directed towards the comprehensive development of the teaching force in all sections of the education service, for the continued improvement of the education of children, young people and adults.

It will be noted that the recommendations for good practice are addressed not only to teachers.

THE GTC AND A EUROPEAN PERSPECTIVE

One of the least-noted virtues of the Green Paper is that it makes proposals for 'external development' (§§ 134–5), including a target for teachers to have some form of international professional development and to learn from other school systems. Completely ignored, however, has been the post-1992 European accord through which mutual recognition of qualifications are intended to give access to professional mobility across EU countries, and the prospect of an EU Green Paper on Teacher Education. The immediate context of the GTC will be a European one, as part of a global perspective.

As teachers have different status in different European countries and in different sectors of education with different traditions, there are different approaches to CPD needs, responsibilities, requirements and entitlements. Examples of CPD practices from a selection of European countries may be cited and the alternatives or interactions may be delineated of:

(a) national requirements and provision: targeted priorities and funding;
(b) local or institutional employment: local or school budgets and CPD in relation to other priorities; staff and organization development;
(c) frameworks for professional responsibility.

European trends in education, e.g. towards a quasi-market in education, new technologies, political and social change, student and professional mobility, have to be set against these approaches, and implications analysed, in terms of control, effectiveness, and professional culture. We all have to move from background national confines towards a more common future.

BACKGROUND TO CPD IN BRITAIN

I was quoted recently from a 1974 article in which I was repeating the observation that 'training is from without, development from within' (Gold, 1998). At the 1994 ECER conference in Bath, twenty years later, the international seminar group came to the same conclusion: that professional development is the responsibility of the teacher.

In the White Paper of the incoming government (DfEE, 1997), there was scant reference to teachers' professional development and in-service training, and not one question in the consultation process.

> Alongside changes to initial training we need to ensure that the 400,000 serving teachers have access to training and advice. High quality in-service training is the key to raising standards through updating teachers' skills and enabling them to keep pace with best practice. Many of the proposals set out in this White Paper will need to be supported by specific training. In particular there will be a major emphasis on training to underpin our drive on literacy and numeracy and to raise teachers' competence and confidence in using IT. (*Excellence in Schools*, p. 48, §16, DfEE, 1997)

The government then welcomed its own Teacher Training Agency framework for teachers' professional career development, and announced the intention to establish a 'virtual' teachers' centre in the national grid for learning, linked to the new 'university for industry'.

There is no evidence from the past that the quality or quantity of CPD opportunities is improved by giving CPD greater attention in policy discourses. From the mid-1960s to the late 1970s, there was a flowering of INSET activity and institutionalization: the teacher-led Schools Council for Curriculum Development and Examinations; 600 teachers' centres, funded curriculum development; the social sides of schooling in new forms of school organization; funding associated with the raising of the school-leaving age, first in anticipation of the intended date 1968, then of the actual deferred date 1973–74; James Committee Report, ACSST and ACSET; the golden age.

Yet I had to record in the 1980s that, as far as could be identified by research,

1. the number of days in the year spent on INSET by teachers declined rather than increased from an average in the mid-1960s of four days per year;
2. the level of identified INSET for teachers was about 1 per cent, with some decline by the late 1970s;
3. secondments for full-time long courses declined, at least until:
4. 'pooled' provision was exploited by some local authorities at the expense of others;
5. INSET activities undertaken by teachers outside school time declined from an estimated two-thirds of all INSET to virtually nil in some areas;
6. grants from central government for INSET were perceived to have been diverted increasingly to maintain systems (teachers' centres, advisory services) which could not otherwise be sustained in times of cutback;
7. discrepancies between LEAs increased while co-ordinating machinery declined;
8. the custom of school release for short-term INSET without supply staffing became increasingly unacceptable;
9. supply staffing previously undiagnosed in separate LEA budgets, became attached to the LEA budget, drastically cutting real delivery of INSET;
10. Other activities associated with professional development though not budgeted as INSET suffered a sharp decline.

Since then, it is likely that:

1. the three of five required days introduced from the 1987 Education Act in line with practice in some other European countries will have had some positive and negative effects;
2. the seizure by central government of powers for the first time to fund its INSET priorities will have tilted the balance towards training and away from development;
3. the technical and vocational initiatives from another Ministry in the 1980s will have been a major source of CPD until their recent conclusion;
4. long courses have declined dramatically;
5. most teachers' centres have closed;
6. the use made by schools of INSET funding in their budget remains to be charted.

THE NEEDS OF A MOBILE TEACHING PROFESSION IN EUROPE

By now, the investigation has to be extended to Europe:

Competencies may well involve certain approaches and attitudes conducive to the kind of society for which schools and colleges are to help learners to prepare. In addition to the obvious criteria of effectiveness, there are expectations in the national and international contexts of the widening European Union, including preparation for the exercise of democracy and human rights, and the will to promote active participation in this wider context. The new inclusion of school education and teacher's continuing development in programmes funded by the European Union has not just curricular but professional dimensions. European networks of training institutions have already been working together on European dimensions of teacher training. It is essential that the whole teaching profession becomes involved in such developments. (Sayer, *The Needs of Teachers*, 1996)

Before we can accept that challenge, we shall need some agreement on what we are talking about. The Eurydice (EC, 1995) survey of in-service training of teachers in EU and EFTA/EEA countries categorized the following definitions:

1. teachers' personal and professional development;
2. improving the quality of education systems, of the education provided, and of teachers' teaching techniques;
3. (some countries only) knowledge of the social and environmental milieu.

It identified as main features: providers; central or local; university or non-university; compulsory or optional. (Differences across countries and within them across sectors.)

It showed a wide discrepancy in national share of budget: 2 per cent to 0.12 per cent (the UK return suggested this was 'not relevant', meaning that there was no firm knowledge available). The percentage of teacher time spent on INSET was not usually available. The country with 2 per cent of national budget shows 8.1 per cent primary/lower secondary teacher time and 3.9 per cent upper secondary. Teacher participation ranged from 73 per cent to 19 per cent, though many countries responded 'no statistics available'. Within countries, there are wide differences across sectors of education. Interestingly, although the figures would be difficult to verify, participation appears to be highest where INSET is voluntary; 'right and duty' countries are among the lowest. Eurydice also shows the variety of qualifying training for promotion, salary increase, specialization.

This is just an illustration of divergences in public understandings and provisions: it needs enlarging to include the future EU members. Within each of our school systems, and perhaps even more across them, the purposes and notions of the very words *school* and *teacher* are wildly divergent. Among the stakeholders in the school, the differences are at least as strongly polarized. We know that in our different school systems, whether within one country or in different countries, the actual work done by teachers is different. How far does the provision of CPD opportunities attune with the kind of work that teachers actually do, or what it is intended that they might do?

GENERAL ISSUES DRAWN FROM AN ACSTT EXAMPLE

In 1978 a working group of ACSTT (Advisory Council on the Supply and Training of Teachers), in which I took part as a school leader, along with teacher-trainers, researchers, professional association leaders, and an observing inspector, offered the now familiar ground that post-experience teacher learning can be usefully considered at different levels: the needs of individual teachers; the needs of functional groups within the school; and the needs of the school as a whole. It suggested that 'INSET is a voluntary professional activity which depends for its success upon the goodwill of teachers'. The most notable aspect of the document (DES, 1978) is that it was written by a cross-professional working group, accepted by the whole profession's advisory council, then published by the DES and, at that time uniquely, distributed to all schools. Later, schools were to be bombarded by unwanted and totally unagreed and largely unread ministry pamphlets. But this was the time of 'the thinking school' and 'the continuous staff meeting', and the year when the government at last accepted a financial plan for 3 per cent of the schools' budget to go on CPD, the year before another party came to power and changed all that.

The different aspects, or levels, of individual teacher need, functional group need, and school organization need, could be seen to be all subordinated to either the needs of learners or the policy of national, local or institutional government. These will each in varying emphases be concerned with the teacher's personal education, professional knowledge, career development and job performance, whether individually or in a group.

These emphases change also according to horizontal and vertical viewpoints, by which I mean reviewing needs at any one moment or reviewing teacher education as a continuum through from initial preparation to induction and through into a third cycle (James, 1972).

> It is self-evident that pre-service education and training, together with the probationary year, can be no more than a foundation. In that initial period it is impossible to foresee, let alone provide for, all the demands that may fall on the teaching profession in future, or on individual members of it during their careers.

We have all gone along with this basis of learning needs, in different categories, and have tried to find ways to identify needs, by consulting or interrogating or inspecting individuals, functional groups, schools. We have sought ways to check individual perceptions against others' perceptions of their needs. On the whole, it has been at least superficially easy enough to find areas of overlap between the identified needs of individual teachers, groups, and the organization. Where there is that overlap, organizations can prioritize the agreed need in its overall budgeting, and be accountable in the economic language of schooling. Where there is not, individuals or groups are left to their own devices.

But some individual needs defy prioritizing. It is all very well, in the effective school jargon, to help staff do their job more effectively, keep up to date, encourage a positive response to intended change; but much less easy to enable a teacher to fulfil lifelong wishes; to investigate a particular personal professional interest; to have a refreshing rest from the routines of teaching; to increase job satisfaction; to prepare to do something different in another workplace.

If we really believed in achieving a balance between individual, group, institutional and government policy needs, we would probably organize our lives, our schools and our finances in that way. The rhetoric suggests that CPD is a good thing, the more the better and the better the more. School realities usually suggest the opposite. CPD is an interference to school routines, it is not fair to students and it is not fair to colleagues; or if it is squeezed in as an extra it is not fair to the teacher concerned. There is great pressure from schools, parents, pupils not to desert them for INSET in school hours. There is great pressure from families not to desert them out of school hours. That is likely to affect those with strong family commitments, and becomes a gender inequality too. But I have seen a Flemish school in which working groups of teachers are timetabled for staff and curricular development into the weekly timetable, and this is not in conflict with the school routine, because it is an essential part of it. I have suggested elsewhere that modular school programmes, to correspond with significant learning phases, would enable longer CPD episodes to be timetabled in without interference or conflict. But school organizations rarely take the subject seriously; instead of looking at ways to build CPD into the organization of schools, the Green Paper can only offer to throw money at out-of-hours training.

As for financing, there is no way that a school, however enlightened and however committed to long-term development, is going to sacrifice immediate benefits to pupils for indirect long-term benefits which may come from teacher development, except in individual crisis cases. The idea of an education voucher seems to be appropriate enough for adult education generally, and for the individual professional needs of teachers in particular. So there would be, in addition to an individual entitlement, a school budget for INSET related to school priorities, and a government funding for specific national developments, to match the categories of need. The proposal that individual needs can be identified through annual appraisal appears to put a narrow interpretation on individual needs: those which will improve the individual's school performance.

Each of these categories develops its own professional discourse: pedagogical discourses related to children's needs; others related to curriculum delivery; others to institutional effectiveness; others to the economics of education; and yet more related to policy. What is singularly difficult is to bring these discourses together. This is our hope for the General Teaching Council.

Categories may equally relate to the stage of professional career, in that continuum which might be seen as from initial preparation to induction, full competence and mastery. There is actually no clear agreement on what those categories would be. There are further categories related to re-training for change of role, promotion, or return to teaching after breaks in other careers, notably family commitment.

Within each of the categories, there are different kinds of aims and objectives. To cite a Czech colleague from CDVU, Masaryk University, Brno:

1. Transformation of both the school and the educational system.
2. Innovations in education.
3. Professional and personal development of the teacher .
4. Qualificational training:
   a) training of school management staff;
   b) training of people working in the education system.
5. Requalificational training.
6. Continuing lifelong training of teachers and people working in the education system (Beran, DSDE 1995)

FUTURE NEEDS

Needs are a mixture of responses to the inevitable and consequences of policy direction, determined by the sort of society or societies we want in Europe.

There will be three essential conditions for social living:

1. To recognize that instead of factory work, big business and large industries, there will be a more and more important role for the practice and effects of smaller human scale activities assisted by new technologies.
2. That secure careers and unproductive unemployment must be replaced by more flexible, less secure and self-generated work, as well as creative leisure periods.
3. That increasingly our activities will be organized around projects and programmes, and less and less around permanent institutions.

Here are some related hopes and aspirations:

1. That inventions and changes may serve ecological needs rather than growth and profit.
2. That authoritarian management systems for static, rigid hierarchies and separate organizations, or again concentrations of power in elites based on wealth, birth or indeed monopolies of knowledge, should be replaced by capabilities and access to knowledge available to all.
3. That general management posts as boss, leader etc. become less significant than collaborative management and shared responsibility for particular activities.
4. That stronger connections – across existing social divisions and lines of organization – should be made between particular activities, which after all come together to influence the same people.

For education, the effects could be expected to be:

1. Openness to languages, cultures and aspirations of the whole human race, whether in a local community or in the global village; priorities not of the nation-state but of the general good.
2. Ecology as a core study of the curriculum.
3. Developing capabilities of problem-solving, rather than prescriptions of general content from previous knowledge.
4. Education as a person for transactions among persons, not for previous roles in yesterday's work and social strata.
5. The right of access to information, in order to be able to make decisions at the point of action.
6. Learning as a lifelong process, not just compulsory years of childhood.
7. Schools not as learning factories but a basis for personal and group work, whether at home or in meeting places like school.

For that to happen, the shape of schooling and education would have to change drastically. These, it seems to me, are core concepts common to all countries and all situations. That is why they are also the main points to be addressed if in Europe school is to relate to the development of a new Europe-wide democracy. They have to be addressed from many directions, but one of the first must be for them to become the priorities for the professional development of teachers.

However, when translating that into action, we continue to assume that continuing professional development is related to a continuing professional career in some kind of progression: initial training, induction, and various phases of professional development extracted from Shakespeare's seven ages of man. If we are not careful, that could fly in the face of what has just been proposed for the future: that secure careers and unproductive unemployment must be replaced by more flexible, less secure and self-generated work, as well as creative leisure periods, and that increasingly our activities will be organized around projects and programmes, and less and less around permanent institutions. The phases of professional development often proposed assume individual development in a career which if not stable is at least predictable. Perhaps we should instead be developing our preparedness for the uncertain, the unpredictable, with a sure knowledge only that the skills and competences we acquire will more and more rapidly become outmoded, and that all of us will be in some senses beginning teachers. In a learning society, this should be projected as a strength, whereas in the hierarchies of experience it could be considered a debilitating weakness.

Yet another issue in practice is that long-term needs for the future may best be identified and adopted by sharing insights among teaching practitioners and those who are looking for future trends, but that resourcing is likely to come from institutions bent on immediate priorities and short-term survival. Teachers under pressure are also likely to sacrifice long-term perceptions to current classroom expectations.

A lot of preliminary work has been done and is being done: Council of Europe, OECD, EU, UNESCO, ILO have all contributed in their way. European and international professional bodies have supported work on the teaching profession in Europe, and have tried to formulate charters for teachers. Professional bodies make statements of ethical principles including the continuing development of competence, skills and understandings. Their work is not being brought together to inform teachers, their institutions, their public, European or national policies. There is a desperate need for research across our countries but at the same time across the different understandings of the classroom, of the school, of the stakeholders, of the economics of education and the funding mechanisms, of education policy in relation to the social policy generally across Europe. These are major issues for the GTC.

3. PREPARATION, TRAINING AND QUALIFICATION FOR SCHOOL AND SERVICE LEADERSHIP

The Green Paper appears to offer the prospect of a coherent coverage of training for school leadership, following a period of fragmented provision and the recent introduction of a voucher scheme for newly appointed headteachers, TTA Headlamp courses. The intention in the Teaching and Higher Education Act to extend required qualification for heads is also a significant departure. But even more significant is the

Green Paper's projection of a new framework to include a potentially broader leadership group on a new leadership pay spine. It will be for governing bodies to determine the size and nature of the leadership group and of individual salaries and progression within it. Those in the leadership group will not be covered by the working time restrictions in the teachers' contract.

Much will depend on the nature, scope and governance of the National College for School Leadership, with whose general direction the GTC should be expected to be identified and involved. This college will serve both as a flagship and as a nerve centre for the regional leadership training network. To be welcomed also is the intention that it should have an international dimension, have a capacity to commission research, have links with leading business schools, universities and with the education officers' virtual staff college.

The desire for such a college has been articulated since the 1960s (Michael, 1967), was particularly strong in the early 1980s (SHA, 1982), and was not properly met by the much more modest government schemes of the mid-1980s, when a national cascade model of one-term training-the-trainer opportunities in thirteen designated centres was supplemented by shorter courses, with a communication and co-ordinating centre at Bristol. Subsequent initiatives for headteachers' training have been no substitute for a coherent scheme, which could now embrace the wider vision of leadership expounded in the Green Paper and give scope for the development of good practice across the education service and related services.

The national college will be directly controlled from the DfEE, not by the TTA. Whatever the locus of control, in order to ensure that the college realizes its full potential, it should have some form of governing body representative of the teaching profession, of bodies having international standing in the development of leadership, and of those who will most clearly participate in its activities. It has been proposed since the 1980s (e.g. SHA, 1982) that a General Teaching Council once established should be significantly involved in such a body, since the GTC will represent all leading interests in and around the education service, including business, and since it has the duty to advise on continuing professional development at all levels.

Arrangements will have to be put in place to ensure that the General Teaching Council is in a position to exercise its statutory responsibilities to be the source of advice on these new developments, as well as those already in train, on behalf of the whole teaching profession and the public interest. For the development of school leadership, as for other key areas of the GTC's advisory responsibility, it will be essential for the GTC itself to have a strong international, and in particular European dimension. In the pre-Council planning stage the future links of the GTC have been considered with other regulatory authorities both in Europe and in other English-speaking countries; a decision had still to be taken whether the GTC should become the competent authority under the EU First Diploma Directive, and its complementary role was envisaged to advise teachers on working abroad and on comparability of qualifications. This vision for the GTC must extend to best practice across Europe for continuing professional development, school management and leadership training.

Chapter 12

Recognition of Professional Status and Agreed Professional Ethics

Previous chapters have mentioned both the controversy about professional status and the difficulty which has been experienced in reaching agreement on professional ethics or a code of conduct. It will now be for the GTC to bring together the insights and understandings which exist about teaching as a profession, and to determine what should be articulated as professional expectations, in what form and for what purposes.

RECOGNITION OF PROFESSIONAL STATUS

Elsewhere, I have dwelt on the understandings we have of status and recognition (Sayer, 1995). Status, or its near-synonym standing, tends to be about place in society, and is used generally about high placing or the wish for it. A status symbol, for example, would probably not be about the underclass. There is a permanence about it. The word is linked to 'estate' (or in German *Stand*, French *état*), with the pre-democratic upper crusts of society. Professional status has that background, further developed since the nineteenth century in those countries where the national government had not taken control of services requiring high qualification and incorporated them into the civil service. It is conferred on groups of people with highly trained skills and qualities founded on a recognizable body of knowledge and research, who take a large measure of responsibility for an essential service performed in the public interest. That responsibility is vested in a professional body with publicly recognized powers to determine what are the required levels of good practice and who is fit or unfit to exercise it. We could not describe philately as a profession: it may have highly trained skills and a recognizable body of knowledge, but it does not require a long period of high-level training beyond apprenticeship/experience; and above all, it would be difficult to argue that it performs an essential public service.

In the ways we use the word 'recognition', there are at least two distinct elements, of identity and of appreciation (or the lack of either or both). The identity of teachers as a body has to do with the need of individual teachers to identify with each other, and to identify their individual work with that of teachers generally. It also has to do with a need to be accurately identified by the wider public. If the word 'teacher' is used, what does it suggest: dedication, trustworthiness, learning, pedagogical skills; or in the plural, perhaps through media headlining, the word may equate more closely with discontent, short hours, disputes, the cause of economic decline and indiscipline. The image of the teacher is not that of teachers collectively. There is no collective body to reflect the distinctiveness of teaching as experienced by individual teachers, or to communicate with the public about the core of the teacher's identity and role, by which a teacher can be recognized.

Secondly, it means appreciation: in French, *reconnaissance* means also gratitude, acknowledgement; in German, *Anerkennung* is an extension of recognizing. By appreciation, we may mean gratitude and acknowledgement; or we may just mean having an understanding of what it is about. Both of these are needed by teachers in the public domain, just as they are by anyone else working for others. Professional recognition is to be distinguished from social and economic recognition.

These days, 'profession' is increasingly 'graduate profession', with a research base in a university-level discipline. For some, the word presents difficulties as being either outmoded or overused or abused; however, for teachers in England and Wales it has a particular force in terms of status, because in England and Wales and in Ireland they have been until now the only major profession without such a professional body, and without powers to exercise their professional responsibilities collectively as well as individually. The need is felt for parity of esteem with other callings, along with the peculiarly British professional class. Statutory bodies for other professions and differences among them provide examples of what a GTC could be, but also examples of what it ought to avoid. In other countries, professional status is not a necessary or even understandable notion, where teachers are part of the civil service structure, and aspects of their status relate to that.

Teaching is seen as both a calling and a craft. Its activities are related to generally recognized definitions of a 'profession'. In this chapter, the gap is explored between present circumstances and those necessary for public recognition as a profession. A full educating profession will not be confined to those teaching in schools. The distinction is to be drawn between traditional professionalism and an open professionality more appropriate for present expectations.

Teachers need to have professional scope and space, to educate according to trained insights into students' learning. They need to have ownership of the teaching task. They need to feel responsible and professionally accountable for the quality of service provided. It may well be, as some sociologists have argued, that profession is a term so variously defined that it is incapable of general definition and of little scientific value. However, it is certainly a symbolic label for a desired status; it is certainly a term which has meaning to people who apply it to themselves; it has felt reality, and that is a prevalent if not universal feeling among teachers.

The Monopolies and Mergers Commission attempt in 1970 to summarize the characteristics which distinguish the professional is now generally referred to in Britain. It sets out seven key characteristics. Professionals:

- possess a specialized skill enabling them to offer a specialized service;
- undergo intellectual and practical training in a well-defined area of study;
- maintain detachment and integrity in exercising personal judgement on behalf of a client;

- establish direct, personal relations with a client, based on confidence, faith and trust;
- collectively have a particular sense of responsibility for maintaining the competence and integrity of the profession as a whole;
- tend or are required to avoid certain manners of attracting business;
- are organized in bodies which, with or without state intervention, are concerned to provide the machinery for testing competence and regulating standards of competence and conduct.

This is not, however, an entirely insular approach incapable of extension in Europe. In recording the UCET-hosted agreement (Sayer, 1989) it was possible to use a similar Scandinavian formulation, at that time part of the professional discourse among European teacher associations:

- a body which performs an essential public service;
- exercising a high degree of responsibility in the way it fulfils the objectives formed by the community of which it is part;
- its work being founded upon a systematic body of knowledge and research;
- its members governed by a code of conduct and professional ethic;
- its required lengthy period of initial training being complemented by in-service growth and development.

To that it was possible to comment:

> the teaching profession seen as a whole embraces and performs an essential public service, directly affecting all young people, and directly or indirectly touching the lives of all adults. It requires for most of its activities a lengthy period of graduate initial higher education and training complemented by INSET. Its work is founded on a massive accumulation of knowledge and research. The work of teaching requires constant exercise of responsible decision-making on fundamental issues. There are general assumptions of a public service ethic. The ingredients are all there: but for want of any one focus of professional leadership they are being kept apart by historical accidents. A large measure of control over its own conduct is an essential part of exercising responsibility in a public service. Recognition and registration as a teacher is one important means of exercising control of professional standards.

There are those who question the systematic body of knowledge and research. It should also be remarked that the statement was about teaching seen as a whole; some were delineating schoolteaching as a sub-profession. What anyone could see was missing was a governing council for the profession and a means of making explicit the professional ethic which teachers knew was implicit in their work.

Distinctions have been drawn between the service motive and the profit motive: in the first, people take reward in order to enable them to provide a service; in the second, they provide a service in order to secure a reward. It would be difficult to ascribe altruism to all recognized professions, however much they would consider it a duty to put the interests of the client first; among teachers, many would recognize altruistic dedication to learners, whilst others would caution against allowing this to be exploited by employers or the State. The distinction drawn between the profit motive of business enterprise and the service motive of the non-profit-making public sector has at best been one of relative tendencies, and in recent years the public sector has been so encouraged or required to emulate business incentives or to be replaced by them that it may not be held to be a distinction which with confidence can now be applied collectively, however much it may explain individual motivation.

A further distinction is between the older, 'liberal' professions and salaried employment in large organizations or the State civil service. That may have been more applicable in Britain where the State was a latecomer to control of services like education and where teaching was more clearly a 'free' profession than it has been since the 1980s. On the other hand, it may become more applicable in those societies which seek to move from a command economy and to shed teaching from civil service or local government security; the more the frontiers of the State are rolled back, the more applicable will be the professional self-regulatory approach which developed in Britain and countries influenced by its institutions. However, recent forms of denationalization or privatization have in Britain been accompanied by increasingly severe State regulatory powers over private practice, in which the State may be seen not to have relinquished its power but to have harnessed private enterprise within its control. Elements of this tendency can be seen in the build-up to a GTC, and it remains to be seen whether or not the State will relinquish further powers, such as recognition of qualifications, discipline of child protection cases, the large number of Secretary of State appointments to the Council, or the proposed national code of practice which the government expects to be underpinned by the GTC.

Social control over professions is emphasized at a time when the professions appear to be less than rigorous in their protection of the public interest; the State is presented as having a duty to protect the unwary client from exploitation or negligence. The more closed a profession has become, the more necessary that intervention may appear. On the other hand, what may be called 'open professionality' will recognize the context in which special skills are exercised, and will draw into the self-regulatory body those related services and client interests which can then be protected from inside, in the case of teaching as co-educators.

A distinction frequently heard in teaching is between the teacher's professionalism (or professionality, to distinguish it from unacceptable usages of the word) and the teacher as technicist. Otherwise formulated (Elliott, 1972), the professional applies broad theoretical knowledge to non-routine tasks requiring judgement in decision-making according to ends decided for the benefit of society or the individual client, whereas the technicist applies a craft skill to routine programmed tasks, with decisions made according to ends decided by society or the customer. The profession forms a corporate identity, in which the work becomes a central life interest and the basis for individual recognition and achievement through entry qualifications, extensive education and corporate expectations beyond the individual work situation; the technicist has other motivation, the work becomes a means to other ends, and the role or job is defined, limited and specific.

In teaching in England and Wales, the last twenty years have been generally felt to have been de-professionalizing; it is hoped that the GTC represents a move to a new relationship of the profession and public authorities, whilst at the same time representing what has continued despite all to be felt to be a professional relationship between teachers and their clients.

It is suggested, as the GTC comes into being and as it seeks to assert its responsibility both to advise and to regulate, that its authority will have to be earned. That is true, but it raises the questions already being voiced in the 1970s and referred to in Chapter 1. If the independence and further development of a GTC depends on its behaviour, does it mark no more than a return to what Grace identified as partial social democratic and professional consensus (1940s–mid-1970s) legitimized by compliance with government? Would the GTC's earned legitimacy then be seen as neutering other forms of pressure on state and employers? That is the danger in the Green Paper notion of the GTC's professional code underpinning a government-devised national code of practice. It is vital that the GTC should be seen to be responsible, if necessary challenging government proposals.

STATEMENTS OF ETHICS: A CODE OF CONDUCT

Differences of perspective about what constitutes a teacher or the profession of teaching emerge most strongly when attempts are made to make explicit assumptions of teachers and the public of right and wrong professional behaviour. This emerged strongly in deliberations leading to the GTC. Previous chapters have noted both the objective set for GTC (England and Wales) and the difficulties encountered when working on a code of professional ethics between 1992 and 1997.

The first difficulty was ownership. Without first establishing a GTC to determine what statements should be made on professional ethics and to have some control over how these statements should be used, it was seen by some that a code of conduct could be misused by a hostile government, and would be a hostage to fortune. It was also a matter of sensitivity that some associations already had a code of conduct for their own members, and others might not wish to be seen to adopt or adapt from them. So it appeared at first that instead of proceeding to a short statement of the obvious, perhaps a pick-and-mix of existing codes, what would be most helpful would be a more searching foundation of ethical principles on which such a code could be based. The GTC (England and Wales) Trust was generously supported by the Comino Foundation in commissioning such work, invited two of its most active GTC advocates to undertake it, and was fortunate in being able to engage one of them, Meryl Thompson, to pursue the project.

Over two years, the issues drawn from previous thinking and raised by members were brought to GTC forums and Directors' meetings, and the work was modified with every possible effort made to accommodate different viewpoints, indeed cast in a mode which set out the pros and cons of each route being explored. Three fundamental ethical principles were proposed, explored and revisited: the ethic of care, the ethic of commitment, and the ethic of competence. The ethic of care excited considerable debate, there being a continuing resistance to the teacher as social worker and doubts over the peculiarly British and peculiarly ambiguous legal responsibility of the teacher or school *in loco parentis*. The ethic of competence was subject to the anxiety that statements could be used to intervene in the employer–employee relationship in which a GTC should not be directly involved. Another c-word, conscientiousness, had emerged as a dilemma in research conducted for two of the member-associations to ensure that assumptions were not being made about the occupation of teaching which do not correspond to current reality or future probability. After a considerable gap from 1974 (the last major study of the teacher's day (Hilsum and Strong, 1978)) these studies gave a fair picture of what actually happened to a teacher's time in the 1990s. Recent commissioned surveys of what actually goes on (NAS/UWT 1990, 1991 and AMMA, 1991) present generally similar pictures and may serve as illustration, and the most recent of them (Campbell and Neill, 1991) is used here, a survey conducted through the Policy Analysis Unit of Warwick University of secondary schoolteachers' time, following a similar study with similar findings of infant teachers. The survey includes time on and off school premises, including weekends, having been recorded on seven consecutive days. It does not include the school holiday periods. On this basis, the overall finding is that in seven consecutive days the overall average occupation of teachers totalled 54.4 hours. Of this time, 14.7 hours were taken with work away from school. Allowing for times when teachers were engaged in more than one activity at once, teaching contact-time took 16.9 hours, preparation 12.9, administration 18.1, in-service activity including meetings 5.3, and other activities 4.1 hours. Overall contact-time, including registration, supervision and assembly, accounted for 37 per cent of time spent (or in an alternative presentation 39 per cent), whilst actual teaching was just over 30 per cent. The time taken with work away from school was closely associated with what the researchers termed 'conscientiousness', as measured by the teachers' views of what constitutes a reasonable level of 'non-directed' time in the terms of the 1987 and then 1990 Pay and Conditions of Service Documents. The researchers saw it as a moral dimension to teacher motivation, and what teachers deemed reasonable ranged from below five hours a week to above 25, with 9.3 as an average, compared to the 14.7 actually spent at work away from school. They dwell on the diffuse nature of teachers' responsibilities, and come to the conclusion that 'the ethic of care as a central value in teachers' occupational culture contributes to work overload' and look for ways to control conscientiousness. It is not surprising that the GTC Trust deliberations on the ethic of care remained unresolved.

The deeper the debate, the more tempting it became to go for the more superficial general statements of the obvious, or indeed if people did not wish to be seen to borrow from particular teacher associations, then to borrow from related services. Indeed, those who had at first not wished to work straight to a code or statement were now taking the view that this would be preferable to the revealing depths of exploration into which we had been drawn. This was indeed a strong temptation when, at St George's Windsor, the GTC Directors and Members of Parliament were engaged in joint exploration and drawing on the UKCC as a catalyst. A back-of-envelope adaptation of the UKCC code of conduct for nurses, midwives and health visitors was drafted and would have presented little difficulty, but nobody could have pretended that this was the intended consensual result of discussion and debate among teachers.

A draft consultation document in 1996 was reformulated as a statement of ethical principles for the teaching profession, and views sought both on the statement itself and on ways in which a future document might be offered. Though welcomed by some associations, agreement to proceed could not be reached in the Forum of 1997. Meryl Thompson's study was published in its own right (Thompson, 1997) in the hope that it would stimulate discussion in all parts of the education service, as it certainly had in its negotiated stages. The work that went into it and its result now await the attention of the GTC, which has the responsibility to advise on standards of conduct for teachers as it thinks fit or as the Secretary of State may require. Meanwhile, there have been additions to the existing repertoire of codes, not just for particular associations. The RSA Inter-Professional Colloquium in 1996 initiated a continuing investigation. UCET (1997) has published a code of ethical principles for the teaching profession. In its own shorthand, it extends across intellectual and vocational integrity, moral courage, altruism, impartiality, human insight, responsibility for influence, humility, collegiality, partnership, public vigilance on professional responsibilities and aspirations, and provides a useful outline of context and further readings in values in education. Both FENTO and ILT have formulations ready for their 1999 launch.

Last and not least, the GTC for Scotland has drafted a code of conduct, having managed for three decades without doing so, and has put it out to all teachers for comment, with about 85 per cent of respondents being favourable. The draft document for consultation opens with a clear and concise introductory preamble, and statements of purposes and professional obligations echo the exploration south of the Border; it repeats the three ethical principles of care, competence and commitment, but wisely these do not appear as headings in the draft code itself, which is set out below. The real exercise, no doubt, comes with bridging the gap between 85 per cent and 100 per cent. There will be plenty for the new GTC to draw on.

In doing so, it will benefit from the experience of pitfalls. It is most unlikely merely to follow the Green Paper and underpin any code of practice emanating from government or its agencies. The experience of the GTC Trust indicates the need to define even more carefully than has been achieved before what it is that is sought and for what purposes. The wording of the Act is that regulations may make provision for authorizing the Council to issue and from time to time revise 'a code laying down standards of professional conduct and practice expected of registered teachers'. The regulations drafted for consultation in April 1999 have now to be finalized. Nigel Harris (1996) in his encyclopaedic directory of codes of conduct in the UK attempts to distinguish broadly between codes of ethics, codes of conduct and rules of practice, whilst observing that each expression is variously used. Codes of ethics will be short sets of broad ethical principles; codes of conduct will be more detailed and specific; codes of practice govern the way duties are performed. He observes that relatively few codes distinguish between rules which articulate fundamental moral principals to be observed in any circumstance and rules which set down detail of how duties should be performed in order to ensure consistency of practice. He notes, moreover, the increasing importance of securing international agreement, particularly as the free movement of workers takes effect across the European Union. The GTC will be able to work in the European context.

Harris rightly insists on a distinction between the benefit to the public and the benefit to members of the profession. A code of conduct will be of most benefit to the public if it is a requirement on those exercising a profession, if it is published, and if it can be enforced by disciplinary procedures. Teaching is now to join those few professions in which all these conditions apply. The GTCs have statutory powers and duties through registration to investigate and apply discipline which can involve withdrawal of the right to teach. In the public interest, it must be only a matter of time before this applies in any school and not only the majority covered by the Act. The benefit to members of the profession is in the immeasurable terms of trust, confidence and reputation both among the public and among themselves. It may protect them against unreasonable demands to act in ways that are considered and explicitly stated to be unprofessional, for example to conceal or to condone practices which are harmful to the client, to the public or to fellow-teachers. It is also a safeguard against passing moods of antagonism to behaviours which may seem in moments of fervour or hysteria to be associated with misconduct but which on reflection are not of that order.

The GTC will have to clarify not only its own thinking but that of the political language of the day. What, for example, is meant by the word to which successive governments have declared total commitment: standards? The government have introduced the legislation for a GTC to contribute to the government drive for standards. That somewhat subordinating imperative could be expressed as a shared concern: but it is easy to be so lost in repeated rhetoric that the meaning is lost or that there are so many different meanings as to render it meaningless. Leaving aside the botanical or ornithological connotations, a standard is a flag or figurehead raised to indicate a rallying-point. Etymologically it has to do with both extending and standing. It is sometimes used to mean that to which we aspire, with superlatives attached: the highest standard. At other times it may mean the generally accepted norm, as in standard measurement, or the average. Or yet again, it may be used to mean the lowest acceptable level. Translated into a code of conduct, the first of these might be the values which inform a profession, the second would be norms on which work can be done to change them, and the third would have to do with professional unacceptability. Translated into codified rules of practice, the focus would be the third, where the word 'standards' is uttered with a growl and the point is reached at which unacceptable practice becomes professionally actionable. The immediate political pressure will be for the GTC to work on unacceptable behaviour and practice, in a self-regulatory discipline mode. It would, however, be disastrous if this became the main thrust of a GTC. The GTC must be constantly vigilant in reviewing and advising on acceptable and attainable norms as well. Above all, it must be creating new vision, new aspiration, and in that sense be the standard-bearer and flagship of the profession; this cannot be left to minority voluntary groups such as the College of Teachers, UCET, or particular associations, however much they may contribute to the general vision. For the public good, it must be a corporate activity representing all teachers.

There has to be early resolution of the differing views already noted about involving the GTC in disciplinary regulation of the c-for-competence. The debates in Parliament, consultation documents and regulations from the Act show that the government wishes the GTC to use its powers to deal with cases of 'serious incompetence', and in parliamentary debate it was clarified that GTC procedures in such cases would be preceded by and therefore not doubly prejudice procedures between employer and employee. Serious incompetence presumably indicates unfitness to teach in any situation. It could be a mechanism for dealing with that dwindling minority of older teachers who did not have to qualify by pedagogical training and are deemed seriously incompetent in practice; or those whose qualifications from other contexts appeared to warrant registration but who have proved otherwise. But it is much more likely to be teachers who have at some stage successfully completed a course of training but are now referred to the GTC as seriously incompetent. The draft business plan estimates on past DfEE evidence that there will be up to 250 misconduct cases per year, with up to 40 involving a full hearing;

whereas there is no experience of dealing with cases of serious incompetence, which are thought likely to be much lower.

Whatever the result of consultation on this point, it would be wrong for a GTC to enter into regulatory proceedings without formulating and disseminating a clear understanding of what constitutes serious incompetence, and what could be done about it. The media attention is bound to be on 'getting rid of incompetent teachers', whilst the responsible approach would be across a range of alternative measures. The ILT in its over-hasty but nonetheless worthwhile 1999 consultation has proposed that teachers in higher education should be able to demonstrate that they 'remain in good standing' by use of a portfolio of evidence of updating and continuing professional learning and development. Incoming schoolteachers are already to hold profiles passed through from initial training and to build on them through induction, and a similar procedure to the ILT proposal would be feasible. The GTC could certainly recommend professional expectations and procedures to ensure that skills are updated, and could where necessary withhold registration if it is satisfied that this has not been adequately attended to; but this has to do with the professional duty to try to develop and update; levels of competence are more a matter for the employment itself. In the area of competence and incompetence, it seems essential that the GTC influence should extend across all three interpretations of 'standards': advising and inspiring teachers to aspire to the highest achievable standards; advising the Secretary of State on norms and the best ways to provide for them; and setting out what are unacceptably low levels of competence which it may deal with after and beyond employment procedures. Statements or codes should not be confined to the last of these. It may well be, moreover, that a GTC composed not only of teachers but of related public interests, employers and other providers will wish to reflect this open professionality in the coverage of its statements; certainly GTC (England and Wales) Trust has found it appropriate to set out expectations not only on teachers but at the same time on heads, governors, employers and government to ensure that the opportunities exist for teachers to meet their professional obligations.

GTC FOR SCOTLAND DRAFT DOCUMENT FOR CONSULTATION OCTOBER 1997

4. Professional Code for Teachers

A registered teacher shall be committed to carry out all professional responsibilities in such a way as to:

- safeguard and promote the interests and well-being of learners and, in so doing, have regard to the interests of others affected by the service provided;
- exercise due care and diligence in all matters affecting the welfare of learners;
- recognize and respond appropriately to the fact that learners are susceptible to being influenced by the example of their teachers;
- show proper and impartial respect to each learner as an individual with distinctive needs and capacities – and adapt the service offered, so far as possible, to match their personal needs and aptitudes;

- involve the learner and, where appropriate, others whose interests are affected, in considering suitable provision;
- observe professional confidentiality in a manner consistent with legal requirements, wider public interests and the interests of the individual learner;
- maintain, at all times, appropriately professional relationships with learners;
- ensure that professional knowledge and competence to practise are maintained at a level sufficient to ensure a high quality service;
- co-operate and collaborate with teacher colleagues and other professionals in promoting the learner's welfare;
- have a working knowledge of his or her pastoral, contractual, legal and administrative responsibilities which is reasonable in all circumstances;
- justify public trust and confidence, and enhance the esteem in which the profession is held.

Chapter 13

Not to Conclude – Pursuing the Future

This is a new beginning, in a new context. The immediate task will be to make the GTC work as an organization, establish confidence and build capability. The plans prepared for the Council are already challenging, and the expectations even in the short term are high. The Council itself will wish to add to those immediate objectives. The first two years will be a testing time. They will also be the period in which the Council will determine what are its middle-term priorities and longer-term objectives, to present to the professional electorate and the public before the GTC election of 2004. Whether short, middle or long-term, the Council will be finding a balance between its internal and external, operational and developmental, advisory and regulatory responsibilities. This chapter draws together some of the negotiations on hold, some of the aspirations already recorded, some of the gaps between present and potential scope.

MAKING THE GTC WORK FROM THE START

The outline plan made ready for the first Council and the administration already being formed assumes a support staff of up to 100, to service the Council. It is to be hoped that Ministers can be persuaded of the priority for a strong infra-structure. Work is already well advanced on the database for teacher records and registration, and the Council will have to be confident that it is capable of providing the range of information needed for all Council purposes, including advice on teacher supply priorities. Each of the GTC standing committees, whether for advisory or regulatory functions, will have to be effectively supported. Communications within the Council, to teachers and the public, with government and other public bodies, will be a constant priority. The range of professional and administrative skills and levels will be extensive, across organizational, financial, legal, publicity capabilities, as well as working credibly and supportively across all facets of the education service.

The database will maintain records of about one million qualified teachers, at least half of whom will be registered by 2001. Annually the GTC team has estimated that there will probably be up to 40,000 newly qualified teachers to register provisionally, most of them to be confirmed as registered on completion of the induction period, perhaps 35,000 other new registrations by teachers returning or arriving from elsewhere, 100,000 changes of details, annual registration fees to be recorded and acknowledged from September 2001. These are operations which will have to work unobtrusively well. Ease of access to the general information must be a priority; privacy equally must be maintained on individual files. As shown earlier, the opportunity must be seized to gather and keep updated information which at present does not exist, such as the whereabouts and potential availability of teachers not currently teaching or teaching abroad.

It was asserted in Chapter 8 that for the GTC to establish credibility and confidence, teachers and the public should expect within the first two years substantial position, discussion, consultation or guidance documents on each of the advisory areas. So too, the handling by the GTC of disciplinary cases will possibly be in the public domain, and will be dealt with the openness and transparency now properly expected rather than behind the scenes as has been previous practice. The intention may well be modified that the GTC will deal with induction appeals as soon as it starts to meet in September 2000, but it must certainly be ready at an early stage. For these outputs to be possible, and for advice to have been produced with the considered advice of the whole Council and decisions affecting registration with fair and firm judgement pre-supposes a very rapid sorting out of shared understandings among the newly appointed members, of sorting out roles, of establishing what support is needed and available from the staff, some already appointed, some to be specified. The preparations made in the previous months by the temporary Chair, chief executive and pilot staff will themselves have to be agreed or modified by the Council. That first year or two is going to be a challenge to the Chair, the members and the officers combined. The combining and binding into a cohesive and effective Council must be a first priority.

COMMUNICATION

Initial and continuing communication with teachers is going to be a major challenge: not only information to them, for they are over-supplied with one-way paper and media messages; but the capacity to receive and exchange, to prompt and be accessible to communications from teachers and elsewhere. At the moment this book is appearing, there is a multimedia exercise through websites, press advertisements, circular letters and via teacher associations and other organizations to encourage registration by those entitled but not at this stage required to register, to invite nominations for elected and appointed places on the first Council, and to ensure that all who are eligible are in a position to cast their vote. Consultative documents on the GTC in 1998 and 1999 attracted hundreds, but not thousands of responses, most of them it is true from organizations representing the majority of teachers; this has to be turned into six-figure responses, and teachers individually have to be aware of their new opportunities and responsibilities, not least when it comes to the first registration fee payable either via employers or individually in September 2001. The GTC is for teachers to celebrate. It is no good expecting professional morale to be raised just because a GTC exists 'out there'; it has to be 'in here'.

That question of location starts by being symbolic: the GTC has to be in London, visibly at the heart of policy-forming. It will now be in two locations, although there will be no significant economy and all the disadvantages of a divided organization to add unenviably to the start-up problems. In the middle term, however, the organization must work from where teachers are in physical and professional senses. It has already been noted that in the initial proposals for Wales, for good reason, there were to have been electoral regions, and these are proposed also in the Republic of Ireland; but in England, where the numbers are so much larger and the need for a more local presence so much more obvious, the regional dimension was mentioned but not proposed in the consultation documents. If the GTC is to engage hearts and minds, if it is to bring together the insights of teachers and related services as active participants, it will have to develop a regional and local presence. CATE had just recognized this before it was disbanded; its initiation of area professional committees of training institutions, schools and LEAs to maximize teacher training resources was ended abruptly; but it made good sense, and even more a GTC which has a much wider brief, which is the voice of the profession and which is to have an enhancing effect on teachers' lives will not do that from London alone. If it is to be about a participative profession, it has to start from where teachers are. This could be considered as part of future electoral arrangements to ensure regional representation on the Council; or it could be promoted through regional field officers for development work. There is good practical reason for the starting operation to be centralized, and it may well be that a regional dimension will be best considered when it becomes clearer what is the future of regional government in England; but in the long term there are strong grounds for a regional presence, and it should be feasible early in the life of the Council to hold regional conferences, promote development projects in a variety of local settings, and to find an equivalent of local 'surgeries'.

For teachers to communicate with the Council – and they will be involved only when the communication is *from* as well as *to* them – its meetings will have to be accessible. The Secretary of State has the right to observers in Council and committee meetings and to minutes from them; the same right should be there for teachers and the public, unless there are compelling reasons for reserved business, and their presence should be encouraged. There must be opportunities through a GTC periodical and website for participative communication, and ways must be found to enable Council members to have constant exchange with their electoral constituencies.

The composition of the Council has been arrived at according to the balance of interests which is most conducive to its aims. This is not only a representational spread of interests; that same balance can be conducive to communication with teachers, the concerned public, and employers. It is to be hoped that bodies represented can help to reach and help to involve people with innovative ideas and deep concerns, as part and parcel of their professional activity. It will not happen overnight, and it would be all too easy to be exasperated by low voting percentages or widespread unawareness of GTC developments. After all, how many teachers could name without hesitation the body which runs the National Curriculum, the agency for funding the education and training of teachers, the meaning of OFSTED, the title of the latest Green Paper or the name of the Minister for Schools? It is only when people feel actively involved that national bodies are part of their consciousness.

EXTENDING REGISTRATION AND ACTIVE MEMBERSHIP

The Act and subsequent regulations confine the definition of 'teacher' to those qualified to work in schools. Registration is required of those in all maintained schools and non-maintained special schools. Others may register and may then vote; they may stand for election to the Council if they are teaching young people up to the age of 19 in any setting, which could include independent schools or sixth-form and other further education colleges. This is not yet the GTC constituency which has been proposed. The GTC is about the protection and trust of the public, about the quality of education and the skills and qualities and morale of teachers. How is the public protected until all teachers are required to be qualified and to register?

The professional requirement and the public interest to register with the GTC as a condition for the entitlement to teach is applicable to schools of all kinds. In the particular contexts of the UK, it is understandable that independent schools have negotiated the right not to require registration while it is in the hands of the State, i.e. in the pre-Council phase, although even here to require registration for one sector of independent schooling and not another is anomalous. However, it is strongly to be hoped that the ISC and others will ensure that registration for teachers in independent schools becomes an expectation as soon as it is in the control of the professional council, and it may well be that the GTC could assist by providing a form of certification for those schools which do require their teachers to be registered. The GTC is there to bring teachers together, not divide them; and the memory is still there of the failure at the start of the twentieth century to set up a Council for which elementary schoolteachers were to be required to register whilst secondary teachers could do so voluntarily.

A second constituency of teachers who should be expected to register are those engaged in the professional education and training of teachers, and the GTC must have a responsibility to advise on their work. Ideologies in the 1980s and 1990s about teacher training were based on pre-1970s experience of school; in order to undermine the 'educational establishment' or 'traditional' routes', it was necessary to label higher education teacher-trainers as 'theorists' as opposed to 'practitioners', whereas in fact from the acceptance of ACSET recommendations in 1983 they had been required to have 'recent, relevant and substantial experience of teaching in schools', and any who had less than that were going back into the classroom. What was developing (indeed from the 1970s) was a much stronger partnership of school and training institution, without the later government intervention and agency pressures which can be seen to have undermined professional partnership whilst using its rhetoric, and which in parallel through research and assessment exercises across higher education generally have driven teacher training into a subsidiary role to research and publication in universities. However that may be, the case remains for requiring registration with the GTC for all who have a major input to professional teacher training.

A third group, and by far the largest, who should be drawn into some form of registration with the GTC are those qualified to teach but not currently doing so. The numbers of 'professionally inactive teachers' may approximate to the numbers in teaching employment. It has been noted in previous chapters how badly those are treated who wish to return to teaching, whether through supply or part-time re-entry or by resuming a full-time commitment. Proper provision for them is one of the keys to improved recruitment, retention and retrieval of teachers. It is not an adequate solution to wait for them to resume and then offer or require updating; in their professional interests and the interests of the public, re-entry programmes have to be available to encourage and prepare for their return. Their retention on the GTC register, together with information about their intentions and needs, should become the foundation for advice to them and to employers on re-entry.

The recent extension of entitlement to pre-school education, whether in schools or in nursery education, should bring another significant sector of education under the aegis of the GTC, and it should be represented there too; there may well be a variant form of registration needed here. Exploration of wider access routes into teaching, including gradation from learning support assistant roles to training for qualification as a teacher also suggests a form of registration or pre-registration, together with the involvement of teaching assistants in GTC deliberations and advice about their role and their training needs. It is to be hoped that teachers drawn into non-school education work, such as local authority advisory and officer roles or further training as educational psychologists, will be strongly encouraged and professionally expected to retain their GTC registration.

FURTHER AND HIGHER EDUCATION

There remain the two major post-school sectors of the education service, further and higher education, and their extension in adult education. For the GTC as now constituted, they present issues both of internal and of external management. Internally, those in higher education involved significantly as teacher-educators should be on the GTC register, whatever may be the other developments in higher education; and the estimated one-third of teachers in further education who are qualified to teach in schools should be strongly encouraged to register and should be as a next stage represented on the GTC; again, whatever the parallel developments affecting all further education may be.

However, as things stand, the further education sector has from 1999 its own national training organization, FENTO, establishing professional development systems and expectations, including a code of practice drawn up by its steering group with inputs from the GTC movement. Higher education now has the ILT, also started in 1999, with standards of good practice designed to ensure that new entrants to higher education teaching receive some training, and by voluntary registration to encourage higher education teachers to 'remain in good standing' through demonstrating their updating of teaching skills by portfolios of continuing professional development. The ILT planning group also has articulated the long-term objective that its standards should become expected of 'all those with teaching and learning responsibilities in HE'. So the GTC must work with them as equal partners with a common concern for teaching quality, and systems of liaison and cross-representation must be established to ensure that this partnership flourishes. If it does so, the future may be one of federal association, in which the whole profession of teaching is represented while each sector has its distinctive focus. Adult education, which in terms of lifelong learning should be the most prominent in all these developments, is at the moment the most neglected, and an initiative from the GTC, not least from its community school coverage, may be needed here.

GOVERNMENT AND ITS AGENCIES

The two agencies with functions closest to those of the GTC are the TTA and OFSTED. When the TTA was established in 1993, it was against the opposition of most in the education service and especially in higher education, and as seen earlier the proposals for a GTC were drawn into the debate as a better alternative. So it has been generally recognized that the respective roles of GTC and TTA must be sorted out. The TTA has meanwhile secured and carried out much wider functions than those determined in statute, which are 'to fund teacher training in England; to provide information and advice on teaching as a career, and to carry out such other functions as the Secretary of State may by order confer or impose'. The Teaching and Higher Education Act places with the GTC the duty to provide advice on the purpose, standards and nature of initial teacher training, induction and continuing professional development. So there is no overlap in primary legislation, but only in some of the functions conferred on the TTA by the Secretary of State, in the absence of a GTC. These include advice on ITT and CPD, including preparation and development for school leadership; whilst the accreditation of training institutions or programmes could go to either or neither. The 1999 quinquennial review of the TTA has been conducted with particular regard to the impending establishment of the GTC, and has gone some way to clarify that, as we proposed, once established 'the GTC should be seen as the prime source of advice across the spectrum of teacher training and development'; the views of the TTA, as an active participant in the initial training process, would then inform the GTC.

Just before the review, however, the Secretary of State (3 February 1999) had commissioned the TTA or rather confirmed its work on three further immediate tasks announced in the 1998 Green Paper: to propose and pilot a numeracy test for ITT trainees (a proposal which many found demeaning to teachers and to the supposed improvements in qualifications and achievements under the National Curriculum); to develop proposals for new modular courses of postgraduate teacher training; and to develop proposals to extend pre-course/in-course study for teacher training, all to be ready before the closing date for responses to the Green Paper! The second and third set of proposals would then become the basis for further consultation.

On the other hand, in the 1999 quinquennial review, the TTA is now to make a priority of its recruitment activities and the operation of ITT, and to narrow its brief. It was made clear to the TTA that it would not take charge of the new leadership college, over which the DfEE would 'take a more direct lead', as it would over the new 'fast-track scheme' for the teaching profession, on designing and piloting individual learning accounts for school staff, reviewing and launching existing scholarship and international development opportunities for teachers and launching new programmes 'drawing on advice from the TTA and others'. The DfEE would oversee the initial piloting of paid teacher associates in EAZs and establish the basis for further extension. David Blunkett had asserted before taking office that he wanted the DfEE to become the engine room for change. This will have a strong bearing on the GTC task of advising on best practice.

Another source of advice are the Chief Inspectors of Schools, whose powers to inspect and report on initial teacher training institutions in England and Wales are extended to Scotland, and in all three territories also to inspect and report on providers of in-service training of teachers and (in England and Wales) specialist teaching assistants for schools. The inspections have the purposes of informing the TTA's decisions on funding and accreditation, and 'to provide advice to the Secretary of State with respect to initial teacher training and in-service training and development' (DfEE Notes on Sections of the Teaching and Higher Education Act).

So here is another source of potential confusion; it is one thing for the Chief Inspectors to report on institutions, but what is the nature of advice to the Secretary of State when this has been vested in the GTC? It has to be established early on that whilst the duty of OFSTED in particular is to report on individual training institutions, general advice is the statutory task of the GTC, informed also by OFSTED reports. What would be unsatisfactory would be for the Secretary of State to be presented with contradictory advice from different sources which should be working together. In the longer term, the GTC will have the task of demonstrating by the quality of its advice that it becomes the prime source of advice on the matters within its remit. The interpretation of 'general' advice should be as indicated by the Minister in Parliament, that which does not relate to individual cases.

FUTURE PRIMARY LEGISLATION

It will be remembered that the Minister indicated in debate that the Government might have recourse to further primary legislation in the next session of Parliament. For that to happen, careful thought will have to be given in the Council's first year or two to what would be necessary and desirable. The scope of the GTC's functions will, after the initial period of taking on and managing well the initial responsibilities, have to be extended either by further powers conferred by the Secretary of State (and in some cases therefore withdrawn from the DfEE or its agencies) or by the further primary legislation which Parliament was assured could be envisaged.

There is one apparently minor change to legislation which would give scope for future development without pre-supposing it. It is a change which was urged on parliamentarians during the progress of the 1997 Bill, but was not incorporated. That is the definition of the word 'teacher', which at present is confined to the limited coverage of the 1988 Act section 218, for those qualified to teach in maintained schools and non-maintained special schools, and indeed has become even more confined since sixth-form colleges were removed from the schools sector. The definition proposed by the GTC movement and incorporated in the 'Thornton Bill' was:

'Teach' means teach in or on behalf of a school or other educational establishment as defined in the 1996 Act or as extended by order, and 'teaching' and 'teacher' shall be construed accordingly. (Section 19)

This was intended to give scope for extension by order rather than by recourse to further primary legislation, which would now be necessary to include pre-school teachers, independent schools or all or parts of further and higher education. More controversially, it would now seem appropriate to enable an extension to cover teaching assistants.

A second amendment to primary legislation would be the schedule enabling the retention by the Secretary of State of powers to consider any cases which involve a child protection dimension. In debate this was used by the Minister first to justify retaining all disciplinary powers, and then to justify this power being retained because it applies not only to teachers as narrowly defined but to assistants and to further education teachers too. To this the long-term answer would be to extend the definition of teacher, and to recognize the new GTCs as responsible guardians of public protection as is the GTC for Scotland. There is no long-term justification to the argument that some cases are too important for the GTC to deal with.

To undertake the responsibility of advising the Secretary of State, the GTC must have access not only to the information which the DfEE considers it needs but the information the GTC itself considers it needs in the form it needs. If may not prove necessary to amend legislation to secure this, but it might nevertheless be prudent. Other amendments may be contextual, for example dealing with the roles of agencies if they are seen to overlap or detract from GTC responsibility. There may have to be further attention to the definition of words and expressions. What for example is covered by the new use of language reflected in Section 2 (2) (d) of the Act, the Council to advise on 'the training, career development and performance management of teachers'? Subsequently, the 1998 Green Paper shows that performance management means to the DfEE the new arrangements for appraisal, and it is proposed that these will be linked with career development in the sense of remuneration. Because appraisal as at present understood is not solely to do with identifying needs for professional development, but also with negotiated remuneration, not everyone has wished advice in this area to be the province of the GTC; but appraisal *is* about professional development, and that aspect of appraisal must be subject to the scrutiny and advice of the Council.

It is reasonable to suppose that these clarifications and amendments can be negotiated with good will within the four-year span of the first Council. Some of them can be dealt with by amendment to regulations, whether or not they have to be presented to Parliament for affirmative resolution. The number of appointments to the Council by the Secretary of State could for example be scaled down after the first Council. At some stage, when mutual confidence has grown, the provision that the Secretary of State must 'consult' the Council before changing regulations affecting entry and QTS qualifications may have to be strengthened. It may confidently be expected that the new Council itself, in a rapidly changing context and with an eye to the future, will bring forward further proposals for legislation so that it can work more and more effectively in the public interest.

BEYOND NATIONAL CONFINES

On 29 March 1999 a meeting described as '4-Nations GTC' was held among officers working on GTC proposals for England, Wales, and Northern Ireland, and the Registrar of GTC for Scotland, to share progress reports and identify matters of common concern. This can be confidently expected to lead to regular exchanges; not only are the Councils for England and Wales required in law to exchange information, but they will wish to examine the best ways in which they can combine distinctive and common features. They will also be expected by teachers to do so, in order to work economically. The carefully estimated costs for the Republic of Ireland suggest a registration fee of £50 as compared to the £20 at present in Scotland and likely to be the fee in England and Wales. Is it necessary for England and Wales to have separate databases in order to be distinctive, or to work separately on each area of advice, or to deal separately with the machineries of discipline and appeals? Is it desirable for access to teacher training and opportunities for professional development to be open to all across the UK, and for QTS recognition to be mutually agreed? Teachers and the public would rightly expect the Councils to resolve such questions, and it will require constant attention, probably through a high-level standing committee and also by cross-representation or co-option for particular purposes. The case of Scotland is distinctive, both because of its seniority and because of the different school and teacher-training systems and legal framework, but a federation of GTCs must be on the agenda for the benefit of all.

By extension, in professional terms this could and should involve the Republic of Ireland, set to have its GTC ahead of England, Wales and Northern Ireland, and having shared thinking in formulating its proposals with the GTC for Scotland and the GTC movement in England and Wales. Good practice in the profession of teaching both transcends and accommodates to national confines. This in turn leads to the European and international dimensions within which the teaching profession practises. First and most obviously, the GTC must now be confirmed as the nominated body within the terms of the EU First Diploma Directive; this already is the position in Scotland. The role of the GTC both to promote and to regulate professional mobility and the interchange of international experience and best practice will be of increasing importance. Recognition of comparability of overseas qualifications is the task of the profession. It should be expected that a forthcoming EU Green Paper on Teacher Education and responses to it will do more to fashion the future quality of teaching than individual national preoccupations.

The trends in Europe, particularly in countries reacting from a command economy, are erratic but on the whole away from State and central control of teaching towards devolution and self-regulation. Accords on professional mobility and awareness of individual responsibility sit uneasily with civil service regulation of teaching. Even in France, who would have credited a generation ago the development of the regions and, for teaching, the impact of the more local academies? Teachers in Central Europe in particular are beginning to form professional associations and are looking for models to accord with devolution. There are other European models of statutory professional responsibility beyond the Republic of Ireland and the UK: the Flemish Education Council is one of them. The GTC development may have sprung from a particular background; but it could well represent a much wider future, which has to do with the European principle of subsidiarity, with a participative profession actively engaged in democratic contexts, engendering and not just meeting the challenge of change. The principles of open professionality not only acknowledge that teaching is set in social contexts; they engage the whole context in recommending on the teaching role; far from diminishing the strength of advice given, this prior involvement of the public ensures that advice to governments is heeded. In countries where the State is trying to claw back its lost powers, that consensus is also a vital protection. Wherever the GTC has come from in the twentieth century, that I believe is where it will be pointing in the next one. The European Union and Council of Europe networks immediately and UNESCO fundamentally are the forums beyond each national system in which the values of education and the best principles and practices of teaching will be shared, and from which they will be interpreted in context by the teaching profession in the service of the public.

Documentation

Chapter 1
Documentation
Teaching and Higher Education Act 1998. London: HMSO.
Teaching and Higher Education Act 1998. Notes on Sections. DfEE.
Teaching Council (Scotland) Act 1965. Edinburgh: HMSO.
GTC Partners Progress Reports and Minutes, 12 December 1998, 22 February 1999, 10 May 1999.
Draft Regulations for the Composition of the Councils, March 1999.
DfEE Consultation Paper on Registration and Deregistration, April 1999.

Chapter 2
Unpublished documentation
Joint Council of Heads, NAHT, SHA notes, journals and position papers, 1975–81.
NAHT (1978) A Professional Code of Conduct for Teachers.
NAHT/JCH (1981) A Professional Code of Conduct for Teachers (amended).
Scott, L. (1978) unpublished correspondence.
Joint Four, NUT, NAHT meetings 1978–79.
CATEC (1981) News-sheet.

Chapter 3
Documentation
Morgan, I. (1983) *A General Teaching Council: A Personal Paper* for UCET.
Conference Position Papers for 3 October 1984 AMMA, AUT, CNAA, CP, Institute of Mechanical Engineers, NAHT NAS/UWT, NUT, PCET, Sayer, J., SCETT, SCOP.
Papers to Working Party. Harrison, G. and Morgan, I. (1984) *Relations Between a General Teaching Council and National and Local Government Agencies, Advisory Committees, other Professions, Interested Bodies and the Public*. Blenkinsopp, D. (1984) *Financing a GTC*. Sayer, J. (1984) *General Professional Council*. Middlebrook, W. (1984) *General Teaching Council: Role and Function*. Balchin, R. (1985) *The Composition of a General Teaching Council*.

UCET Minutes of Meetings and Conferences of Associations
1984: 26 April, 3 October.
1985: 12 March, 25 September.
1986: 10 March, 26 September, 10 December.
1987: 17 February.
1988: 15 March, 27 June, 7 November.
1989: Invitational Review Conference, 3 July, 31 October, 21 November.
1990: Extended Forum, 5 February. Forum, 6 February, 30 April, 25 June, 2 October.

Memoranda
1985: from Alec Ross to associations, 13 May.
1986: from Alec Ross to associations 10 October .
1989: from John Sayer: *Summary Report of GTC Regional Seminars.*
1989: *Preliminary Findings from College of Preceptors Enquiry into the Acceptability and Purposes of a General Teaching Council.*
Press Releases
1984: 12 October.
1985: 30 September.
1989: 13 and 15 February, 1 March, 9 May, 8 June.
Working Party Notes
1984: 29 October, 6 December.
1985: 30 January, 21 May, 10 July, 25 September, 21 November, 4 December.
1986: 23 January, 26 February, 18 September.
1987: 19 January.
1989: 21 November.
Working Party Reports and Drafts
1985: 15 February, 14 May, 25 September.
1986: 23 January, 10 March, 25 March, 18 July, October.
1987: 27 January, 17 February.
1988: March, June, October.
1989: July.
Association Responses to Working Party Reports
1985, July, NAHT, PAT, NATFHE, AMMA, GSA, CDP, UCET, NUT, PCET, SCETT, SHA, CP.
1985: November, GSA, NAHT, NAS/UWT, PAT, SCETT, NATFHE.
1986: AMMA, NATFHE, SEO.
1986: December, AUT.
1988: GTC (England and Wales). *Memorandum and Articles.* Companies House.
Education (1989) *Parliament:* extracts from House of Lords debate (9 June).

Chapter 4
Unpublished documentation
Sayer, J. (1990) Briefing Paper to Labour Front Bench and Education Advisory Group, July.
Sayer, J. (1991) *Leaping Forward Together,* address to RSA, 26 March.
Sayer, J. (1991) Update to Labour Front Bench and Education Advisory Group, July.
GTC Correspondence with Secretaries of State and others.

UCET-hosted Forum meetings Minutes: 5 and 6 February 1990.

GTC (England and Wales) Directors' Meeting Minutes, 1990: 9 July, 17 September, 5 November. 1991: 14 January, 28 February, 23 April, 3 June, 26 September, 19 November. 1992: 14 January, 5 May, 22 June, 26 September, 19 November.

GTC (England and Wales) Forum of Associations, Extended Forum and AGM 1990: 6 February, 30 April, 25 June, 2 October. 1991: 4 February, 1 July, 10 July, 29 October. 1992: 3 February, 1 June, 27 October.

GTC (England and Wales) Working Papers Revised Document of Agreement, February 1990, May 1991. Proposals to Hamlyn Foundation for GTC regional investigation and dissemination, June and July 1990, February 1991. Proposal to Directors: 'Funding the Forum', October 1990. Update and Progress Report to Member Associations, July 1991. A Communications Programme, April and July 1991.

GTC (England and Wales) Memorandum and Articles of Association.

GTC (England and Wales) Press releases: 1990: 9 May, 8 June, 17 July, 9 October. 1991: 5 May, 5 July, 16 July, 21 September, 5 November. 1992: 19 March.

GTC reponse to six questions by the Secretary of State, 19 November 1991.

GTC ten-point action plan 1992: *What are we doing in 1992?*

Sayer, J. (1990) *Towards the General Teaching Council: a Self-Managing Profession?* Paper to BEMAS Annual Conference, June for September 1990.

Tomlinson, J. Opening Address, GTC Extended Forum, 1 July 1991.

Tomlinson, J. Opening Statement from the Chair, GTC Forum, 1 July 1991.

Chapter 5
Documentation

DfE (1991) School Teacher Probation: consultative letter, Teachers Branch, 17 September.

DfE (1992) School Teacher Probation: DfEE letters and press announcement 96/92, including 'The abolition of the pointless probationary year', 4 March.

DfE (1992) Letter, Administrative Memorandum 00/90 and Guidance on Induction of Newly Qualified Teachers, 22 July.

GTC (England and Wales) Directors. 1991: 26 September, 19 November. 1992: 14 January, 5 May, 22 June, 26 September, 19 November.

GTC (England and Wales) Forum of Associations, Extended Forum and AGM. 1991: 10 July, 29 October. 1992: 3 February, 1 June, 27 October.

GTC Correspondence Files 1991–2: with DES and Ministers; with Member Associations; with Parliamentarians; with interested bodies.

Proposals to Hamlyn Foundation for GTC regional investigation and dissemination, February 1991.

Technical Working Party: *Promoting an Agreed Scheme,* January 1987, updated for March 1988.

Update and Progress Report to Member Associations, July 1991.

A Communications Programme, April, July, November 1991.

What are we doing in 1992? The ten-point plan.

Press releases 1991: 10 May, 16 July, 5 November.

Correspondence and Proposals to National Commission on Education 1991–92.

Updating paper to Labour Front Bench team and Education Advisory Group, 16 July 1991.

GTC papers to BEMAS Annual Conference, September 1992.
GTC Correspondence with NCE, 1992.

Chapter 6
Documentation
Secretary of State (Kenneth Clarke) (1992). Speech for the North of England Education Conference, 4 January.
GTC (England and Wales) (1992) *Advice and Comments on DES 'Reform of Initial Teacher Training'* 19 March.
DES (1992) *Articled Teacher Scheme: Arrangements for Primary Courses w.e.f. 1993* (5 June).
Education Council (1992): *An Introduction.* Education Council Interim Committee. London.
Hansard: House of Lords 23–24 March, 20 April, 10 May, 7 December 1993, 2 February, 10 March 1994.
Barber, M. (1993) *GTC England and Wales: Future Directions.* Paper for GTC Forum 15 June.
GTC (England and Wales) *The Initial Training of Primary School Teachers: Summary of Advice and Comments.* 30 July.
GTC Forum Minutes. 1992: 3 February, 1 June, 27 October. 1993: 9 February, 15 June, 20 October. 1994: 8 February, 16 June.
GTC Directors Minutes, 1992: 14 January, 5 May, 22 June, 1 October, 19 November. 1993: 11 May.
GTC Press releases. 1992: 19 March.
GTC Parliamentary correspondence 1992–94.
GTC/CATE correspondence 1992.
GTC Newsletter 10/92, 6/93, 10/93.
Teacher Education Alliance Briefing Papers 1993–94.
GTC Requests for Amendments to the Education Bill, 13 December 1993.
Times Educational Supplement leader: *Send for A GTC,* 12 November 1993.
First Report from the Delegated Powers Scrutiny Committee House of Lords, 9 December 1993.
Note of meeting at the Department of Education and Science, 4 June 1992. John Hedger, Robert Horne, John Tomlinson, John Sayer.
From the Northern Ireland Teachers Council GTC initiative, 11 May 1993.

Chapter 7
Documentation
GTC (1995) *You are a Parent.*
Warnock, M. (1996) *Who is a Teacher?* Paper to GTC Forum, 11 June.
GTC Forum Minutes. 1995: 7 February, 13 June, 19 October. 1996: 6 February, 11 June, 15 October. 1997: 4 February.
GTC Directors' Minutes. 1995: 8 March, 11 May, 5 July. 1996: 16 January, 14 March, 9 May, 17 July, 19 September, 21 November. 1997: 16 January, 13 March.

Chapter 8
Documentation

DfEE (1998) *Teaching: High Status, High Standards The Composition of the General Teaching Council: a Consultation Document.*

Welsh Office (1998): *Teaching: High Status, High Standards General Teaching Council.*

GTC (England and Wales) responses: June, July 1998.

DfEE (1999) *Composition of the GTC. Summary of Consultation Responses and Main Decisions Made.*

Chapter 9
Documentation

Dodds, J. (1992): 'Will teacher supply continue to boom?' *Education,* Vol. 180, No. 23, p. 456, 4 December 1992. London: Longman.

GTC (England and Wales) Trust (1999) *The General Teaching Council and Teacher Supply.* Commissioned paper (J. Howson).

National Commission on Education (1993): *The Case for a General Teaching Council for England and Wales.* Briefing Paper. London, NCE.

Roe, I. (1999) 'No daughter of mine is going to be a teacher', *The Independent,* 28 January.

Scottish Office Education Department (1992): GTC for Scotland Policy Review 1992–93. Edinburgh, Scottish Office.

Chapter 10
Documentation

TTA (1998) *Induction for Newly Qualified Teachers. Recommendations on Monitoring, Support and Assessment Arrangements. A Consultation Document.* London: TTA.

DfEE (1991) School Teacher Probation: consultative letter, Teachers Branch, 17 September.

DfEE (1992) School Teacher Probation: DfEE letters and press announcement 96/92, including 'The abolition of the pointless probationary year'. 4 March.

DfEE (1992) Letter, Administrative Memorandum 00/90 and Guidance on Induction of Newly Qualified Teachers, 22 July.

GTC for Scotland (1997/98) *Link,* Nos 27 and 28.

GTC for Scotland (1997) *Study of Probation and Supply Teaching.*

GTC (England and Wales) (1998). Induction for new teachers: Response to the DfEE Consultation Document .

Note of meeting 8 January 1999, GTC/TTA/DfEE, re: induction.

Chapter 12
Documentation

ILT (1999) *The National Framework for Higher Education Teaching.* London: CVCP.

GTC for Scotland (1997) *A Professional Code for Teachers.* Edinburgh: GTC.

GTC for Scotland (1998) *A Professional Code for Teachers.* Summary Leaflet, Edinburgh: GTC.

GTC (England and Wales) (1996) *A Statement of Ethical Principles for the Teaching Profession* (draft for consultation with member associations).

Inter-Professional Colloquium (1996) *Changing Society: Changing Professional Cultures?* London: RSA.

College of Preceptors (1992) *Code of Professional Conduct* in CoP Newsletter.

UKCC (1992) *Revised Code of Professional Conduct,* London: UKCC.

British Association of Social Workers (1987) *Revised Code of Ethics for Social Work,* Birmingham: BASW.

Professional Association of Teachers (1988) *Code of Professional Conduct.* Derby: PAT.

National Association of Headteachers: *Code of Conduct for the Teaching Profession,* Haywards Heath: NAHT (also adopted with one amendment by Joint Council of Heads 1981).

Education Council (1994) *The Code of Conduct,* Billericay: The Education Council.

1994 Draft Code of Professional Conduct for Teachers based on UKCC code, for discussion of GTC Directors.

AUCL *Code of Practice for Members* in AUCL constitution.

Chapter 13
Documentation

Correspondence: Secretary of State to Chair, TTA, 3 February 1999 'TTA and the Green Paper'.

House of Commons Parliamentary Answer: Minister for Schools, 3 February 1999, launching TTA five-year review.

GTC (England and Wales) response to TTA Quinquennnial review, 1 March 1999.

GTC Partners Meeting Progress Report, 22 February 1999.

ILT (1999) *The National Framework for Higher Education Teaching.* Consultation paper, CVCP.

FEDA (1997) Fento: the proposed Further Education National Training Organisation.

FEDA (1998) National Standards for Teaching and Supporting Learning in Further Education in England and Wales.

TTA (1995–99) Annual Reports.

Bibliography

ACSET (1982) *The Initial Teacher Training System*. London: DES.

ACSET (1984) *Teacher Training and Special Educational Needs*. London: DES.

Alexander, R., Rose, J., and Woodhead, C. (1992) *Curriculum Organisation and Classroom Practice in Primary Schools*. London: DES.

Balchin, R. (ed) (1981) The Teacher and Professionalism: A Consideration of the General Teaching Council. *Education Today*, Vol. 31 No. 3.

Bell, J. (1995) *Teachers Talk about Teaching*. Buckingham: Open University Press.

Bentley, D. (1998) Intellectual Regeneration: A New Direction for Teachers. *Education Journal*, Issue 28.

Beran, J. and Kohnová, J. (1995) *Proposal for a Concept of INSET*, in Sayer *et al.* (1995) *op. cit.*

Burgess, T. (1991) Hallmark of a Profession. *TES*, June.

Burgess, T. (1994) A Truly Professional Body. *TES*, 9 April.

Campbell R. J. and Neill, S. R. St J. (1991). *The Workloads of Secondary School Teachers*. London: AMMA.

Campbell R. J. and Neill, S. R. St J. (1994) *Primary Teachers at Work*. London: Routledge.

Campbell R. J. and Neill, S. R. St J. (1994) *Secondary Teachers at Work*. London: Routledge.

Carr, D. (1992) *Four Dimensions of Educational Professionalism*.

Casey, T. (1981) Professional Status at Last? *NAS/UWT Journal*, December.

Cashdan, A. (1993) The Easy Option? *Education*, 9 July.

Circular 1065 (1999) *The Education (Induction) Arrangements for School Teachers* London: HMSO.

Command Paper 1148 (1990) *The Government Response to the Second Report from ESAC: The Supply of Teachers for the 1990s*. London: HMSO.

Cross, C. (1978) Having a Say in Who Teaches. *Observer*, 15 April.

Dempster, C. (1986) Softly, Softly for 100 Years. London: *Times Educational Supplement*, 3 January.

DfE (1987) *Excellence in Schools*. London: HMSO.

DfE (1992) Circular 9/92. *Initial Teacher Training (Secondary Phase)*. London: DfE.

DfE (1993): *Guidance on Audits of Teaching Staff.* London: DFE.

DfEE (1997) *Excellence in Schools* (White Paper). London: HMSO.

DfEE (1998) *Induction for New Teachers: A Consultation Document.* London: DfEE.

DfEE (1998) *Teachers Meeting the Challenge of Change.* London: DfEE.

DfEE (1998) *Teaching: High Status, High Standards: The Composition of the General Teaching Council.* London: DfEE.

DfEE (1999) *The General Teaching Council for England: The Register of Teachers.* London: DfEE.

DfEE (1999) *Quinquennial Review of the Teacher Training Agency.* London: DfEE.

DENI (1997) *A General Teaching Council for Northern Ireland.* Consultation Paper: Bangor, Co. Down: DENI.

DENI (1998) *Lifelong Learning: A New Learning Culture for All.* Bangor, Co. Down: DENI.

DES (1970) 'The Weaver Report'. *A Teaching Council for England and Wales.* London: HMSO.

DES (1978). *Making Inset Work.* London: HMSO.

Downie, R. S. (1990) Professions and Professionalism. *Journal of Philosophy of Education,* Vol. 24.

Draper, J., Fraser, H., and Taylor, W. (1991). *A Study of Probationers.* Edinburgh: Moray House.

Elliot, J. (1991) A Model of Professionalism and its Implications for Teacher Education. *British Education Research Journal,* Vol. 17.

Elliott, P. (1972) *The Sociology of the Professions.* London: Macmillan.

European Commission. Eurydice (1995). *Report on the Professional Development of Teachers in Europe.* Strasbourg, EC.

Freidson, E. (ed.) (1971)*The Professions and their Prospects.* Beverly Hills: Sage.

Gallie, D. and White, M. (1993) *Employment Commitment and the Skills Revolution.* London: Policy Studies Centre.

Gold, A. (1998) *Head of Department: Principles and Practice.* London: Cassell.

Gordon, P. (ed.) (1983) *Is Teaching a Profession?* Bedford Way Paper 15. London: Institute of Education.

Gosden, P. (1972) *The Evolution of a Profession: A Study of the Contribution of Teachers' Associations to the Development of School Teaching as a Professional Occupation.* Oxford: Blackwell.

Gouldner, A. (1979). *The Future of the Intellectuals and the Rise of the New Class* London: Macmillan.

Grace, G. (1987) Teachers and the State in Britain: A Changing Relation, in Lawn, M. and Grace, G. (eds) (1987) *Teachers: The Culture and Politics of Work.* Brighton: Falmer Press.

GTC (England and Wales) Trust (1992). *The Induction of Newly Appointed Teachers: Recommendations for Good Practice.* Slough: NFER.

GTC (England and Wales) (1992) *Proposals for the Statutory General Teaching Council.* London: GTC (England and Wales).

GTC (England and Wales) (1996) *Proposals for the Statutory General Teaching Council.* London: GTC (England and Wales).

GTC (England and Wales) Trust (1993) *The Initial Training and Education of Teachers.* London: GTC.

GTC (England and Wales) Trust (1993) *The Continuing Professional Development of Teachers*. Swansea: University College of Swansea.

GTC (England and Wales) (1996) *Revised Proposals for the Statutory General Teaching Council*. London: GTC (England and Wales).

GTC for Scotland (1990) *Assessment of Probationer Teachers: Guidance for Headteachers.* Edinburgh: GTC for Scotland.

GTC for Scotland (1990) *The Management of Probation.* Edinburgh: GTC for Scotland.

GTC for Scotland (1993) *Assesssing Probationers: An Opportunity for Professional Development.* Edinburgh: GTC for Scotland .

Handy, C. (1994) *The Empty Raincoat: Making Sense of the Future.* London: Hutchinson.

Hansard (1989) House of Lords Official Report, 5 April. *Teaching Council Proposal,* London: HMSO.

Hansard (1991) House of Lords.

Hansard (1997) House of Commons Standing Committee D, 16 January. London: HMSO House of Commons Education Bill, 28 January: London: HMSO.

Harris, N. (1996) *Professional Codes of Conduct in the United Kingdom: A Directory* (second edition). London: Cassell.

Helsby, G. (1995) Teachers' Construction of Professionalism in England in the 1990s. *Journal of Education for Teaching*, Vol. 21, No. 3.

Hilsum, S. and Strong, C. (1978) *The Secondary Teacher's Day.* Slough: NFER.

HMI (1982) *The New Teacher in School.* London: HMSO.

HMI (1983) *Teacher Quality.* London: HMSO.

HMI (1987) *Quality in Schools: The Initial Training of Teachers.* London: HMSO.

HMI (1988) *The New Teacher in School.* London: HMSO.

HMI (1988) Initial Teacher Training in Universities in England, Northern Ireland and Wales. *Education Observed* 7. London: DES.

HMI (1991) *School-based Initial Teacher Training in England and Wales.*

HMI (1992) *The Induction and Probation of New Teachers.* London: HMSO.

HMI (1992) *Review of Local Management of Schools 1989–1992.* London: DFE.

House of Commons Education, Science and Arts Committee (1990) *The Supply of Teachers for the 1990s.* London: HMSO.

Hoyle, E. (1969) *The Role of the Teacher.* London: Routledge and Kegan Paul.

Hoyle, E. (1980) Professionalization and Deprofessionalization in Education, in Hoyle, E. and Megarry, J. (eds) *World Year Book of Education 1980: The Professional Development of Teachers.* London: Kogan Page.

James, E. (1972) *Report of the Commission on Teacher Education and Training.* London: HMSO.

King's Fund (1991) *Report of a Working Party on Osteopathy*, chaired by Rt Hon. Sir Thomas Bingham. London: King's Fund.

Kogan, M. (1975) *Education Policy-Making: A Study of Interest Groups and Parliament*. London: Allen and Unwin.

Larson, M.S. (1977) *The Rise of Professionalism.* University of California Press.

Lawrence, I. (1992) *Power and Politics at the Department of Education and Science* London: Cassell.

Maclure, S. (1993) *A General Teaching Council for England and Wales?* NCE Briefing

Paper No. 11. London: National Commission on Education.

McGuinness, S. (Chair) (1998) *Report of the Steering Committee on the Establishment of a Teaching Council.* Dublin: Stationery Office.

Michael, P. (1967) *The Idea of a Staff College.* London: HMA/HMC.

Millerson, G. (1964). *The Qualifying Professions.* London: Routledge and Kegan Paul.

Monopolies and Mergers Commission (1970) *The Supply of Professional Services* London: HMSO.

NAEIA (1991) *The Induction of New Advisers.* London: NAEIA.

National Commission on Education (1993) *Briefings.* London: Heinemann.

National Commission on Education (1993) *Learning to Succeed.* London: Heinemann.

NUT (1979) Teaching Council: Talks Break Down. *The Teacher,* 12 October.

Ozga, J. and Lawn, M. (1981) *Teachers, Professionalism and Class.* Brighton: Falmer.

Ozga, J. (ed) (1988) *Schoolwork: Approaches to the Labour Process of Teaching.* Buckingham: Open University Press.

Ribbins, P. and Sherratt, B. (1997) *Radical Educational Policies and Conservative Secretaries of State.* London: Cassell.

Roe, I. (1999) No Daughter of Mine is Going to be a Teacher (Education Supplement) *The Independent,* 28 January.

Ross, A. and Tomlinson, S. (1991) Teachers for Tomorrow, in *Teachers and Parents,* Education and Training Paper No. 7. London: IPPR.

Sayer, J. (1980) Managing the Teaching Profession, in *Local Government Studies,* November/December.

Sayer, J. (1983) Time for a Professional Step. *TES,* 16 December.

Sayer, J. (1984) Towards a General Teaching Council. *Education,* 5 October.

Sayer, J. (1985) What Price Professionality? *Dialogue,* Issue 2.

Sayer, J. (1985) Time to go for the Grand Design. *TES.*

Sayer, J. (1986) The Teachers, in Ranson, S. and Tomlinson, J. (eds) *The Changing Government of Education.* London: Allen and Unwin.

Sayer, J. (1989) *Towards a Shared Purpose for the Education Service Education,* 8 September.

Sayer, J. (1989) *Towards the General Teaching Council.* London: EMU.

Sayer, J. (1990) *Towards the General Teaching Council: A Self-Managing Profession?'* Invited Paper to Annual Conference of British Educational Management and Administration Society.

Sayer, J. (1991) Proposal for a General Teaching Council. *Learn,* June 1991.

Sayer, J. (1991) A Professional Move. *Education,* 8 February.

Sayer, J. (1992) We Cannot Wait. *Education,* 24 January.

Sayer, J. (1992) *Background and Current Moves towards the GTC.* Invited Paper to BEMAS Annual Conference.

Sayer, J. (1992) The Case for the General Teaching Council. *Education Review,* November.

Sayer, J. (1993) *The Future Governance of Education.* London: Cassell .

Sayer, J. (1993) The General Teaching Council and Teacher Supply, in Fidler, B., Fugler, B. and Esp, D. (eds) *The Supply and Recruitment of School Teachers.* London: Longman.

Sayer, J. (1994) Political Control and Professionality, in *Pedagogisch Tijdschrift,*

November. Belgium: Leuven.

Sayer, J. (1994) Mission for Tomorrow: The General Teaching Council, in Lawrence, I. (ed.) *Education Tomorrow*. London: Cassell.

Sayer, J. *et al.* (eds) (1995) *Developing Schools for Democracy in Europe.* Wallingford: Triangle.

Sayer, J. (1996) The Need for Recognition and Professional Status, in McClelland, V. A. and Varma, V. (eds) *The Needs of Teachers.* London: Cassell.

Scottish Office (1963) *The Teaching Profession in Scotland:* Report of the Committee chaired by Lord Wheatley. HMSO: Edinburgh.

Scottish Office (1993) *Guidelines for Teacher Training Courses.* Scottish Office: Edinburgh.

SHA (1982) *Towards Coherence.* London: SHA.

Sockett, H. (1976) Teacher Accountability. *Proceedings of the Philosophy of Education Society of Great Britain,* Vol. 10.

Smith, P. (1991) Action is Harder. *The House* [of Commons] *Magazine,* 3 June.

Sockett, H. (ed.) (1980) *Accountability in the English Education System.* London: Hodder and Stoughton.

Sockett, H. (1990) Accountability, Trust and Ethical Codes of Practice, in Goodlad, J. *et al.* (eds) *The Moral Dimensions of Teaching.* San Francisco: Jossey-Bass.

Strike, K. A. and Ternasky, P. I. (eds) (1993) *Ethics for Professionals in Education.* New York: Teachers' College Press.

Teaching and Higher Education Act 1998. London: HMSO.

Teaching Council (Scotland) Act 1965. Edinburgh: HMSO.

Thompson, J. (Chair) (1991) *Only a Teacher . . . ? An Enquiry into Science Teacher Provision.* Joint Working Party, ASE, BAAS, Royal Society. Hatfield: ASE.

Thompson, M. (1997) *Professional Ethics and the Teacher: Towards a General Teaching Council.* Stoke-on-Trent: Trentham Books.

Tomlinson, J. (1991) Why a General Teaching Council? Opening Address, GTC Forum, 1 July. *Education Today,* Vol. 41, No. 4.

Tomlinson, J. (1992) A Matter of Professionals. *Junior Education,* February 1992.

Tomlinson, J. (1995) Professional Development and Control: The Role of the General Teaching Council. *Journal of Education for Teaching,* Vol. 21, No. 5.

Tomlinson, J. (1997) Professional Development and Control: A General Teaching Council, in Bines, H. and Welton, J., *Managing Partnership in Teacher Training and Development.* London: Routledge.

Tropp, A. (1957) *The School Teachers: The Growth of the Teaching Profession in England and Wales from 1800 to the Present Day.* London: Heinemann.

TTA (1998) *Induction for Newly Qualified Teachers: Recommendations on Monitoring, Support and Assessment Arrangements. A Consultation Document.* London: TTA.

UCET (1997) *Code of Ethical Principles for the Teaching Profession.* Occasional Paper No. 7. London: UCET.

UKCC (1993) *Consolidated Version of the Nurses, Midwives and Health Visitors Acts 1979 and 1992.* London: UKCC.

UKCC (1993) *Complaints about Professional Misconduct.* London: UKCC.

Whitbread, N. (1987) General Council, *NATFHE Journal,* February.

Wou, T. (chair) (1990) *Code for the Education Profession of Hong Kong.* Hong Kong: Preparatory Committee.

Name Index

Subject Index

Great Astronomers

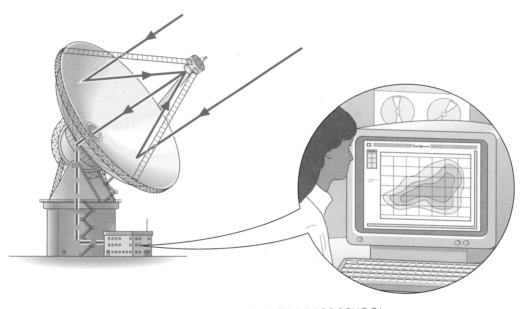

ST LAURENCE CHURCH JUNIOR SCHOOL
BUNBURY ROAD
NORTHFIELD
BIRMINGHAM B31 2DJ
TEL: 0121 475 6499

Jenny Armstrong and Mike Roberts

OXFORD
UNIVERSITY PRESS

Great Clarendon Street, Oxford OX2 6DP

Oxford University Press is a department of the University of Oxford.
It furthers the University's objective of excellence in research,
scholarship, and education by publishing worldwide in

Oxford New York

Auckland Bangkok Buenos Aires Cape Town Chennai
Dar es Salaam Delhi Hong Kong Istanbul Karachi Kolkata
Kuala Lumpur Madrid Melbourne Mexico City Mumbai
Nairobi São Paulo Shanghai Taipei Tokyo Toronto

Oxford is a registered trade mark of Oxford University Press
in the UK and in certain other countries

British Library Cataloguing in Publication Data

Data available

ISBN 0 19 917455 5

Also available as packs

The Earth in Space Inspection Pack (one of each book)
ISBN 0 19 917458 X

The Earth in Space Class Pack (six of each book)
ISBN 0 19 917459 8

10 9 8 7 6 5 4 3 2

Designed by Alicia Howard at Tangerine Tiger

Printed in Hong Kong

Acknowledgements

The authors would like to thank Reverend Tymothy Edge for his advice on this project.

The Publisher would like to thank the following for permission to reproduce photographs:

AMANDA Project: p 28 (bottom right); Apache Point Observatory: p 30 (top); Astronomical
Society of the Pacific: pp 21, 27, 28 (bottom left); Bridgeman Art Library: pp 5 (top left and
right), 8 (top), 17 (bottom); Carnegie Institute, Washington: p 24 (both); Corbis UK Ltd: p 16
(top); Corbis UK Ltd/Bettmann: pp 6, 10 (both), 12 (left), 13, 15, 20 (top); Corbis UK Ltd/
James Sugar: p 16 (bottom); Corbis Uk Ltd/Paulo Ragazzini: p 9; Corbis UK Ltd/Roger
Ressmeyer/NASA: p 29 (bottom right); Corbis UK Ltd/Janet Wishnetsky: p 4 (right); Corbis UK
Ltd/Adam Woolfit: p 4 (left); John Frost Newspapers: p 23 (left); Heritage Image Partnership: pp
14, 19 (top); Hulton Getty: pp 11, 19 (middle & bottom), 20 (bottom); MACHO Project: p 28
(top); NASA: pp 29 (top), 30 (bottom); Photodisc: p 5 (bottom); Popperfoto: p 22; Retrograph: p
23 (right); Ann Ronan Picture Library: p 26; Scala: p 17 (top); Science Photo Library/
Jean-Loup Charmet: pp 12 (right), 18; Science Photo Library/NASA: p 29 (bottom left);
Martin Sookias: p 25 (both).

Front cover: Heritage Image Partners

Back cover: Apache Point Observatory

Illustrations are by: Stefan Chabluk, Richard Morris and Thomas Sperling.

To Ben and Lizzie

Contents

Introduction

When we look up into the night sky, we see, more or less, what people saw 10,000 years ago. But although our picture is very similar to theirs, our understanding of it is very different.

In the ancient world, people believed that the Earth was the centre of the Universe. They used the **stars** to monitor the seasons, to help them navigate across the seas, and to predict what was going to happen on Earth. The Ancient Egyptians noticed that the stars moved in a regular pattern every 365 days, so they divided up the calendar year into 365 days.

Today, we know that Earth is just one **planet** in one **solar system** in one **galaxy** in the whole Universe. We also know that the Universe is enormous and expanding; the distance between stars is measured in **light-years**, and what we see is just a tiny fraction of what is actually out there. The more we find out about the Universe, the more we realize how little we know about it.

This book looks at some of the great astronomers who have helped us expand our knowledge of the Universe. Their theories were not always correct. Sometimes their ideas made them unpopular, or put them in great danger, but without these pioneers we would not have the knowledge that we have today.

▲ The remains of Stonehenge in Wiltshire, England. Some people think that prehistoric stone circles, built thousands of years ago, were set up to track movements of the Sun and Moon, and also the seasons.

▶ This stone beehive-style building in Korea, in South-East Asia, may be the earliest surviving **observatory**. It has a central opening in the roof, for looking at the stars.

▲ This astrolabe was invented more than 2000 years ago by Hipparchus, an Ancient Greek astronomer. It measured the positions of the Sun, Moon, and stars, and was often used to navigate across seas.

▲ This picture, from a 14th-century Arabic manuscript, shows an astrolabe being used.

◀ Today, we can see more through a pair of ordinary modern binoculars than Galileo or Newton could see through their most powerful telescopes.

Aristotle (384–322 BC)

The ideas and writings of the Ancient Greek philosopher, Aristotle, helped to shape the way people thought about the Universe for nearly 2000 years.

Learning and teaching

As a young man, Aristotle was sent to study at the academy in Athens, where he was taught by the brilliant philosopher Plato. He continued his studies abroad and then took up teaching. One of his pupils was Alexander, son of the ruler of Greece. Alexander was to become a powerful leader, later known as Alexander the Great.

▲ Aristotle, like many Ancient Greek philosophers, tried to explain the Universe through logic and reason, rather than through myths and legends.

Earth at the centre of the Universe

In his books *On the Heavens* and *Physics*, Aristotle explained his beliefs about the Universe. He thought the Earth was at the centre of the Universe, surrounded by the starry heavens in the shape of a sphere. Whereas the Earth was full of change and turmoil, he believed the heavens were fixed and unchanging. The heavens became known as the **firmament**. Between the Earth and the heavens, Aristotle described the Sun, Moon, and **planets** as rotating around the Earth.

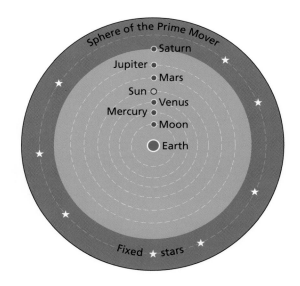

▲ Aristotle's **geocentric** (Earth-at-the-centre) view of the Universe

Wandering planets

"Planets" means "wanderers" in Ancient Greek. They were named "planets" because early astronomers saw that they moved in irregular patterns – they appeared to "wander" in the night sky (see pages 14–15). Although puzzled by these movements, few people doubted that the Earth was fixed at the centre of the Universe.

Aristarchos

One of the few astronomers who questioned Aristotle's geocentric view of the Universe was Aristarchos. In about 290 BC, Aristarchos put forward a **heliocentric** (Sun-at-the-centre) view of the Universe. He suggested that the Earth **orbited** the Sun, and spun on its axis.

However, Aristarchos' ideas were laughed at by others who argued:

1 If the Earth spun on its axis, why didn't objects fly off the Earth?

2 If the Earth was moving, why didn't it leave behind birds flying in the air?

3 If the Earth was moving round the Sun, why did the stars appear to stay in the same relative positions (i.e. why was there no parallax effect)?

The parallax effect

The parallax effect is when an object appears to move if you view it from different positions. For example, try viewing a finger with one eye shut and then the other eye shut: the finger appears to move. The further from your eye, the smaller the apparent movement.

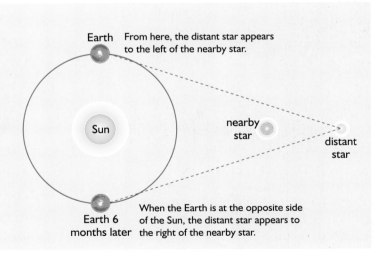

Earth — From here, the distant star appears to the left of the nearby star.

Sun

nearby star

distant star

Earth 6 months later — When the Earth is at the opposite side of the Sun, the distant star appears to the right of the nearby star.

Aristotle's views were accepted for 2000 years, until scientists gained more understanding about the laws of motion and **gravity** (see pages 18–19). It was not until better astronomical instruments were developed that people could see there was a parallax effect. It was just too small to see with the naked eye.

Claudius Ptolemy

(AD 100–170)

Known as the "Prince of Astronomers",
Ptolemy was the greatest astronomer of his time.

Life and work

Ptolemy lived in the Egyptian city of
Alexandria. He was an able scientist, whose
work covered geography, **optics**, and
astrology, as well as **astronomy**.

When the Roman Empire collapsed in the
4th century, much learning was lost as
libraries and books were burned by the
invaders. Fortunately, Ptolemy's work had
been translated into Arabic. While Europe
was plunged into the **Dark Ages**, the
science of astronomy was kept alive in the
great civilizations of Islam.

▲ This medieval painting (AD 1475) shows
Ptolemy holding an armillary sphere,
designed to show how the **planets**, the
Sun, and the Moon circled the Earth,
which, at that time, was believed to be in
the centre.

▲ This extract from a 16th-century translation
of the *Almagest* lists the **stars** in the Orion
constellation, gives their positions, and rates
them according to their brightness.

The *Almagest*

Ptolemy's most important work was a
collection of 13 books known as the
Almagest. In this work, Ptolemy wrote: "We
shall try to note down everything which we
think we have discovered up to the present
time … to avoid undue length we shall
merely recount what has been adequately
established by the Ancients. However,
those topics which have not been dealt
with by our predecessors at all will be
discussed at length to the best of our
ability."

The *Almagest* explained Aristotle's ideas
of a **geocentric** Universe, predicted the
positions of the **planets** for many years to
come, and also contained a catalogue of
1028 **stars**.

Imperfect orbits

Although the planets' **orbits** were drawn as perfect circles, astronomers had been puzzled for centuries by observations that showed these orbits were irregular. Sometimes the planets appeared to move backwards, then forwards again. Also, their brightness varied. Ptolemy explained the "imperfect" orbits with a theory that the planets moved in **epicycles** (small circles) within their orbits. He also suggested that the Earth was not always fixed at the exact centre of the planets' orbits.

▲ Medieval scholars showed Ptolemy's model of the Universe as a series of circles, representing the orbits of the planets around the Earth. The outer circle showed the stars that were believed to be the boundary of the Universe.

▼ The orbits and epicycles of the planets

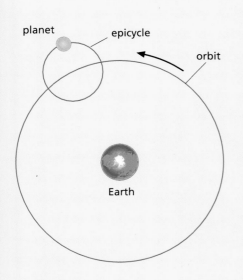

planet
epicycle
orbit
Earth

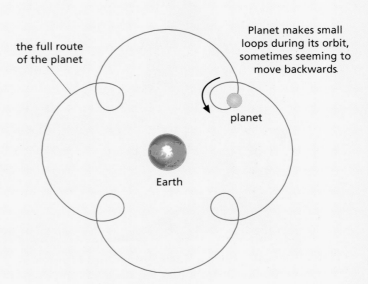

the full route of the planet

Planet makes small loops during its orbit, sometimes seeming to move backwards

planet

Earth

Nicolaus Copernicus

(1473–1543)

*Nicolaus Copernicus brought **astronomy** out of the **Dark Ages**. He suggested that the Sun, not the Earth, was the centre of the Universe. Although Copernicus' work was not recognized in his own lifetime, it led the way for important discoveries in the future.*

Early life

Copernicus was born in Poland and from childhood he took his studies very seriously. He was interested in mathematics, Greek, medicine, and church law. He became a priest, but he spent much of his spare time studying the **stars** and reading works by the Ancient Greek astronomers.

▲ Copernicus became a canon (an important clergyman) in a cathedral, but refused to become a bishop as he felt it would leave him too little time to study astronomy.

Sun

Earth

zodiac

▲ Copernicus' **Solar System**. This 17th-century print shows Copernicus' theory about the six known planets moving around the Sun.

10

The Copernican revolution

Copernicus' ideas were based more on his reading than his observations. What puzzled him most about Ptolemy's idea of the Universe was why the planets' movements were so irregular. He took up Aristarchos' theories about the Sun-centred Universe (see page 7). If the Earth and other planets **orbited** the Sun, this would explain some of the "wanderings" in the planets' movements. Copernicus pointed out that, if it took the Earth 24 hours to rotate (turn on its axis), this would explain night and day.

In some ways, Copernicus was an unusual "revolutionary". Although his ideas about the Solar System, with the Sun at the centre, were startling, he talked about them with just a few people in private. He did not publish his book *De Revolutionibus* until he was dying, in 1543. However, his assistant persuaded him to write down his ideas, which were then given to people anonymously (without his name on).

The Christian Church

The Church had accepted Ptolemy's idea that the Earth was the centre of the Universe, as it fitted in with the Church's understanding of Creation at the time. Copernicus knew that his new ideas might anger the Church, which was why he was reluctant to publish his work. Like most medieval scientists and scholars, Copernicus depended on the support of the Church for books, work, and money.

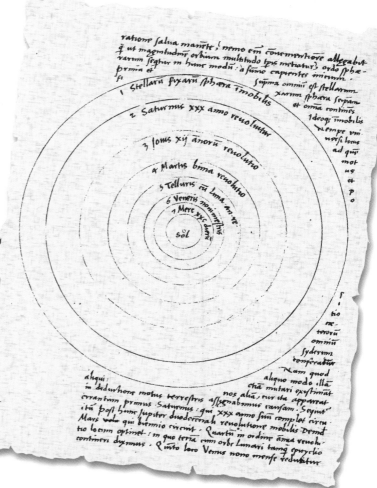

▶ This is a page from an early manuscript version of *De Revolutionibus*, before it was published. It was written in Latin, which was the language of learning at the time.

Tycho Brahe (1546–1601)

*Tycho Brahe observed and catalogued over 1000 **stars**. He did this by building sensitive scientific instruments that enabled him to see more than ten times the detail of any previous observations.*

▲ Tycho Brahe was impulsive and competitive. An argument with another student about who was the better mathematician led to a duel in which Brahe lost part of his nose. Afterwards, he wore an artificial one made of gold and silver.

Early life

Tycho Brahe was the eldest son of a wealthy Danish family who sent him to university, at the age of 13, to study law. However, when he saw an **eclipse** of the Sun in 1560, he became fascinated with **astronomy**, particularly with predictions about the movements of the **planets**. Despite his family's disapproval, he spent most of his time and money on astronomy.

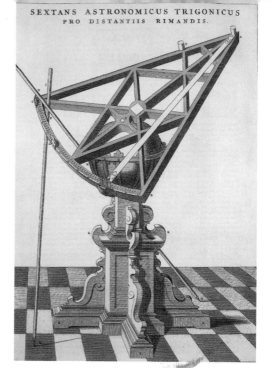

SEXTANS ASTRONOMICUS TRIGONICUS
PRO DISTANTIIS RIMANDIS.

▲ Before **telescopes**, astronomers used measuring instruments, such as this sextant, to map the stars.

A new star

In 1572, Brahe noticed a brilliant new star, so bright that it could be seen in daylight. The nova (new star) caused great surprise as people believed, since the time of Aristotle, that stars were fixed and unchanging in the heavens. Brahe used his newly built, large **sextant** to measure the position of the new star. He proved it was far beyond the Earth's **atmosphere**.

The Castle of the Heavens

Brahe gave lectures and published his work. By 1575, he was famous throughout Europe. Proud of his achievements, the King of Denmark gave Brahe the island of Hven and money to build an **observatory**. Brahe built his "Castle of the Heavens", which contained several observatories, a laboratory, and a library. In the library, Brahe installed a brass globe, 1.5m in diameter. During the next 20 years, as he measured and observed the stars, he engraved them onto the globe.

In Brahe's study a huge **quadrant** was set up next to a window, through which he could make his observations. With a team of assistants, many sets of instruments, and clocks, Brahe recorded more accurate measurements of the stars than had ever been made before.

By 1597, Brahe had argued with the new Danish king, so he left Hven and went to Prague in Bohemia.

Although many of Brahe's ideas were wrong (for example, he believed that the Sun moved around the Earth), he was correct in thinking that the other planets moved around the Sun. His careful measurements and records of the stars and planets were important to future astronomers.

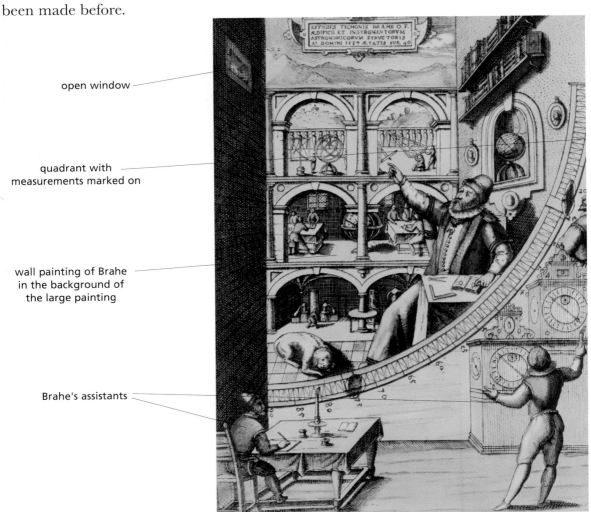

open window

quadrant with measurements marked on

wall painting of Brahe in the background of the large painting

Brahe's assistants

▲ A painting of Tycho Brahe in his observatory

Johannes Kepler

(1571–1630)

Johannes Kepler had a brilliant mind. By looking carefully at some of Tycho Brahe's data, he made some startling discoveries.

Early life

Johannes Kepler was born in south-west Germany. At university he proved himself brilliant at mathematics and **astronomy**. His tutor, Michael Maestlin, taught astronomy according to Ptolemy's theories (with the Earth at the centre of the Universe), but he privately believed in Copernicus' theories (with the Sun at the centre). Kepler began to support Copernicus' ideas, but this made him unpopular with the university authorities.

Drawing an ellipse

Push two pins into a board and link them with a loop of thread. Place a pencil inside the loop and stretch it, moving it round both pins. This makes an **ellipse**. Each pin is called a focus. In each planet's elliptical **orbit** in the **Solar System**, the Sun is at one focus.

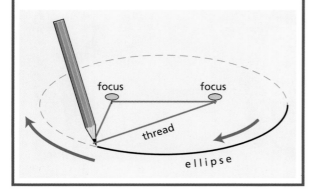

▲ Kepler believed that his own work confirmed Copernicus' theories about the Sun being at the centre of the Universe. He urged fellow astronomers, such as Galileo, to publish their work to support these ideas.

Discovering how planets move

In 1600, Kepler was invited to work as Tycho Brahe's assistant in Prague. Brahe was the best-known astronomer of his time and Kepler was eager to see the huge amount of information that he had collected. However, Brahe kept most of his records to himself and suggested that Kepler just look at the information he had collected about Mars. This, in fact, was all Kepler needed to make the calculations that led to an important new discovery – that the orbit of Mars was elliptical (oval-shaped) and not circular.

▲ Kepler explaining his discovery of planetary motion to his sponsor, Emperor Rudolph II

This discovery was important because it explained the wandering movements of the **planets** that had puzzled astronomers since ancient times (see page 6). In Ancient Greece, Ptolemy had explained them with his theory of **epicycles**, but Kepler, using Brahe's data, proved this was wrong.

Kepler's laws

Brahe died in 1601, and Kepler immediately took possession of all his books and records. Using Brahe's data, Kepler worked out three mathematical laws that explained the movements of the planets around the Sun. He showed that their orbits were elliptical and that their speed changed during orbit. He also linked the distances of the planets from the Sun with the time they took to make a single orbit.

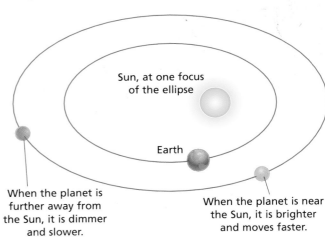

Sun, at one focus of the ellipse

Earth

When the planet is further away from the Sun, it is dimmer and slower.

When the planet is near the Sun, it is brighter and moves faster.

▲ Kepler discovered that the speed of each planet varies during its orbit.

Galileo Galilei (1564–1642)

*Galileo was the first astronomer to use a **telescope** to study the **stars**. What he saw changed people's view of the Universe for ever.*

Galileo's telescopes

Galileo was a mathematics professor at Padua University in Italy when he heard that a new scientific instrument had been invented. The instrument was a tube with two **lenses** (curved pieces of glass) that made things look bigger. Galileo was fascinated by this idea and soon made his own instrument (a telescope). He turned it towards the stars and found that he could see the **planets** and stars more clearly than ever before.

Galileo's first telescope made objects look three times larger than usual. Later, he made more powerful telescopes: one of them made objects look thirty times larger.

▲ Galileo was a brilliant and brave scientist. His new ideas challenged the Church's teachings and put him in great danger.

New discoveries

With his telescope, Galileo made some startling discoveries. He saw four moons circling the planet Jupiter; the "ears" of Saturn (which we now know are rings of ice particles); sunspots on the Sun; and mountains and craters on the Moon. He also observed the planet Venus changing shape gradually, like the Moon, from a full sphere, to a crescent, and back again.

Galileo realized that all these things proved that the Church was wrong in teaching that the Earth was the centre of the Universe with all the planets circling around it in perfect spheres. Clearly, Jupiter was being circled by its own moons, Venus appeared to change shape because it was circling around the Sun, and the variations on the surfaces of the Sun and Moon meant they were not perfect "heavenly bodies".

▲ One of Galileo's telescopes

▼ Galileo drew these ink sketches of the Moon, after a series of observations through his telescope. They were published in his book *Messenger of the Stars* in 1610.

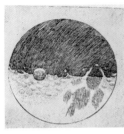

▼ This 19th-century painting shows Galileo in the Church Court in 1616. Although the court imprisoned Galileo, it could not stop news of his discoveries from spreading.

The Church fights back

Although a few other scientists, such as Copernicus, had suggested that the Earth was not the centre of the Universe, the Church had not been alarmed as the idea seemed so unlikely. Galileo, however, was seen as a dangerous threat because he was a highly respected scientist and people believed him. He published his work in Italian, so that ordinary people could read about his discoveries, rather than in Latin, which was the language used by the Church and universities.

In 1616, the Church forced Galileo to appear in court. They threatened to torture him unless he said that his ideas were wrong. Galileo had no choice but to agree. His books were banned and he was imprisoned in his house for the rest of his life.

Isaac Newton (1642–1727)

More than any other scientist, Isaac Newton increased our understanding of how things move on Earth and in space. He has been described as "the father of modern science".

Laws of motion

While Isaac Newton was Professor of Mathematics at Cambridge University in England, he made detailed studies and calculations about how things moved. He came to the conclusion that objects moved according to three main ideas (these became known as Newton's "laws of motion"). At the centre of these laws was the idea that any object will keep moving in a straight line unless it is interrupted by a force, and that when an object is still, it has stopped moving because of a force. For example, a ball stops rolling because of air resistance and friction.

DÉCOUVERTE DE LA THÉORIE DE LA GRAVITATION UNIVERSELLE.

▲ Watching an apple fall to the ground may have started Newton thinking about gravity, but he had to make long mathematical calculations to prove his theories.

Gravity

Studying how and why things moved led Newton to a theory of **gravity**. He proved, through observations and calculations, that all objects are pulled together by a force (gravity). Smaller objects are pulled towards larger objects (for example, an apple is pulled towards the Earth). Massive objects in motion, such as **planets** and moons, can be pulled by gravity into **orbit** around larger objects. Without gravity, the Moon would travel through space in a straight line.

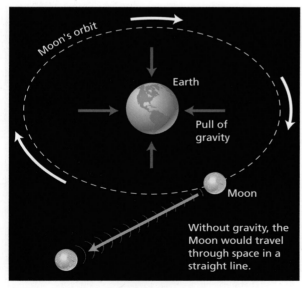

Moon's orbit

Earth

Pull of gravity

Moon

Without gravity, the Moon would travel through space in a straight line.

▲ Gravity keeps the Moon in orbit around the Earth.

Newton's telescope

As well as studying the movement of objects, Newton was also interested in light and **optics**. He developed a new type of **telescope**, using mirrors made from polished metal instead of **lenses**.

◄ Newton's telescope was shorter than previous ones and gave a clearer image. Details of the invention were published in 1671 and Newton became famous throughout Europe.

Edmund Halley (1656–1742)

Newton was encouraged in his work by a fellow British astronomer, Edmund Halley, who was particularly interested in **comets**. He studied records of their appearance and traced their orbits, using Newton's ideas about gravity.

One comet, in particular, fascinated him – it was seen in 1066 during the Battle of Hastings and recorded on the Bayeux Tapestry. Halley proposed that some of the comets were, in fact, the same comet reappearing at regular intervals. His theory was proved when he predicted, correctly, that the 1066 comet would reappear in 1759. It was named Halley's Comet in his honour.

▲ In 1066, William the Conqueror thought the comet was a sign that Harold would lose the Battle of Hastings.

▲ Halley's Comet, photographed in 1910. It was last seen in 1986.

William and Caroline Herschel

(1738–1822 and 1750–1848)

*Unlike other astronomers of their day, William Herschel and his sister Caroline were not content with observing just the nearby **planets**, the Sun, and the Moon. They wanted to look further into space, but to do this they needed more powerful **telescopes** – so they made their own.*

A new planet

The Herschels ground and polished their own mirrors to use in their telescopes. The larger the mirror, the more light could be collected and the more detail could be observed.

In 1781, using his own telescope, William identified a new planet, which he named Uranus. It was the first planet to be discovered since prehistoric times, and William became famous.

▲ Caroline and William were talented musicians from Hanover in Germany, but they gave up their music to devote more time to astronomy. In their **observatory** near Bath, England, they frequently worked through the night, one observing the stars through the telescope, the other taking notes.

▲ In 1845, Lord Rosse built a 183 cm telescope at Birr Castle, Dublin. He used it to observe that some nebulae (now known to be galaxies) had a spiral shape.

Luminous nebulae

Through their powerful telescopes, the Herschels studied what appeared to be luminous clouds (**nebulae**) in the sky. While some astronomers thought these clouds were a glowing milky fluid or gas, the Herschels identified individual **stars** within them. They suggested that groups of nebulae might be very distant star systems (now known as **galaxies**).

Henrietta Leavitt

(1868–1921)

Henrietta Leavitt discovered how to measure the distance to stars a long way from Earth. Her method of measurement was important for working out the real size of the Universe, and it is still used today.

"Winking" stars

Much of Leavitt's work was on **variable stars**. These stars are sometimes bright, sometimes dim, so appear to be slowly "winking" over time. Leavitt identified over 2400 variable stars, about half the known stars in her day. However, her most important contribution to **astronomy** was her work on cepheid variables. These are

▲ Leavitt spent most of her working life at the Harvard College Observatory in the USA. This is one of the few photographs of her at work.

stars whose brightness varies in a regular pattern. She worked out how to calculate the distance of these stars, using the speed at which they appear to flash on and off, and allowing for the fact that more distant stars are less bright than close ones.

The Great Debate

In the 1920s, an official debate (discussion) took place at the Smithsonian Institution in Washington DC, in the USA. Some astronomers (led by Harlow Shapley) argued that the Universe was one big galaxy, while others (led by Heber Curtis) argued that the Universe was made up of many galaxies like our own.

There was disagreement until Edwin Hubble used Leavitt's methods of calculation while studying distant nebulae and confirmed that these were distant galaxies, not just clouds of dust and gas (see pages 24–25).

Albert Einstein (1879–1955)

*Albert Einstein was one of the greatest scientists of all time. He challenged Newton's laws of physics, suggesting that time, space, and **gravity** were all interlinked (related). These **relativity** theories changed the way people thought about the Universe.*

Early life

Einstein was born in Germany but followed his family to Italy in 1895, and then completed his education in Switzerland. He was a brilliant, but unusual, student. Although he was very clever, Einstein often fell out with his teachers and was unpopular with many academics. In 1902, he started work in the Patent Office, studying projects by Swiss inventors. In his spare time, Einstein worked on his own scientific ideas.

Relativity

In 1905, Einstein published a paper (later known as the special theory of relativity) outlining revolutionary new ideas about time and space. He argued that the speed of light is the same whether the source of light is moving or not, but that time varies according to the speed of the person measuring time. The faster someone travels, the less time will seem to pass.

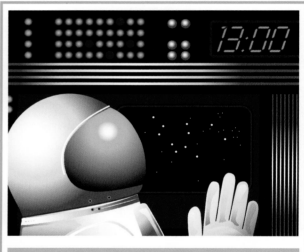

▲ According to Einstein's theory of relativity, astronauts on a voyage travelling close to the speed of light will find that time passes more slowly for them than for people on Earth.

Ten years later, Einstein completed his work on relativity with another paper (now known as the general theory of relativity). This proposed that the effects of gravity are due to the curvature of space around objects, a bit like the way a trampoline curves when there is a weight on it.

▼ Einstein's general theory of relativity was proved correct during the **eclipse** of the Sun in 1919. The light from a star was seen to be curved by the gravity of the Sun.

$$E = mc^2$$

This famous equation was worked out by Einstein. Understanding the relationship between energy (E), matter (m), and the speed of light (c) was crucial to future work on atomic fission (splitting the atom) and fusion (joining atoms). Atomic fission and fusion are used in nuclear weapons and the manufacture of nuclear power.
    Atomic fission and fusion give the Sun its light and heat.

actual position
of star

apparent
positions
of star

light bent
here

Sun

Moon

Earth

Fame

In 1921, Einstein was awarded the Nobel Prize for physics. He became famous not only for his scientific achievements, but also for his stance against the Nazis, and his promotion of peace, freedom, and justice.
    Einstein believed that scientists have a great responsibility to other people. He said: "Never regard your study as a duty, but as the enviable opportunity to learn [for your own pleasure] and to profit the community to which your work belongs."

▲ Einstein's scientific ideas and political beliefs made him a popular public figure. His photograph was often in newspapers and magazines.

Edwin Hubble (1884–1953)

Edwin Hubble proved that the Universe was far bigger than anyone had previously thought.

Early life

Born in Missouri in the USA, Edwin Hubble trained as a lawyer, but his interest in **astronomy** drew him to work at the largest **observatory** in the world. This was at the top of Mount Wilson, near Los Angeles in California.

▼ Hubble looking through the Hooker **telescope** at Mount Wilson, which was famous for its 250 cm mirror.

Measuring distance in light-years

Using the giant Hooker telescope, Hubble studied other **galaxies** and **nebulae** (clouds of dust and gas). In 1923, he examined the Andromeda galaxy and discovered "winking" **stars** similar to those studied by Henrietta Leavitt (see page 21). Using Leavitt's methods of calculation, Hubble worked out that the Andromeda galaxy was so far away that it was impossible to calculate the distance in kilometres. Instead, he measured it in **light-years**. A light-year is the distance that light travels in one year – about 9500 billion kilometres. Hubble worked out that the Andromeda galaxy was more than one million light-years away.

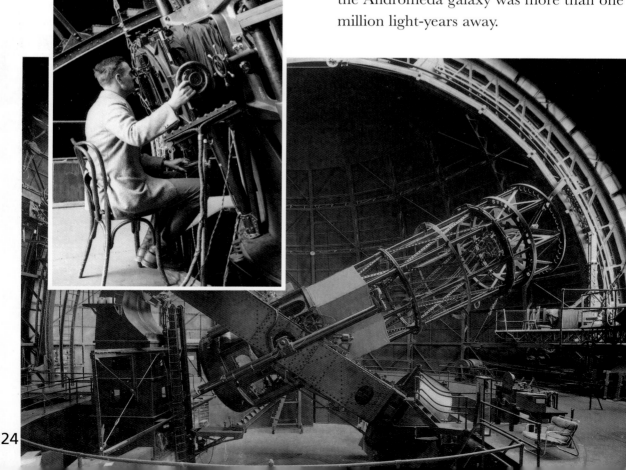

The expanding Universe

As Hubble began to map the Universe, galaxy by galaxy, he also measured how quickly the galaxies were moving. Those furthest away seemed to be moving most quickly. This became known as Hubble's law. Hubble concluded that the Universe was expanding.

The Big Bang theory

Many scientists refused to believe that the Universe was expanding. However, in 1927, a Catholic priest, Georges Lemaître, proposed that the Universe began about 15 billion years ago, with a huge explosion. This explosion marked the beginning of space, matter, and time, and led to the creation of galaxies, stars, and **planets**. The Roman Catholic Church supported this theory as it fitted in with its belief in a single moment of creation.

A meeting of great minds

Lemaître believed that the idea of the **Big Bang** brought together Einstein's theories of **relativity** with Hubble's theory of the **expanding Universe**. The three men met and Lemaître explained his ideas in detail. Einstein remarked that the Big Bang theory was, "the most beautiful and satisfying interpretation I have ever listened to".

▲ The theory of the expanding Universe can be shown with a balloon. Mark some stars on a balloon, then watch them move further apart as the balloon is inflated. The stars more distant from one another move away from each other fastest.

25

Radio astronomers

The light we can see with our eyes is called visible light. It can be split into different colours, as in a rainbow. However, there are other "colours" that humans cannot see, in the same way that there are sounds that humans cannot hear (for example, a dog whistle).

Early astronomers could only observe the Universe using visible light. However, the development of radio **telescopes** in the mid-20th century meant that astronomers could look beyond visible light and begin to learn more about the Universe.

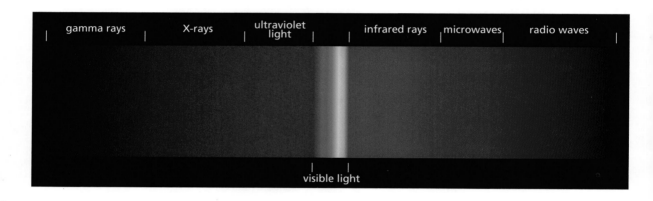

gamma rays   X-rays   ultraviolet light   infrared rays   microwaves   radio waves

visible light

Karl Jansky (1905–1950)

Karl Jansky was an American engineer who worked for Bell Telephone Laboratories. His job was to find out what was causing interference with telephone communications. Jansky built a huge antenna receiver (the first basic radio telescope) and analyzed all the signals he detected. In 1931, he discovered that some radio interference was actually coming from **stars**.

◄ Jansky building his antenna receiver

Grote Reber (born 1911)

Another American engineer, Grote Reber, developed Jansky's work and built the first dish-shaped radio receiver. This could detect radio noise coming from **galaxies** so far away that they were invisible to the naked eye. Jansky began to map out more distant galaxies.

Arno Penzias (born 1933) and Robert Wilson (born 1936)

In 1965, American scientists Penzias and Wilson were doing experiments with a very sensitive radio receiver, but they kept detecting a hissing interference. They realized that the hiss was due to the low level of radiation astronomers had predicted would have been left throughout the Universe after the **Big Bang**. This was the best evidence, to date, that the Big Bang had occurred.

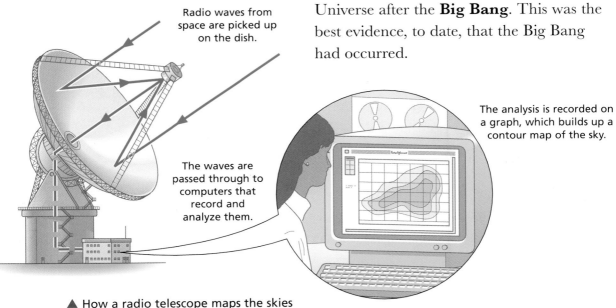

Radio waves from space are picked up on the dish.

The waves are passed through to computers that record and analyze them.

The analysis is recorded on a graph, which builds up a contour map of the sky.

▲ How a radio telescope maps the skies

▼ A rare photograph of Jocelyn Bell at work

Jocelyn Bell (born 1943)

Jocelyn Bell was a young Irish student working with her tutor, Anthony Hewish, at Cambridge University in England, when she noted regular radio signals from space. Some people wondered whether these could be signals from other life forms, but Bell discovered they were coming from rapidly spinning new stars – now known as **pulsars**. Pulsars throw out radio signals as they spin (in the same way that a lighthouse gives out a beam of light at regular intervals).

27

Dark matter astronomers

Vera Rubin (born 1928)

Until the 20th century, astronomers thought that they could see everything in the Universe with modern instruments. But in the 1970s, an American astronomer, Vera Rubin, suggested that we see only 10 per cent of what actually exists. The other 90 per cent is invisible and is called dark matter.

Rubin's measurement of the speed of rotating galaxies led her to believe in dark matter – a halo of invisible material surrounding galaxies. Although at first many scientists doubted Rubin's theory, today it is widely accepted. Several teams of astronomers are trying to find out more about dark matter.

▼ Vera Rubin

MACHO

The MACHO (Massive Compact Halo Object) team is looking for huge **stellar** bodies with great mass and weight, or massive **black holes**. This project involves astronomers working with **telescopes** set up in Australia and the USA.

▲ The MACHO team

WIMPS

Another team of scientists believe that the dark matter may be WIMPS (Weakly Interacting Massive Particles) – tiny particles smaller than atoms. These particles can be studied not just by looking at the sky, but by reading sensitive equipment buried deep in the Antarctic ice. This equipment can detect these tiny particles (neutrinos) that have come from outer space.

▶In the AMANDA (Antarctic Muon and Neutrino Detector Array) project, detectors are lowered more than a kilometre below the surface of the Antarctic ice.

George Smoot

(born 1945)

One of the greatest challenges for astronomers has been to get clearer pictures of space by setting up telescopes outside the Earth's **atmosphere**. The atmosphere can distort light and radiation, so telescopes are less effective on Earth.

The American George Smoot led a team of scientists who wanted to study the cosmic radiation left by the **Big Bang**. They first tried mounting telescopes on rockets and balloons, but they achieved real success with the *Cosmic Background Explorer* (*COBE*) in 1989.

By 1992, *COBE* had detected an irregular pattern in the background radiation in the Universe (first identified by Penzias and Wilson, see page 27). This "ripple effect" was further evidence that the Big Bang had taken place. Scientists agreed that the irregular strings and clumps of radiation had led to the formation of **galaxies**, **stars**, and **planets**.

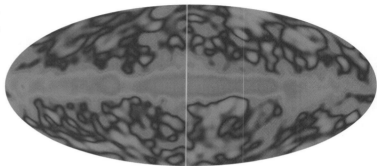

▲ This computer image from *COBE* shows the variations in the radiation from the Big Bang.

▼ *COBE* was a radio telescope attached to a satellite.

The *Hubble Space Telescope*

▲ Astronauts repairing the *Hubble* telescope in 1993

The *Hubble Space Telescope* was launched into Earth's **orbit** in 1990, to take pictures of the Universe outside Earth's distorting atmosphere. It is so powerful that if it were above Washington DC in the USA, it could see a firefly in Tokyo, Japan! It was named as a tribute to Edwin Hubble's work.

The future

Great astronomers have expanded our view and understanding of the Universe. We can now look further and further into space, although we know that whatever we see is probably just a small fraction of what is out there.

As technology has advanced, we are able to build powerful, sensitive, and more specialized scientific equipment, but this is very expensive. Individual countries are unable to afford the expense. As a result, more and more astronomical projects are set up jointly by two or more countries. For example, the USA and Japan have set up the Sloan Digital Sky Survey, in order to map more than 100 million **stars**, one million **galaxies**, and 100,000 **quasars**.

▲ The 2.5 m telescope on Apache Point in New Mexico, USA (part of the Sloan Digital Sky Survey), can see to a distance of 1.5 billion **light-years** from Earth.

▲ Part of the Hubble Deep Field image, which shows more than 3000 galaxies, all at different stages of evolution. It is a glimpse of the history of the Universe!

It may be that the most important astronomers in the future will be robots – the **probes** that are sent into space to travel to distant planets and stars. So far, probes such as *Venera*, *Viking*, *Voyager*, and *Galileo*, have explored the giant **planets** in our **Solar System**. Maybe others will travel further afield one day.

Alternatively, the future may lie with space **telescopes**, such as the *Hubble Space Telescope*. In 1995, the *Hubble Telescope* spent ten days collecting images from one tiny patch of the sky. The images were put together by computer and the final picture is like a snapshot of the entire history of the Universe. Teams of astronomers around the world are now studying all the information contained in this one amazing picture, the Hubble Deep Field.

Glossary

astrolabe An ancient instrument used for measuring the positions of the stars, Moon, and Sun.

astrology Study attempting to link the movement of the stars and planets to what happens on Earth.

astronomy The study of the stars, planets, Sun, and Moon.

atmosphere The layer of gases around the Earth or other planet.

Big Bang A theory about the Universe being created in one explosion.

black hole A place in space into which everything nearby, including light, is drawn in.

comet An icy object surrounded by gas and dust which develops a tail of gas and dust as it approaches the Sun.

constellation A pattern of stars in the sky.

Dark Ages A time in European history (AD 476–800) after Roman civilization broke down, when much learning and culture was lost.

eclipse A movement which hides the object behind.

ellipse An oval.

epicycles Small circles around the circumference of a larger circle.

expanding Universe A theory that the Universe has been growing (and still is) since the moment of creation.

firmament An ancient name for the night sky.

galaxy A collection of stars in space.

geocentric With the Earth at the centre.

gravity A force that pulls objects together.

heliocentric With the Sun at the centre.

lenses Curved pieces of glass or other transparent material that focus light.

light-year Distance travelled by light in one year.

nebula (plural **nebulae**) A faint, cloud-like collection of stars or gas.

observatory A place for viewing the stars.

optics The science of light.

orbit The path of a planet (can be used as a noun or verb).

planet A large body that orbits around a star.

probes Spacecraft that travel far into space to explore, without human crew.

pulsar A star that gives off pulses of radio waves.

quadrant An instrument for measuring angles between stars.

quasar A luminous object in space that may be the centre of a distant galaxy.

relativity A theory linking time, energy, and mass.

sextant An instrument for measuring angles between stars.

Solar System The Sun and the planets, moons, asteroids, and comets which move around it.

star A massive globe of hot gas.

stellar To do with, or looking like, a star.

telescope An instrument to make distant objects look bigger.

variable star A star whose brightness changes.

Books for further reading

John and Mary Gribbin, *Eyewitness Science: Time and Space* (Dorling Kindersley, 1994)

Robin Kerrod, *Learn about Astronomy* (Anness Publishing, 1996)

Peter Lafferty, *Pioneers in Science: Astronomy* (Heinemann Educational, 1992)

Kristen Lippincott, *Eyewitness Science: Astronomy* (Dorling Kindersley, 1994)

Fiona Macdonald, *Albert Einstein* (Exley Publications, 1992)

Fiona Macdonald, *Groundbreakers: Edwin Hubble* (Heinemann Library, 2000)

Simon and Jaqueline Mitton, *The Young Oxford Book of Astronomy* (OUP, 1994)

Patrick Moore, *The Guinness Book of Astronomy* (Guinness Publishing Ltd., 1992)

Phillip Wilkinson and Michael Pollard, *Scientists Who Changed the World* (Dragons World Ltd., 1994)

The Children's Space Atlas (Quarto Publishing, 1991)

The Dorling Kindersley Science Encyclopedia (Dorling Kindersley, 1994)

Index